John Jacobus    Twentieth-Century Architecture: The Middle Years 1940–65

John Jacobus **Twentieth-Century Architecture
The Middle Years 1940-65**

Frederick A. Praeger, Publishers, New York · Washington

BOOKS THAT MATTER

Published in the United States of America in 1966
by Frederick A. Praeger, Publishers
111 Fourth Avenue, New York 3, N.Y.
Copyright 1966 by Verlag Gerd Hatje, Stuttgart
Library of Congress Catalog Card Number: 66–12526
Printed in Germany

# Contents

To the Memory of my Mother

# Preface

"A picture," wrote Proust, "is a kind of revelation of some small part of a mysterious world of which we know various other aspects, which are canvases by the same artist." Similarly, a building conceived in the spirit of creative adventure results in a unique, ordered, yet otherwise unknowable world of space and form, one whose meaning is enhanced through experience with other works produced by the same creative imagination. Although the palpable, encompassing space of architecture is more immediate than the physically impenetrable world of a painting, it is no less mysterious in its total impact.

Every building presented in the following pages does not, of course, attain such an ideal of space and form. Too many are mere stylish artifacts of our contemporary world, automatons produced by fashion and largely devoid of authentic creative spark. A number of these artifacts, however, are of considerable historical and stylistic significance. Although they were not brought into being by a unique creative insight, nevertheless they were produced by architects committed to the continuing relevance of a revolutionary twentieth-century design idiom.

The quarter century of modern architecture under specific review here—the period from about 1940 to the present—has been derivative in style to a large extent. It is, essentially, a period of secondary creativity which has sustained a revolution reaching back half a century for its architectural forms and even farther for its theoretical origins. Consequently, the recent goals of modern architects have been considerably different from those of the radical generation that dominated the crucial years 1918–39. The first of these recent concerns has been to continue, even while expanding and reforming, the modernity of style and technique established by the earlier avant-garde, architects of Expressionism and the International Style. A corollary aspect of this continuing revolution has been the resurgence of individuality and personal style as a reaction against the communal, anonymous shapes of the 1920's and 1930's. This development was by no means a denial of International Style design, as some critics and architects have been inclined to assume, but was rather a conscious attempt to emphasize the positive and idiosyncratic features of the new architecture at the expense of its once-important self-effacing qualities. Historically, this shift from a unanimous style toward more diverse expressions has many precedents. The early years of the sixteenth century in Italy, when the idealized High Renaissance style of Raphael gave way to the diverse trends of Mannerism, provides but one instance of stylistic evolution proceeding from the general and universal to the particular and individual.

Unfortunately, in contrast to the development from High Renaissance to Mannerism, the recent expansion of the modernist idiom has tended to procede without a clearly focused taste, and without a basic clarification of the unique principles of the new architecture. With only a few exceptions, contemporary architects have wavered, seemingly lost for want of a neat, concise set of laws or an established repertoire of details such as those previously furnished by the academic tradition. Many have fallen back on a real or feigned opulence of material, or upon a prodigality of novel yet meaningless detail, the better to mask the absence of quality in both plans and interior organization. While much of today's most conspicuous "modern" architecture seems to reflect our affluent age, the true growth of a fundamental contemporary style has virtually no causal relation with the tremendous expansion of the speculative building industry over the past two decades. The style of today's genuinely significant building owes but little to the social and economic factors which are, it is true, responsibile for the proliferation and vulgarization of modernism as a fashion. The serious critic or historian of contemporary architecture must begin by separating the authentic monuments from the chaff, unless his aim is to write social history rather than an account of the buildings themselves.

There are several possible ways to write a history of this hectic quarter century of modern building. One of them could be based mainly upon sheer quantity, dwelling upon the variety of buildings that either aspire to the epithet contemporary or that, at least, ape the mannerisms of the fashionable pace-setters. An intriguing book could be written of our roadside, resort, and merchandising architecture, and I earnestly hope that someone is already gathering and preserving material related to this aspect of contemporary culture. A companion volume could also be written about the collective failure of our master-architects to alter the totality of our visual environment. The author of such a study could begin with the Utopian dreams of the architects of the 1920's and then go on to enumerate the progressive vulgarizations by which opportunists (or fools) managed to dishonor a once-noble vision. He might conclude with a diatribe against the proliferation of junk and refuse across our landscape, whether urban or rural.

In contrast, the approach of this volume is neither of these but, rather, a history of style. I am concerned with the latter-day evolution of modern architecture as a totality, beginning just before 1940, when the heroic epoch of discovery was over. This study is meant to encompass the subsequent ebb and flow of confidence and creativity in the recent quarter-century, concluding in the mid 1960's with the dawn of what may prove to be a new age of fulfillment and creative expansion.

Many readers will challenge the validity of history written from so close a vantage point, a fact that, of necessity, causes the use of a perspective system based more on breadth than on depth. True, the picture of mid-twentieth-century architecture that unfolds in the following pages will often seem uncomfortably two-dimensional, closer to an antique processional relief or a Chinese scroll painting than to a compactly framed Renaissance painting. Depth, particularly in recent history, must come primarily from contrived juxta-positions and brusque changes of scale, from the use of artificial conventions and styli-zations. To situate the individual buildings of our epoch in a proper historical framework, it is frequently necessary to refer to some remote and seemingly irrelevant period, or to discover an analogy of shape or purpose in the works of another creative field. Only in this way can contemporary history hope to rise above simple journalism. The risks are obvious. They are justified, I believe, because a masterpiece is most clearly separable from its lesser contemporaries only when the apparatus of historical and stylistic criticism is brought to bear upon it and because, in the last analysis, it is only with those buildings which reveal "some small part of a mysterious world" that we are concerned. Historical criticism is not an infallible, nor a necessarily exclusive, method, but without it we fail to be aware of the qualities characteristic of, and hence peculiar to, our own times.

Since first conceiving this book in the winter of 1959–60, I have accumulated indebtedness to a multitude of helpful friends and associates, often for a fact and sometimes for a basic idea. To enumerate them all would risk omission, and it has therefore seemed wiser to acknowlede this indispensable accumulation of advice and assistance with a single expression of grateful appreciation. Nevertheless, I am aware that many of the basic forces that have shaped this study are, to a considerable degree, the result of the teachings and guidance that I have received from Paul Parker, Carroll L. V. Meeks, and Henry-Russell Hitchcock. Such quality as may exist in the following pages is in large measure the conse-quence of their patience and friendship. I have one other special debt to Vincent Scully, whose lectures at Yale in 1952 and 1953 first revealed to me the vastness and complexity of the modernist tradition in architecture, and whose publications since then have already anticipated many aspects of my own work.

The scope of this book is largely due to the initiative of the German publisher, Gerd Hatje, who, together with his staff, has significantly helped the author in his work over a considerable period. In particular, I am indebted to Wolfgang Pehnt for the illustrations and the layout, to Antje Pehnt for the German edition of the text, to Eugenia Robbins for help in refining and untangling the original manuscript, and to Ruth Wurster for seeing the book through the press. My wife and daughter have willingly borne with the numerous crises that have gone into the making of the book, and are therefore due special and affectionate recognition.

This book has been written at various intervals over the past six years, during which time I have received generous support from the Graham Foundation and from the American Council of Learned Societies for research in various related areas in the history of modern architecture. Indirectly, their aid has materially helped the progress of the present study.

Finally, I would like to express my appreciation to the many librarians who, by the diligent attention lavished on their collections, have made my task of research and writing one of unending discovery. These librarians include those of the Marquand Library at Princeton University; the Avery Architectural Library at Columbia University; the Architectural Library of the University of California at Berkeley; the Art and Architecture Library at Yale University; the Hillyer Art Library at Smith College; and the Fine Arts Library at Indiana University.

Paris, January, 1966                                                                          J. J.

# Chapter I
## A Genealogy for Contemporary Architecture

Both the triumphs and frustrations of contemporary architecture stem from the same general cause. For three generations, contemporary design has constantly reiterated a desire to make a new start, to sweep the board clean and begin again without the pretense of timeworn formulas or the clutter of outmoded techniques. Sometimes this longing for unfettered independence has been expressed directly and simply, but more often it has been embedded in such slogans and doctrines as "functionalism," "expression of structure and materials," "organic architecture," or the "machine aesthetic." All of these concepts share one feature: the redefinition of architecture in a pristine, abstract way, quite apart from any sacrosanct stylistic label. Separating themselves from the issues of historicizing architecture as practiced in the nineteenth century, the architects of the twentieth century have welcomed this state of detachment as an opportunity to strike out in new, unexplored directions.

Within the span of a generation, a new architecture came into being and, by the early 1930's, its collective accomplishments were already recognizable as a style. At first, this new style seemed to be completely unique, based upon expressive and utilitarian criteria rather than upon any systematic concept of structural or compositional principles. To a degree this distinction was illusive, but it required the span of yet another generation for the roots of twentieth-century architecture to become visible and for its stylistic character to be revealed as one additional step in the long evolution of Western art. By the middle of the century, modern architecture—like all revolutionary movements—had established itself as a new tradition with special vested interests, particularly a stake in the booming building industry and in thriving professional schools and academies. The turmoil created by the earlier generation, a small band of visionaries who challenged the establishment, the traditional styles and institutions of the profession, has today been replaced by an atmosphere of acceptance or, at least, of accommodation. Contemporary architects are increasingly aware of their immediate heritage and, unlike their predecessors, they are becoming reconciled to many facets of historical tradition that were anathema only yesterday.

Because of the emotional and ideological conflicts that appeared in the wake of modern architecture's early triumphs, its evolution since the late 1930's does not present a well-defined historical pattern. This is in contrast to the relative clarity of purpose and intent that characterizes the earlier, climactic moment in the architecture of the 1920's. Much of the apparent confusion is the result of the vast procedural and technological revolution still incompletely absorbed by today's architects. It must not be forgotten that the buildings of our era, although they are indeed formal and spatial configurations of new vision, are primarily conditioned by new attitudes adapted from the researches of science, technology, sociology, and ethics. In other times, the fruits of these disciplines were not considered to be directly applicable to architecture. The ideals of our architecture are based upon a multifarious assemblage of factual data and subjective prejudices concerning the nature and needs of contemporary man and his relationship to a new and perplexing universe. Furthermore, man is conscious that his physical environment is no longer the exclusive

1. Le Corbusier. Unité d'Habitation. Nantes-Rezé, 1952-57. Pilotis at ground level.

2. Frank Lloyd Wright. Robie House. Chicago, 1909.

3. Adolf Loos. Steiner House. Vienna, 1910.

4. Peter Behrens. A.E.G. Turbine Factory. Berlin, 1908–9.

product of natural conditions, but is becoming more and more a world of his own devising. It is of small wonder that an architecture which consciously seeks to respond to these changing conditions exhibits so much apparent instability.

It would be a mistake to think that simply because of the myriad new conditions under which contemporary architects labor, it is impossible to identify a pattern of evolving architecture similar to those patterns recognized in earlier historical periods. Although the process of evolution has been immeasurably quickened by new pressures from without, and although the separate strands of history that must be brought together are infinitely more numerous, the responses of our major architects have followed a pattern in time that is far from chaotic. If our new architecture has not yet achieved an emotionally mature attitude, this would seem related to psychic rather than stylistic causes. In terms of sheer formal accomplishment, modern architecture came of age long ago.

The twentieth century has already witnessed several separate moments of major creative activity. Although radical theoretical pronouncements sometimes heralded these especially inventive moments, distinction was achieved primarily through the outward stylistic features of buildings and projects. The first of these climactic moments occurred about 1910, the epoch of Frank Lloyd Wright's greatest prairie houses (Fig. 2), of Peter Behrens' Berlin factories (Fig. 4), and of Adolf Loos's strikingly simple Vienna villas (Fig. 3). A subsequent period of clarification centered about the peak years of the so-called International Style, from about 1927 to 1932, years that saw the construction of Mies van der Rohe's Barcelona Pavilion (Figs. 47, 48) and his Tugendhat House (Figs. 6, 7), of Le Corbusier's "machine era" villas at Boulogne, Garches (Fig. 5), and Poissy (Figs. 27, 28, 30, 31, 33), and of Richard Neutra's Lovell House, Los Angeles (Fig. 8). Yet a third climactic period of modern architecture occurred around 1950, when the building boom of post-World War II reconstruction converged with the creative renaissance of Mies and Le Corbusier and was momentarily strengthened as a collective effort by the youthful works of a new generation of designers. A fourth climax seems to be centered about the present—the mid-1960's—and is manifested in the last projects of Le Corbusier, the recent works of Louis Kahn, and the vitality of younger architects as diverse in appeal as James Stirling and Paul Rudolph.

The pattern suggested by these several concentrations of events is one of cumulative growth and maturity, punctuated by a classic denouement every fifteen years or so. At each peak moment, theoretical objectives seem to have been defined by lucid stylistic and structural accomplishments. This visual definition was followed by a period of relaxation and repetition which, in its turn, was succeeded by a new phase of struggle and invention. Beginning in confusion and obscurity, this phase ultimately pointed toward a new cycle of order, renewal, and creativity.

In the short view, the development of modern art in general may seem to have been a succession of endless transformations, of jumps from one extreme to another. Yet if the twentieth century is viewed in relation to its immediate past as well as to the distant historical traditions on which it ultimately has drawn, certain common features become evident. These features suggest general aims and achievements that pervade the whole century, although occasionally they vanish in the midst of superficial, contradictory, or unrelated fashions. Only with reference to a larger picture can the modern architecture of the two most recent decades be appreciated.

The true ancestry of today's architecture is not limited exclusively to early twentieth-century contributions, but must be traced to many of the innovations in theory and taste that emerged toward the end of the Baroque period. Marking the end of the humanist tradition, one of the mainsprings of European culture since the Renaissance, the Late Baroque epoch provided new ideas about man and his surroundings; these led to the growth of modernist points of view in all fields of endeavor. More than just the conclusion of another style in Western art was involved with the culmination and withering of this three-hundred-year-old tradition in the course of the skeptical eighteenth century. The Baroque absolutist

5. Le Corbusier. Villa Stein, "Les Terrasses." Garches, 1927.

6, 7. Ludwig Mies van der Rohe. Tugendhat House. Brno, 1930. View and plan of the ground floor.

8. Richard Neutra. Lovell House. Los Angeles, 1927–29.

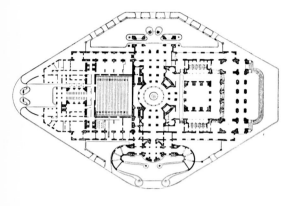

9, 10. Charles Garnier. Opéra. Paris, 1861–74. View and plan.

style in art, architecture, and landscape gardening, which had found its expression in the vast chateaux and gardens of Louis XIV at Versailles, gradually passed out of fashion. In its place came a picturesque vision that contributed to the emerging romantic sensibility, especially in the creation of the artificially contrived "naturalistic" English gardens and in the pastoral, moralistic paintings of Boucher and Greuze.

These new fashions, spawned as inversions of Late Baroque style, undermined the very source from which they sprang. At first, they produced not a new style in architecture but a new way of conceiving of styles. The humanist and academic tradition, which had effectively maintained a monolithic discipline in European arts and letters since the early Renaissance, even in the face of notable and often irreconcilable variations in taste and style, was gradually supplanted in the course of the eighteenth century by an attitude toward the past which was relative rather than absolute. History came to be understood as a series of separate and distinct periods, and the unique values expressed by the art forms of these periods came to be appreciated in their own right without necessarily suffering injurious comparisons to the once-supreme classical tradition.

In effect, "tradition" then ceased to be that monolithic "great chain of being" passed down as an instrument of recognized authority from one generation to the next, as had been the case since the early Renaissance reintroduction of ancient orders as constant, if malleable, instruments in architectural design. While the architects of the Enlightenment did not reject the ancient orders, men such as Laugier or new classicists such as Soufflot, Ledoux, and Soane subjected them to searching scrutiny until, gradually and almost imperceptibly, the tangible form and shape of the order used was considered more important than the accumulated meaning that stood behind its traditional application.[1] In the eyes of these new eighteenth-century architects, expressive external appearance became more important than the intellectual humanist content of an expiring architectural design system that had put greater value in harmonic proportions and ideal forms. Once this new appreciation of form was released from the restraints of Renaissance-inspired theory, a kind of permissiveness resulted which led to a budding interest in other styles. In the mid-eighteenth century, the vast differences between the classic art of Greece and the classicism of Rome, heretofore a matter of some indifference, suddenly became a subject of debate and controversy. Concomitantly, the styles of the Middle Ages gained recognition along with other, more exotic, styles.

If the collapse of humanism[2] was one of the liberating events leading toward modern architecture, the forms presently thought of as "modern"—that is to say, generally non-traditional—did not appear for another century. True, there were certain remarkably original and independent efforts to create a new, unfettered language of architectural form before the eighteenth century was over, notably by Ledoux and his generation, but the most radical of these efforts remained on paper, unbuilt, and for another century there were only intermittent sequels to this inventive flurry. Instead, the bewildering accomplishments of the nineteenth century, its progress in science and technology as well as in the accumulation of historical prototypes, intervened like a kind of purgatory between the demise of one architectural civilization and the appearance of another. This period's output resembled a vast, loosely related accumulation of data, in the fashion of the periodical and encyclopedic literature of the day, rather than a series of interrelated creative events. Along with the introduction of radically new structural methods and new materials, the architectural and scholarly professions added constantly to a burgeoning store of knowledge through an enthusiastic, but sometimes misapplied, study of historical styles. Out of this rearranged fund of raw material emerged a bewildering, overlapping succession of revivals and emulative styles, in effect, congeries of rapidly changing fashions which today seem an inevitable by-product of the period's obsessive fascination with progress, invention, and exploration. If nothing else, this drive toward constant change—change which was infrequently renewal—is perhaps the most far-reaching contribution of the nineteenth century to the vibrant spirit of twentieth-century architecture.

The passage of time has made it possible to revise this impression, to see the frenzied events of the nineteenth century in a more coherent form, but one is still apt to be overwhelmed by its endless variety and disturbing inner contradictions.[3] Sometimes the period impresses us by a dazzling power of invention; at other times its shallow perfunctoriness or glorification of the routine is inescapably depressing. In many of its most characteristic buildings, such as Charles Garnier's Paris Opéra (Figs. 9, 10), superficial brilliance is combined with meaningless hyperbole. In other instances, by virtue of the preponderant role played by technology, a building conveys the feeling that a new architecture was about to come into being. Curiously, however, the striking features of the new, with respect to space, lighting, and technical bravura, were often concealed behind a face of conventionally scaled, if picturesquely handled, details based on contemporary fashion. This is true of the daring 243-foot span of W. H. Barlow's train shed at St. Pancras, London (Fig. 12), which is a ferrovitreous form hidden by a colorful, but small-scale, Victorian-Gothic façade, the work of Sir George Gilbert Scott (Fig. 11). Such inconsistencies indicate the failure of the mid-nineteenth century to integrate and digest its new knowledge, historical as well as technical, and to bring it to bear upon the creation of a new architecture. Part of the difficulty arose because the inventive architects of the Enlightenment, and of the romantic period which overlapped and followed it, had taken over the forms of the past but had emptied them of their original meaning and significance. Consequently, forms came to be used indiscriminately, without reference to necessity, motivation, or expression.

The architects who arrived at creative maturity in the early twentieth century inherited this dubious birthright, a large portion of which they vociferously disowned. The outward forms of the past, which had either outlived their meaningful usage or, in their nineteenth-century revival, had too rarely been infused with new life, were rejected in favor of something new. The nature of this something new (whether it is called the modern movement, new architecture, International Style, or by the most widespread, but totally inadequate, designation, functionalism) has never been comprehensively defined, although there have been a number of significant efforts to do so.[4] At first, this new architectural movement's belligerent iconoclasm, which had been heralded in the Futurist manifestoes of 1909, 1910, 1912, and 1914, found expression in various post-World War I movements of art and architecture: De Stijl, Constructivism, Purism (this movement going so far as to write finis to the then barely decade-old "tradition" of Cubism![5]), and the Bauhaus.

During the 1920's, this new architecture, ultimately christened the International Style when its development was all but over in 1932, produced forms that were almost completely abstract. That is to say, their appearance and expression owed nothing, outwardly, to traditional architectural vocabularies. There were, however, major debts to recent Cubist and post-Cubist painting, especially with regard to the creation of a fundamentally new pictorial system in which space and form ceased to be separate and distinct, but were now deliberately woven together. These startling ambiguities of solid and void produced a deliberate confusion of "within" and "without," most notably in the complex analytical figures and still lifes of Picasso and Braque. These were exploited in appropriately architectonic ways by architects ten and twenty years later.

In architecture, these ambiguities resulted in a style made up of glass-enclosed volumes, with thin, textureless walls independent of the structural frame. These forms ideally were made of steel or reinforced concrete. Architectural elements were customarily worked into a series of seemingly unstable and weightless planes, of hovering forms that often lacked any direct visual correlation to the normal demands of structural stability or to the laws of gravity. Spaces easily flowed around, or sometimes even through, nominal interior partitions, and the design deliberately provided a sense of uncertainty concerning the exact boundaries of interior and exterior. Generally undecorated except for patterns

11. Sir George Gilbert Scott. St. Pancras Station. London, 1865. Façade of former Midland Hotel.

12. W. H. Barlow and R. M. Ordish. St. Pancras Station. London, 1863–68. Train shed.

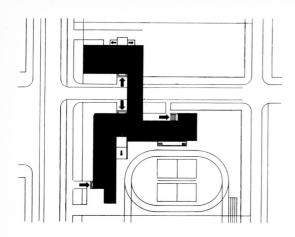

13, 13a. Walter Gropius. Bauhaus. Dessau, 1925–26. Site plan and view.

14. Eric Mendelsohn. Schocken Department Store. Chemnitz, 1927–28.

15. Hans Scharoun. Rest Home at the exhibition "Wohnen und Werken." Breslau, 1929.

inherent in the building material, even major forms defied convention by their impalpability and general avoidance of normal structural expression. Frequently, spaces were indeed conceived in a functional spirit but, in retrospect, much of this simplified design now seems arbitrary and affected. These qualities can be clearly seen in a number of classic International Style buildings: Walter Gropius' Dessau Bauhaus, 1925–26 (Figs. 13, 13a); J. J. P. Oud's Kiefhoek housing project, Rotterdam, 1928–30 (Figs. 17, 18); Mies van der Rohe's Barcelona Pavilion, 1929 (Figs. 47, 48); Le Corbusier's Villa Stein, Garches, 1927 (Fig. 5) and his Villa Savoye, Poissy, 1929 (Figs. 27, 28, 30, 31, 33). So strong was the influence of this spirit of design that characteristics even appear in the work of architects who, at the beginning of the 1920's, had been devoted to the free inventiveness of the subjective Expressionist movement but who, subsequently, developed a more sober style. Among these post-Expressionist designs are Eric Mendelsohn's Schocken Store, Chemnitz, 1927–28 (Fig. 14); Otto Bartning's Steel Church, Cologne, 1928 (Fig. 16), and Hans Scharoun's Rest Home, Breslau, 1929 (Fig. 15).[6]

Curiously, as it becomes possible to see this architectural movement in perspective, it is increasingly difficult to present it only in terms of its proudly independent, isolated rationalism. Even as this movement and its peak period of the late 1920's recedes into the past, it becomes apparent that the architects involved never really rejected the ultimate messages of historical tradition when they put aside the cloak of historical vocabulary. Their rejection was of the literal techniques of revivalism and eclecticism. The historical sources themselves, however concealed, remained as a stimulus for invention, often of the most unexpected and improbable sort. In the work of Le Corbusier, for instance, the influence of the Athenian Acropolis and its buildings, especially the concise nature of the Doric order of the Parthenon, is crucial.[7] These influences, however, led neither to imitation nor to the creation of an equivalent design technique, but rather to the decisive reinforcement of Le Corbusier's own modernist aesthetic. His predisposition toward a post-Cubist, Purist form found parallel stimulae in such diverse sources as automobiles, airplanes, grain elevators, and modern ocean liners. Interestingly enough, Le Corbusier came precariously close to imitating the outward forms of modern ships during the late 1920's in his designs for villas at Garches (Fig. 5) and Poissy (Figs. 27, 28, 30, 31, 33), with the result that the subjective, truly romantic aspect of this machine art now seems to have taken precedence over its nominal rationalism of technology.

When considered in terms of its ideologies, contemporary architecture is full of inner contradictions. Many of these are highlighted by the simultaneous existence of at least two rationalist strains which, in outward appearance, are not compatible. One is the rationalism of structure, with its ancestry going back to the visionary metal and glass architecture of nineteenth-century crystal palaces and to articulate theorists of that period's medieval revivals, among whom Pugin and Viollet-le-Duc were outstanding.

The other strain is a rationalism of form that reaches back even further to theorists of the Enlightenment like the Abbé Laugier and to an initial realization in the forms designed by Ledoux and Boullée. Today, the rationalism of structure finds its adherents in architects as far apart in style as Auguste Perret and Pier Luigi Nervi, whereas the rationalism of form is, or has been, a part of the work of designers as dissimilar in taste as Le Corbusier and Philip Johnson. Only a designer of Mies van der Rohe's particular discipline has successfully combined the two strains.

In addition, there are other major tendencies in twentieth-century architecture which are inimicable to the seemingly pervasive rational attitude. A striking example is the subjective style of Antonio Gaudí, an architect once ignored but now highly regarded. In part stimulated by the structural rationalism of nineteenth-century medievalists like Viollet-le-Duc (Fig. 21a), Gaudí's style, in the last analysis, transcends materialistic limitations with a burst of frenzied, surrealist poetry (Fig. 19). Much of his formal subjectivism favoring molded, curvilinear shapes is also found in the work of Central European Expressionists like Mendelsohn (Fig. 20), Bartning (Fig. 21), and Hans Poelzig, men who enjoyed their greatest success in the early 1920's, just before the triumph of the International Style. While there may be little or nothing conceptually expressionistic intended in the new formalist architecture of the 1950's, its subjective, free forms recently have reappeared in the designs of Eero Saarinen and Jørn Utzon (Fig. 22), as well as in the newer buildings of Le Corbusier and Alvar Aalto. Indeed, the ultimate source of our current rhetorical curvilinear tradition lies in the *art nouveau* architecture of the 1890's, and it is an indication of contemporary taste that this style has regained a measure of respect and popularity during the last decade.

Another factor tending to obscure the rationalism of contemporary architecture, though

16. Otto Bartning. Steel Church. Cologne, 1928.

17, 18. J. J. P. Oud. Kiefhoek Housing Estate. Rotterdam, 1928–30.

19. Antonio Gaudí. Church of the Sagrada Familia. Barcelona, 1883–1926. Transverse section.

20. Eric Mendelsohn. Sketch for a church building. 1921.

less forcefully than the subjective, formal configurations discussed above, is the perennial re-emergence of academicism in one form or another. Although Le Corbusier's intellectual debt to the classic tradition is innocent of real academicism, other French architects, notably Tony Garnier and Auguste Perret, have been very close to this scholarly movement; in yet a different way, it appears in the work of Mies and his disciple, Philip Johnson. The academic point of view played an enormous role even in the individual stylistic development of Frank Lloyd Wright.[8] This is especially true of Wright's early designs, where a form of academicism provided a force of order and discipline to clarify the romantic, picturesque side of both his domestic and monumental architecture. It was Wright who first introduced an integrated twentieth-century style, integrated because it brought together many, if not all, of the varied tendencies of modern architecture. Indeed, it was Wright who first managed to rise above the limitations of his source material to create a personal, contemporary style in which the past was made to serve the present. The suggestiveness of his manner is apparent in the strength of his influence upon other twentieth-century architects, an influence which has reached well beyond the central masters of the International Style.

In retrospect, the International Style may still seem to be a kind of ideal moment, a period of peak inventiveness; but its uniqueness and isolated development no longer strike us as primary characteristics. Our liberation from the rather narrow view of the recent past has led to a more patient and even sympathetic consideration of aspects of nineteenth-century eclecticism. From this has come recognition of the almost sacrificial efforts required from several generations of earnest, determined architects before results could become manifest in a new architecture. Consequently, it is important to recognize the positive relationships that do exist between the ostensibly free architecture of the mid-twentieth century and the historicizing architecture of a century ago. Expansion of architectural modes during the 1950's has stimulated a reinvestigation and reinterpretation of earlier pre-1900 movements while, conversely, the renewed appreciation of these various tendencies has furthered recent creative developments.

Careful study would seem to indicate that there is no single building of the 1890's—the heyday of *art nouveau* and the immediate ancestor of today's radical architecture—that alone represents the specific inauguration of modern architecture. The origins of the self-consciously modernistic *art nouveau* are inextricably tied to the neo-medieval and academic traditions of the period 1860–90 with respect to both design and theory. This holds true whether this movement is interpreted as a simple and decorative period fashion or, instead, as the most significant artistic achievement of the *fin de siècle,* dominating major as well as minor design. However frivolously, *art nouveau* was indeed the first movement to reject the principles of revivalism and eclecticism, principles which occasionally had been challenged, but never effectively supplanted, in the course of the previous decades. In the work of Victor Horta and, to a lesser extent, in that of Henry van de Velde and Hector Guimard, there was an effort to reconcile the new technology of metal and glass with the lavish architectural fashions of the day. This effort certainly grew from a desire to express some sort of order from the fragmentary chaos of building and construction achievements.

During the nineteenth century, there had been a few attempts to synthesize the vast accumulation of historical, social, aesthetic, and technological data that was then becoming available. In effect, there were isolated efforts to reintegrate the rapidly diverging professions of architect and engineer, though none of these met with noteworthy success. This frustration is conspicuous in the writings and buildings of Viollet-le-Duc, whose knowledge of earlier building techniques led him to examine the seeming inability of contemporary architecture to create its own characteristic style. Despite his considerable intellectual insights, Viollet-le-Duc's effort to write a program for the creation of a modern style came to naught, although a detailed theory of structural rationalism was produced

21. Otto Bartning. Project for the "Star Church." 1924.

as a by-product of his labors.[9] His doctrines seem to have provoked a number of important architects active around 1900, and such diverse personalities as H. P. Berlage, Hector Guimard, Perret, Wright, van de Velde, and Horta were probably influenced by his writings. Even more important than this superficial contact between the younger generation of early twentieth-century architects and the writings of Viollet-le-Duc is the fact that the works of each artist represented an effort to make rational use of historical precedents in conjunction with the new possibilities of technology and industry. When this turn-of-the-century merger of old and new is recognized as a potent new creative methodology, the *art nouveau* of Horta (Fig. 24), the concrete structuralism of Perret (Fig. 25), and the prairie style of Wright (Fig. 2) can all be understood as significantly related events of a specific temporal moment in architectural development. This is true despite the extreme variety of surface appearance and individual mannerism found among the individual architects of those early years.

In many respects, the varied architectural innovations of 1900–14 appear to have more in common with the assorted activities of the 1950's and 1960's than with the disciplined ordered International Style of the intervening interwar period.[10] Both the earliest and the most recent phases of twentieth-century architecture supported a plethora of formal invention and were marked by a variety of outstanding personalities. By and large, however, the orientation of these creative developments was many-sided, ambiguous, and even inconsistent. In contrast, the International Style was dominated by a more limited number of individuals who, for a brief period, were working in parallel, if not identical, directions (Fig. 26). The noteworthy buildings of the 1920's—all unified in visual impact—were produced by a few men, whereas the architecture of the decade and a half before World War I was the work of a larger and more diverse group of individuals. This coalescence of architectural activity into relatively limited channels during the 1920's was, of course, the one factor that made it so immediately recognizable as a coherent style, *the* International Style.

21a. Eugène Emmanuel Viollet-le-Duc. Project for a Concert Hall. 1864.

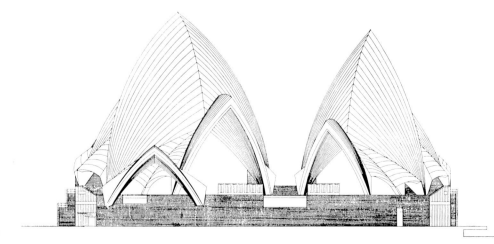

22. Jørn Utzon. Opera. Sydney, 1966 under construction. South elevation.

23. Joseph Maria Olbrich. Art Colony on the Mathilden-höhe. Darmstadt, 1901–8.

24. Victor Horta. Maison du Peuple. Brussels, 1896–99. Demolished 1965.

25. Auguste Perret. Apartment Block, 25bis Rue Franklin. Paris, 1902–3.

In contrast, the variety of personalities producing our contemporary architectural styles, as well as the ebb and flow of design fashions in the 1950's, have made it difficult to characterize the nature of architecture and the directions it has taken since the dispersal of the International Style architects before World War II. Unlike the leading architects of the 1920's, who seem to have had a unanimity of aim and interest, the designers of today seem to be sampling a greater number of possibilities without having developed so strong a concern for consistency or inner logic.

The paradoxes and inconsistencies presently seeming to beset the continued growth of a new style are also found in many of the most characteristic works of the first and second decades of the twentieth century. In the very first years of this century there were a number of remarkably syncretic achievements in radical European architecture. Typical of this many-faceted growth is the loosely related series of buildings erected by Joseph Maria Olbrich on the Mathildenhöhe, Darmstadt, 1901–8 (Fig. 23). Their aesthetic quality is not of the first order; in fact, they are decidedly inferior to even the least outstanding of Wright's contemporary American prairie houses and frequently equaled or even surpassed by the works of European contemporaries such as Charles Rennie Mackintosh, Josef Hoffmann, and Peter Behrens. As a picturesque assemblage of various historical motifs, incompletely digested, casually integrated, and reinterpreted with a seemingly diffident freedom, these Darmstadt Art Colony buildings are especially typical of that period's conflicts. The sources are both German and Italian, alternately medieval or Renaissance, but occasionally are early nineteenth-century romantic-classic in inspiration. The looseness of the ensemble almost seems a gentle parody of the methodology imputed to the masters of nineteenth-century eclecticism. For reasons that are not immediately apparent, however, the buildings possess a simple, relaxed consistency in the adaptation, if not in the choice, of forms, so that the final result also is related to the independent tendencies of later twentieth-century architecture.

To a greater or lesser degree, this permissive, liberal character appeared in most twentieth-century architecture from the turn of the century until World War I. Clearly, architecture of that period was in an experimental stage of stylistic growth. Without having thrown off all the habits of an earlier period, investigation and experimentation in new directions was nevertheless encouraged. From this stage of flux and even of uncertainty emerged the post-World War I wave of architectural radicalism, but with cautiousness replaced by a determination to seize creative initiative to a degree unknown in architecture for more than a century. Unlike contemporary painters, who had an established tradition of radicalism upon which to build—in effect, a revolution in permanence—the young architects of the post-World War I epoch had few precedents from which to develop. Even the fleeting, premature manifestations of *art nouveau* had fallen very much out of fashion at that time.

A cultivated independence and strident rejection of the conventional, often largely commercial, architectural world were among the most obvious aspects of the new work. The severity of its abstract formal discipline was only temporarily rivaled by the rhetorical, bombastic histrionics of expressionism. The inflexibility of its monastic, often anonymous, forms, and the institutional quality of its spatial effects, which were intensified by the use of smooth materials and sparse furnishings, represent the kind of extreme statement that will probably never cease to excite strong reactions. Nevertheless, there are at least occasional instances in which this heavily stressed originality masks a vital concern with the architecture of the past, a concern which operated in the design of a new building on many almost concealed levels. There were at least two architects of the 1920's, Mies van der Rohe and Le Corbusier, who seem to have been preoccupied with messages from the past even while they engaged in the development of an abstract, nonhistorical manner. In this respect, Le Corbusier's Villa Savoye, *Les Heures Claires,* Poissy, 1929–31 (Figs. 27, 28, 30, 31, 33), is especially revealing. As a contribution to the growth and culmination of the International Style, it is virtually without rival or peer, and is very likely the most consequential domestic monument in European architecture since the middle of the eighteenth century. Certainly it is the first European house to challenge successfully the pre-eminence of Wright's great prairie style dwellings of the early 1900's, a style perfected in the Robie House, Chicago, 1909 (Fig. 2).

The intense individuality of the Villa Savoye in no way prevents it from representing the aims of the entire epoch, but rather makes it a kind of ideal figurehead. Seen from a distance, this apparently solid, if flattened, cube, perched on thin, widely spaced stilts, strikes one as clumsy and ungainly, partly because of its unfamiliar proportions. Closer inspection, however, reveals that it is not the solid object it seems; instead, it is a largely open volume with thin surfaces uniformly perforated by a continuous-strip opening, whether the spaces behind are glazed and enclosed or are open-deck and terrace. In effect, the precariously balanced form is not just gravity-defying but is also habit-defying

26. Weissenhof Estate. Stuttgart, 1927. Coordinator: Ludwig Mies van der Rohe.

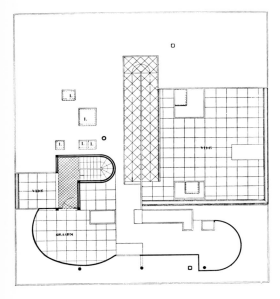

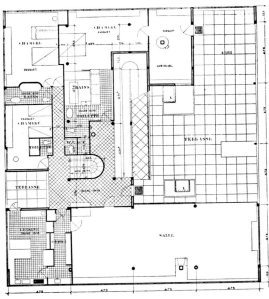

27, 28, 28a. Le Corbusier. Villa Savoye, "Les Heures Claires." Poissy, 1929–31. View, plans of terrace and main floor.

in every respect. The main floor, or *piano nobile,* which is comprised of both interior and exterior spaces (although no variation is introduced in the exterior design to indicate such distinctions), is, from an academic-classic point of view, the nominal "entablature" of the design; the vestigial "peristyle" of slender concrete columns forms a portico sheltering nothing more dignified than the garage, entry, and service areas below. The effect seems self-consciously anticlassical, indeed almost parodistic in intent. Up to this point, every feature has been comprehensible in terms of the particular formal inversions and paradoxes employed by the masters of the new style. Yet, in spite of everything, the Villa Savoye breathes a latent and secret Hellenism which can be explained only by reference to the famous passages devoted to the Athenian Acropolis in *Vers une Architecture.*[11] The entire construction and its setting evoke a variety of stimuli, both architectural and non-architectural, providing a receptive viewer with almost bewildering allusions.

The vocabulary by which Le Corbusier realizes this self-contradictory paraphrase of the classic, Mediterranean tradition is almost literally borrowed from the contemporary forms of an ocean liner's superstructure. The result is a "sea-side villa" in the machine aesthetic sense of the word,[12] but one located far from the shore. Instead, the Villa Savoye stands isolated and unsheltered at the top of a gentle rise of ground surrounded by a tree-bordered meadow. Bearing in mind Le Corbusier's Swiss origins, it is not inappropriate to imagine his house as a steel and concrete version of a neolithic lake dwelling from his homeland, stranded high and dry away from water. At the same time, its volumes and spaces also suggest that period's strong links between architecture and painting. The main deck of the Villa Savoye—Le Corbusier's machine-age answer to the legendary hanging garden—can be compared with the familiar table top in a Cubist still life. The situation here is roughly analogous to a type of picture frequently painted by Picasso and his fellow Catalan, Juan Gris (Fig. 29), during the 1920's. In that type of composition the view to the rear of the picture opens out through a window, providing the spectator with a controlled, regulated view of landscape or seascape beyond. In much the same way, an occupant of the Villa Savoye has framed vistas of "background" surroundings which are determined by the glass wall of the living room and the continuous, banded fenestration which surrounds three sides of the exterior cube.[13]

Under other circumstances, especially with a knowledge of the artist's acknowledged stimuli, this evocation of a Cubist still life with landscape vanishes and is replaced with associations and analogies drawn from many aspects of the classic and pre-classic Mediterranean tradition. The floating deck can be comprehended as an artifical, acropolis-like platform, the court of an imaginary Mycenaean citadel in front of a glass-walled megaron.[14] The ramps moving up within the volume from the lower level to the top recall the narrow, walled approach leading to the propylaea of a stronghold like that at Tiryns. Yet these analogies, so poetically evoked by Le Corbusier's masterpiece, are never so specifically concerned with the incidentals of a given monument or ruin, or even of specific periodic or ethnic types within the Mediterranean architectural tradition, that they make the building historicizing in the conventional sense of the word. Indeed, had the architect himself not written earlier of these antique traditions, such associations would scarcely be justified, for these subtle analogies are as unstable as the reflections of a kaleidoscope.

To take the analysis one step further, the Villa Savoye can evoke Palladio's archetypal Villa Rotonda (Fig. 32) without in any sense translating Palladian ideals into contemporary terms. In effect, the Villa Savoye permits us to see the ideal forms of the central-plan, late-Renaissance house inverted and turned inside out. Whereas each building is an elevated, isolated form, situated at the top of a slope, the staircases of the Palladian monument, opening outward to the four points of the compass, are transformed by Le Corbusier in a concentrated single series of reciprocal diagonal ramps at the center of his volume; the central dome of the Villa Rotonda is replaced by the very real "dome of heaven" that opens above the wind-sheltered hanging gardens of the Villa Savoye. In plan and in section, the spaces of these two villas have literally nothing in common; yet, in spite of this fact, each interior provides a visual framework and bodily shelter for its human occupants that establishes an extraordinarily similar relationship between man and his environment.

The predisposed beholder will of course have other valid associations to offer in this context. The importance of this demonstration, however, goes far beyond the obvious fact that Le Corbusier had so thoroughly imbibed the essence and totality of the Mediterranean tradition that he could stimulate our minds to leap in one step from Tiryns in the second millennium B.C. to Vicenza in the sixteenth century A.D. while meditating upon a single building. Infinitely more significant is the even larger integration of reference and creation that has been effected. In the buildings of Olbrich's Darmstadt Art Colony (Fig. 23), there was a similar variety of historical references, but these were more a matter of surface resemblance than of inner, spiritual suggestiveness. As we have already noted, this earlier series of forms derived from the past (with personal variations) but was barely unified in a tentative and still somewhat re-creative style. In effect, Olbrich deliberately used the past in a series of free, if rather indirect, quotations. The work of Le Corbusier, in

29. Juan Gris. Le Canigou. Oil on canvas, 25³/₄″ × 39⁵/₈″. 1921. Albright-Knox Art Gallery, Buffalo, N.Y.

30, 31. Le Corbusier. Villa Savoye. Poissy, 1929–31. Solarium and main floor terrace.

contrast, sublimates the past to an unprecedented degree; the images function as ideational impulses buried deep within the tightly packed, integrated form. The result is highly original and personal in its outward appearance. Clearly, the degree of stylistic and creative integration, in addition to technical solutions and the expression of a machine aesthetic, is of extraordinary intensity in the Villa Savoye. For this reason, the Villa Savoye illustrates the degree of concentrated classic integration which was momentarily possible at the "high" point in modern architecture even though it went unrecognized at the time, and was a strong contrast to the loose, rambling, still partly eclectic architecture of the period before 1914, exemplified by the works of Mackintosh, Hoffmann, Behrens, Adolf Loos, Hans Poelzig, and numerous others, as well as of Olbrich.

The unusual integration accomplished in the Villa Savoye, however, was fragile and momentary. Perhaps because of its inherent inner tensions, this outspoken clarification of aim and purpose in contemporary architectural terms, even though riddled with secret recollections of the past, was doomed to a brief existence. Perhaps, also, it was fitting (although from a conventional point of view, paradoxical) that at its classic moment of fulfillment modern architecture achieved not serenity but, instead, a tense, precarious, mannerist kind of unity.[15] It was in the nature of its volatile, seemingly unstable forms that the achievement of the International Style never came to rest in a static equilibrium. In the light of subsequent developments, one can speak not of a decline but of a deterioration of ideals which led to a series of new statements and formulations.

The first signs of the approaching rigidity, or the concomitant relaxation, of the new style came with surprising alacrity. One of the innovations of twentieth-century architecture has been the architect's concern with problems of urban design and with the creation of large-scale popular housing. It is in these areas, in works designed as early as the late 1920's, that one can see the reduction of the new mode to the level of standardization. True, architecture is in considerable measure a social art as well as an art intimately related to technological potential; and in many of the large-scale, unexecuted projects of the 1920's—again the proposals of Le Corbusier are practically without peer with regard to imaginativeness—there is a touch of the sublime. Under most circumstances, however, large-scale housing tends to be the prose of architecture. The notable series of German housing projects that came into being during the twilight of the Weimar Republic, culminating not only in the achievements of Gropius, but also in those of Hans Scharoun, Bruno Taut, Ernst May, and Otto Haesler, rival in quantity and occasionally in quality the works of J. J. P. Oud and his contemporaries in Holland. Significantly, none of them reach the aspiring level of Sant' Elia's prewar Futurist projects, or those of Mies van der Rohe and Le Corbusier of the 1920's. Nonetheless, they provide numerous instances of a spontaneous, vernacular International Style, one brought forth with the intent of appealing to popular needs and tastes rather than to the educated sensibilities of an elite whose taste had been formed through contact with contemporary painting and literature. They are probably as historically significant as the knowledgeable *capriccios* of Le Corbusier, like the Villa Savoye; but they can never provide so satisfying an index of the style's potential nor of its ultimate significance.

Unfortunately this line of popular, vernacular development, so promising in German architecture in the early 1930's, was abruptly terminated in 1933 as a consequence of the political upheaval. The almost immediate return to outwardly conventional modes of expression made the situation for modern architects in Germany so hopeless that the greatest figures, Gropius, Mies van der Rohe, and Mendelsohn, became political exiles. Others sought, without lasting success, to pursue their careers in the U. S. S. R. The reactionary reflex, however, was not isolated and was subsequently as ruthlessly sustained under the Russian as under the German dictatorship. In Italy, the Fascists simultaneously seemed to encourage both a modernist and a reactionary trend. Understandably, much of the conservative architecture of Europe of that time did not retreat any further into the

32. Andrea Palladio. Villa Rotonda. Near Vicenza, 1550–52.

past than the ambivalent, quasi-historical architecture of the first decade of the twentieth century, a period which provided most of the "new" formal vocabulary. (One hesitates to speak of "inspiration" in this context, for most of the reactionary work of the 1930's lacked the original creative spark of the early 1900's.) Even in nominally republican France, the hopes for a new architecture were dashed. Le Corbusier's biography of those years reveals a long succession of rejected projects, interrupted only by the Swiss Pavilion of the *Cité Universitaire,* 1930–32 (Figs. 34, 97, 98), and the obscurely located Armée du Salut, 1932–33 (Fig. 35), both in Paris. Consequently, many of the masters of European architecture were largely unrepresented by actual construction throughout much of the 1930's. For most of them, this hiatus occurred at a time when they had reached a degree of maturity and experience that would have greatly profited from an intensified, rather than a reduced, scale of activity. On the other hand, their involuntary withdrawal from construction may well have provided them with an opportunity to rest and reconsider the direction of their efforts, and this interruption may well have influenced the subsequent second blossoming in the work of two of these architects, Mies and Le Corbusier.

Despite the interruption in the work of its originators, the development of the International

33. Le Corbusier. Villa Savoye. Poissy, 1929–31.

34. Le Corbusier. Pavillon Suisse, Cité Universitaire. Paris, 1930–32.

35. Le Corbusier. Cité de Refuge de l'Armée du Salut. Paris, 1932–33.

Style proceeded, but with results that led to a gradual dilution of the style's original severity and balanced inner tension. Probably the most important new personality to emerge from the ranks of continental architects at that time was Alvar Aalto of Finland. His work of the 1930's, in particular, Mairea, a country house at Noormarkku, 1938–39 (Fig. 36), and the cellulose factory and row housing at Sunila, 1937–39, represents a relaxing of the more rigid geometric tensions characteristic of the previous decade. Aalto's personal style offered more varied surface textures, softer, more picturesque silhouettes, and less sharp and clear juxtapositions of forms. From the point of view of the 1920's, it was a retreat from the severity of the original modern discipline; but it was also an enrichment of the style from which other developments would grow in the period after World War II. Furthermore, it was a major symptom of the atmosphere of *détente* typical of the concluding phase of the International Style.

Certain aspects of Aalto's work, an offshoot from the severe geometry of the International Style, were echoed in the work of architects in various parts of Europe in the late 1930's. In Italy, the Tuberculosis Clinic at Alessandria, 1936–38 (Fig. 37), the work of Ignazio Gardella, is, on the exterior, a volume of closed formal regularity that might satisfy the as-

36. Alvar Aalto. Villa Mairea. Noormarkku, near Björneborg, 1938–39.

pirations of Mies van der Rohe. Its departure from the severe International Style is perhaps best illustrated by its principal façade, facing south, which is sheltered by a perforated brick screen and is further punctuated with glazed strip windows of modest size. Areas of glass brick provide further variety within the insistent regularity of the building's silhouette. In Holland, similar modifying tendencies are seen in a different local interpretation of modernism. The 1939 Amstel Station (Fig. 38) in suburban Amsterdam, by H. G. J. Schelling, is a case in point. Here, the familiar glass wall is employed, not in the context of cubic geometry but in a form largely denatured by a conventional pitched roof and by rather intimate, pseudo-romantic detailing. Such compromises seem to anticipate the even more self-effacing architecture of Scandinavia which came to international attention shortly after 1945 under the banner of new empiricism.

No consideration of this terminal phase of the International Style is complete without a look at Frank Lloyd Wright's Kaufmann House, Falling Water, at Bear Run, Pennsylvania, 1936–37 (Fig. 39).[16] This widely publicized and admired house brings together not only the many strands of Wright's personal manner but, equally, the ensemble of nineteenth- and twentieth-century architecture. In Falling Water, the romantic, picturesque, organic tradition of domestic architecture which had formed the mainspring of Anglo-American residential construction for over a century was dramatically blended with the clear, exacting forms of the new continental avant-garde. In addition to being a summation of contemporary *style,* Falling Water represents the abstract, expressive potential of modern design, especially in the defiant gesture of its perch above the water course that gives it its name. Indeed, it represents a technological challenge to the forms and forces of nature in the way that the smooth forms of the cantilevered balconies echo the rock formations. Its combination of concrete with native stone is another endeavor to reconcile machine aesthetic forms with rough-hewn natural materials. Consequently, Falling Water is one of the lyrical achievements of modern architecture, one which, like the Villa Savoye, rises above the workaday level in its expressive and formalistic significance and thus provides a magnified index of the aims and aspirations of its particular moment. There is a detached quality to Falling Water which is not characteristic of the highly personal sensations common in most of Wright's major works. Perhaps the balance between the rational and the organic is so carefully studied that the two forces tend to cancel each other out, and the effects of this house are achieved by an overly self-conscious study and analysis of the problems involved.

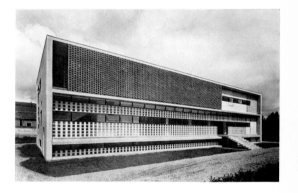

More spontaneous and essentially Wrightian in its poetry is another great house of the late 1930's, his own winter home, Taliesin West (Fig. 42), near Phoenix, Arizona, begun in 1938. The spaces and forms of this rambling house are indicative of Wright's inward, less deliberate response to a set of stimuli, and it therefore seems to be a more fundamental statement of Wright's *personal* inclinations at this time. In addition, the particular cultural significance of Taliesin West and its role as a meeting place for various forces and influences that have decisively shaped its creator's life and work, both American pre-Columbian and western European, is here more inescapably present.[17] Taliesin West goes beyond and behind the expression of the International Style *détente* to a more personal, detached meaning in a way that cannot be matched by the more generalized and impersonal Falling Water, a document more indicative of the general history of modern architecture.

Further modification of the International Style occurred in the U. S. A. during the late 1930's, with the renewed activity of Walter Gropius in association with Marcel Breuer, a former student at the Bauhaus. There is a sense of growing maturity and relaxation in Gropius' own house in Lincoln, Massachusetts, 1937 (Fig. 40), where the austere, planar shapes of the 1920's come in contact with the native New England vernacular tradition of wood frame houses. The results have never been sufficiently appreciated, for the house is perhaps a bit diffident and passive for partisans of an earlier, more deliberately com-

37. Ignazio Gardella. Tuberculosis Clinic. Alessandria, 1936–38.

38. H. G. J. Schelling. Amstel Station. Amsterdam, 1939.

39. Frank Lloyd Wright. Kaufmann House, "Falling Water." Bear Run, Pennsylvania, 1936–37.

posed formalism; in comparison with contemporary work by Aalto or Wright, the Gropius house seems dry and even unimaginative. Nevertheless, it does possess, in a modified fashion, many of the simple, prosaic virtues of earlier Gropius architecture. This house, with its wooden siding painted an abstract and pristine white, is followed by a small vacation house built by Gropius and Breuer for Henry G. Chamberlain in Wayland, Massachusetts, 1940 (Fig. 41), in which a rough, partially organic character is achieved by unfinished vertical fir boarding contrasted with a rough masonry basement. At this point, the geometry of the International Style is all but abandoned, and it is possible to mark the end of a heroic phase of architectural activity with this small, but ultimately influential, house.

If the *détente* in the architecture of the 1930's stood for a dilution or even a retreat from the original modernism of the previous decade, it also inspired enrichments. The borderline between dilution and enrichment is a narrow one, in some measure related to the prejudices and preferences of the critic. Through the direct influence and stimulus of Le Corbusier, the new architecture was exported to South America at roughly the same time that it was brought to the U. S. A. Its first tangible manifestation was in the familiar Ministry of Education and Health, Rio de Janeiro, 1937–43 (Fig. 43), the work of Lúcio Costa, Oscar Niemeyer, Carlos Leão, Jorge Moreira, Affonso Eduardo Reidy, and Ernani

Vasconcelos, with Le Corbusier as the consultant who largely influenced the general character and direction of the building's style. Because Le Corbusier lacked any large-scale commissions of his own at this time, the Rio Ministry was the chief indication before the post-World War II period of the direction in which his monumental style was evolving. It was with this building that he introduced for the first time his modification of the glass curtain wall, a device often unsuitable for interior illumination because of glare and the problems of heat control. Shadow boxes, or *brises-soleils,* produced a kind of "façade in depth" which sheltered the glazed surface from much of the sun's direct rays yet allowed less strong light inside.[18] The outward appearance of the building was thus decisively altered, giving it a more varied surface through the rhythms created by the shadows themselves and by the adjustable louvers. At the same time, this modification and innovation was a strengthening, not a weakening, of the original attitudes and shapes of modern architecture.

If this was the direction in which modifications were taking place in the public side of Le Corbusier's art in the mid-1930's, there was a private and personal development that in a number of ways was a full-fledged negation, even though a temporary one, of the aspirations of the International Style. His small weekend house near Paris, 1935 (Fig. 45), seems disturbing and mysterious in contrast to the extroverted self-confidence of his elevated, earth-liberated forms of the late 1920's and early 1930's. He tells us that the "principle imposed upon this small house situated behind a curtain of trees was that it be as little visible as possible,"[19] in effect affirming our immediate visual impression that this construction is a deliberate contradiction of the principles so boldly realized in the Villa Savoye. Previously the form and space of the house were thrust up above the ground—in effect one lived on an elevated, paved platform floating in mid-air—but the weekend house near Paris willfully inverts this principle. In this house, living goes on underneath a structure of Catalan vaults (about eight feet high on the exterior); on top, there is a new kind of roof-terrace, marked by the undulating extrados of the concrete vaults which have been implanted with turf. The result suggests a subterranean cavern and constitutes a retreat (of formal and spiritual implications) from the exposed, gravity-defying decks character-istic of Le Corbusier's work a decade earlier. Whereas the Corbusian aspects of the Rio Ministry of Education and Health indicated a line of smooth transition from the planar geometry of the 1920's to the more robust, tactile forms of his post-World War II style, the weekend house marks a temporary interruption, a necessary, if passing, phase of

40. Walter Gropius. Gropius House. Lincoln, Massachu-setts, 1937.

41. Walter Gropius and Marcel Breuer. Chamberlain House. Wayland, Massachusetts, 1940.

42. Frank Lloyd Wright. Taliesin West. Paradise Valley, near Phoenix, Arizona, 1938.

introspection and self-questioning. This symbolic withdrawal quickly became the spring-board for a new start, the meaning of which became explicit only toward the end of the 1940's. In some cases Le Corbusier developed the negative theme of the weekend house near Paris as in the Jaoul Houses, Neuilly-sur-Seine, 1952–56 (Figs. 44, 159); in other cases he re-engaged in the development of the air-borne terrace landscape, notably in the roof of the *Unité d'Habitation*, Marseilles, 1946–52 (Fig. 46).

No less interesting is the evolution of Mies van der Rohe during this same decade of the 1930's. His development in the previous decade had culminated in the German Pavilion (Figs. 47, 48) at the Barcelona Exhibition of 1929, a purely decorative structure which, in its own way, was as characteristic an achievement of that decade as was the exactly contemporary Villa Savoye. As a structure, the Barcelona Pavilion was dominated by a horizontal roof slab supported internally on eight thin, chrome columns set to one corner of a travertine stylobate, the remainder of which was occupied by a reflecting pool. Underneath this slab ran a series of marble walls, the disposition of which was only partially determined by the grid of columns. The effect of the trim horizontal and vertical planes was one of ineffable spatial flow suggested by the relations of the openings and the glazed surfaces enclosing this ornamental interior. While the placing of the eight interior columns provided a kind of academic grid pattern to the plan, the whole effect was domi-nated by the apparently ambiguous effects of surface and space which suggested in an elegant fashion the ambiguities and paradoxes that Cubist painters had, earlier in the twentieth century, attributed to the relationship between solid form and surrounding space. In addition, Mies's use of overhanging, hovering planar forms in the Barcelona Pavilion seems equally indebted to the precedents established by Wright in such works as the 1909 Robie House (Fig. 2).

These dynamic qualities are to be found, although in a somewhat more restrained fashion, in the Tugendhat House, Brno, Czechoslovakia, 1930 (Figs. 6, 7), and in a later series of unexe-cuted projects from 1930–35. In these designs, however, the development seems to have been in the direction of more static spaces and less open, more self-contained, forms. The culmination of this development does not become apparent until Mies's move to the U. S. A. and the formulation of his master plan in 1939–40 for the new campus of Armour Institute, Chicago (now the Illinois Institute of Technology) (Figs. 49–51). In contrast to the increasing suppleness and freedom in the forms of Le Corbusier and the growing diffidence and

43. Lúcio Costa, Oscar Niemeyer, Carlos Leão, Jorge Ma-chado Moreira, Affonso Eduardo Reidy, and Ernani Vas-concelos. Consultant architect: Le Corbusier. Ministry of Education and Health. Rio de Janeiro, 1937–43.

44. Le Corbusier. Jaoul Houses. Neuilly-sur-Seine, 1952–56.

45. Le Corbusier. Weekend House. La Celle-St. Cloud, near Paris, 1935.

46. Le Corbusier. Unité d'Habitation. Marseilles, 1946–52.
Detail of the roof.

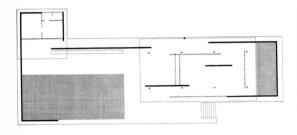

47, 48. Ludwig Mies van der Rohe. German Pavilion at
the International Exhibition. Barcelona, 1929. Floor plan
and view.

relaxation in those of Gropius in the late 1930's, Mies turned to a severe geometric discipline of form and detail, a discipline which developed to peak intensity the one aspect of the original International Style most consistently rejected by other architects in the *détente* of the 1930's. Ignoring the liberalizing, softening tendencies practiced by so many other architects, Mies evolved a stern cubic formalism. Employing the characteristic metal and glass detailing of his earlier work, though more sober and dour in spirit at I. I. T., Mies avoided the picturesque instability and implied movement characteristic of the style of his early maturity.

The final scheme for the Illinois Institute of Technology, evolved in 1940 but tragically modified in subsequent execution, is a remarkably self-effacing group of buildings. These are stern and simple rectilinear volumes fitted to an over-all grid, or module, pattern: $24' \times 24' \times 12'$. Compared to his earlier open style, these new forms are closed and static, anticipations of his rectilinear metal and glass skyscraper designs of the late 1940's and early 1950's. It is significant that this new "late" style of Mies is developed not from sudden inspirations or emotional conflicts, as was the case in the contemporary work of Le Corbusier, but rather from a slowly evolving contraction of his earlier volatile style into something outwardly almost conservative, and certainly more universal, in its application. This steadfast reduction of a relatively complex idiom into one more general and regularized is in remarkable contrast to the more obviously subjective works of Wright and Le Corbusier at that time, and to the looser, less precise forms of Aalto and Gropius. In every respect, Mies's architecture seems out of phase with the dominant trends of the late 1930's and the early 1940's.

Paradoxically, part of the basis for Mies's new style involved as much a retreat to historical sources and an evasion of certain typically new features of the 1920's as did Le Corbusier's altogether different work of this "twilight" decade. The grid system used by Mies for the layout of the Illinois Institute of Technology was, in all probability, derived from the plates

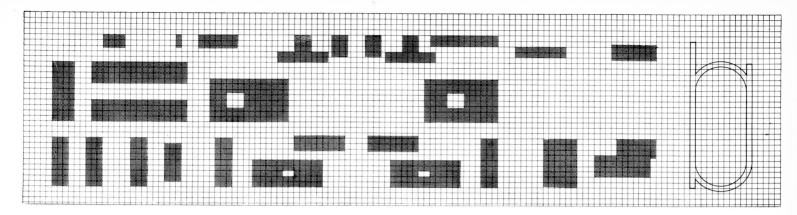

of the *Précis des Leçons d'Architecture* (1802–05), by the French neo-classic architect-theorist J.-N.-L. Durand, Professor of Architecture at the Paris *École Polytechnique* in the early years of the nineteenth century. Mies uses the grid pattern to unify, and there is only the most limited sense of variety. Nor is there any dramatic or suggestive interconnection between either the building forms themselves or the remarkably static, ordered spaces which they surround.

These are only some of the qualities of modern architecture that were apparent on the eve of World War II. The 1930's had been a cooling-off period after the major accomplishments of the International Style during its first hour. The development of architecture over the first forty years of the twentieth century does not follow a constantly rising, or even consistently regular, line of development. Whereas the first generation of architects gradually liberated themselves from many of the excesses of nineteenth-century historicism in order to follow personal lines of development, it required the combined efforts of

49. Ludwig Mies van der Rohe. Illinois Institute of Technology. Chicago. Final site plan of 1939–40.

51. Ludwig Mies van der Rohe. Metallurgy and Chemical Engineering Building, Illinois Institute of Technology. Chicago, 1946.

50. Ludwig Mies van der Rohe. Chemistry Building (left), and Metallurgy and Chemical Engineering Building (right), Illinois Institute of Technology. Chicago, 1946.

the generation that reached full maturity in the 1920's to arrive at a new style that could rival the far-reaching originality achieved in twentieth-century painting and music some years earlier. With the new architectural style scarcely unveiled, and with its popular acceptance far from assured, the 1930's saw a number of ambiguous, tangential, reactionary, and negative developments, which were not always answered by firm, creative responses growing out of the main line of the International Style. Consequently, that decade was a period of readjustment and, in certain quarters, of enervation. The initial burst of enthusiasm was, in part, very quickly compromised, if only because of the abrupt appearance of the new architecture in the previous decade, and its dogmatic, uncompromising severity of form and doctrine. These latter qualities were easily exaggerated and became fuel for a variety of reactions. The war of 1939–45 slowed but did not basically change the pattern of architectural evolution at this juncture.

# Chapter II
## War and Postwar Developments: 1940-50

By 1940 modern architecture, which a decade earlier had seemed on the verge of a major triumph, was in a confused, disorganized state.[1] Exile was the fate of the major German architects Gropius, Mies, and Mendelsohn, while estrangement was the lot of those like Le Corbusier who were able to remain in their habitual places of work. De Stijl had virtually expired with the death of its animating spirit, van Doesburg, in 1931; the Bauhaus was shut down two years afterward; and no new organizations or institutions arose to take their places. As a final insult, dilution and vulgarization of the International Style ideals gradually prevailed in countless designs of the 1930's, many of which were illustrated in periodicals that had heretofore either attacked or ignored the new architecture.[2]

Although the outstanding designers of the 1920's had reached an age of accumulated experience by the following decade, wisdom that should have guaranteed that the 1930's would have been the epoch of their greatest fulfillment, these architects were, in fact, virtually unemployed. Their few small, if significant buildings simply do not compensate for the unrealized monumental projects like Le Corbusier's Palace of the Soviets or Mies's *Reichsbank* (Figs. 52, 52a). Their talents were squandered by a combination of economic, political, and artistic factors at the very moment when their capacities for achievement were at their peak. Consequently, the ultimate personal fulfillments of Mies and Le Corbusier were postponed for a decade and more, and that of Gropius seemingly permanently frustrated.

True, this epoch witnessed the beginning of yet another rejuvenation in the career of Frank Lloyd Wright, whose forceful and still-unappreciated work of the 1920's was largely unrelated to European modernism at that time, even though his earlier designs had exerted an incalculable influence on the formation of the International Style. Now, somewhat belatedly, Wright became a participant in the style itself, beginning with Falling Water, 1936 (Fig. 39).[3] However, Wright's use of the familiar interlocking geometrical patterns of the 1920's at this late date was almost "archaeological." Significantly, he was simultaneously "reviving" the vocabulary of Germanic Expressionism in the offices of the S. C. Johnson Company, Racine (Figs. 56, 57), where tubular glass and pliant, rounded forms evoke memories of several buildings of the previous decade by Eric Mendelsohn. These apparent contradictions in formal vocabulary are indicative of the self-conscious, retrospective nature of modern architecture in the late 1930's—a tendency of great significance for the future. Wright's diverse and even contradictory interests at this juncture are, however, made comprehensible in the light of the varied and occasionally uncertain qualities in the work of Mies and Le Corbusier at this time, features that are often in reaction to their stylistic norms of the 1920's.[4]

Understandably, World War II was a disruptive element of vast magnitude, but it is possible to overestimate its immediate as well as its ultimate impact, since it came at a time when the inner growth of the modern movement was slowed by self-doubt, introspection, and malicious criticism. Furthermore, the political situation had already caused it to become an outcast in most of Central and Eastern Europe. Although by 1950, at the end of the immediate postwar period, there was a marked sense of new and renewed

52. Le Corbusier. Project for the Palace of the Soviets. Moscow, 1931.

52a. Ludwig Mies van der Rohe. Project for the Reichsbank. Berlin, 1933.

enthusiasm for the causes of modern architecture,[5] the situation five years earlier can be characterized as one of marked disenchantment with the severe style of twenty years before. In effect, the post-1945 period was a continuation of the atmosphere prevailing just before the war. It was not a moment of revolution, a break with the past, such as had occurred after the armistice in 1918. The surprisingly conservative tendency after 1945 is discernible in the opinions and ideas expressed in the magazines of the day, as well as in the relatively small number of buildings built during the entire decade.

From the publications of the period, two characteristic phrases stand out. The term "new empiricism," applied to the gentle, self-effacing new architecture of Scandinavia, notably Sweden, was given extremely sympathetic consideration by the editors of the English magazine, *The Architectural Review*.[6] The other phrase, *"architettura organica,"* was an Italianization of Frank Lloyd Wright's well-known ideal, proposed in the title of a widely read book by the historian Bruno Zevi.[7] Both slogans manifested an outwardly romantic point of view, rejecting the formal and theoretical extremes of the 1920's. These rejections of a specific architectural taste grew out of the various tendencies that had appeared during the 1930's, and they indicated an intensified disenchantment with the inherited aesthetic of modernism developed during the 1920's. The message borne by the empiric and organic slogans of the mid-1940's, however, was not the same as that of the reaction governed by ominous, ugly politics of Communism, Fascism, or Nazism in the previous decade. Instead, it was an effort to discover an alternate path toward the creation of a new style that could ignore, rather than resolve, certain pressing demands of the modern situation, especially those relating to industrialism, the city, and to novel concepts of form and space. This somewhat escapist attitude was augmented by a parallel effort, encouraged by the editors of *The Architectural Review,* to stimulate an interest in the English picturesque tradition of the eighteenth and early nineteenth centuries. In all likelihood, this was the first sustained effort in the history of modern architecture to consciously reassess some aspect of the past. In contrast to Le Corbusier's concealed utilization, in the 1920's, of a particular formal configuration from the Mediterranean tradition as a point of departure for some new and unheralded creation (sources that were not recognized at the time) the picturesque "revival" of the 1940's was a more deliberate maneuver. In effect, it sought to emphasize the sources and roots of the new architecture rather than its more iconoclastic and creative aspects.

By the end of the war, the various publications that had carried the message of the International Style a decade or two earlier were, for the most part, defunct.[8] As a widely circulated periodical dealing with ideas and points of view as well as with purely professional matters, *The Architectural Review* virtually had the field to itself. Its development of a new interest in traditional picturesque modes of expression was therefore of immediate influence as well as of scholarly importance. Much of the *Review's* concern for the architecture of the past understandably was stimulated by wartime damage to historical monuments, Gothic, Georgian, or Victorian, in the bomb-torn English cities, and the magazine did not hesitate to assume an editorial position concerning the treatment of the ruins of certain historically important buildings. Deliberately citing eighteenth-century taste with respect to such phenomenon as crumbling architectural remains—a taste which had gone so far as to encourage contrivance of artificial ruins to gratify its thirst for decay—the *Review* called for the preservation without restoration of the actual bombed-and burned-out carcasses of certain of Wren's city churches. "Ruins need not be a disfigurement," it was pointed out; indeed "they can be of great picturesque beauty." In this fashion, the interest in the picturesque point of view gained specific topicality. Together with other similar themes, this point of view was presented in other issues of *The Architectural Review* with the result that a change of values on a broad front was immediately perceptible.[9]

This attitude governed the design and placement of Sir Basil Spence's new cathedral in

Coventry (Fig. 53), completed in 1961, but commissioned as the result of a competition held a decade earlier. The new structure was placed to one side of the landscaped ruins of the Gothic nave and tower of the old cathedral, which had been gutted by the ferocious German bombardment of Coventry. Even in war-torn Germany, a similar effort was made to preserve the façade of an old, mostly destroyed building in the construction of the new Münster Stadttheater, designed by Harald Deilmann, Max von Hausen, Ortwin Rave, and Werner Ruhnau (Fig. 53a). This is especially surprising because it occurred as late as 1954–56, when the neo-picturesque had largely spent itself. Thus, in opposition to the precise, smooth new forms that had been representative of the taste of the 1920's, the postwar years exhibited a preference for something quite the opposite. In its several belated manifestations, this preference ventured beyond the merely coarse and rough to embrace the decayed and ruined.

The significance of this resurrection of the picturesque, which came simultaneously with the debut of new empiricism and *architettura organica,* is manifold. Doubtless, the new interest in the past gave sustenance and encouragement to the empiric and organic tendencies growing out of the *détente* of the 1930's. It is equally clear that these new manners in modern architecture in turn stimulated a renewed exploration of the romantic past. Under these circumstances, the revival of the picturesque in the mid-1940's must be interpreted as a retrospective, though not a reactionary, tendency, conservative in tone if only because of its superficial disagreement with the rigors of rational or functional styles issuing from the 1920's. When seen from a narrow point of view, the picturesque revival may appear to have been a kind of retreat interrupting the development of modern architecture, but when the context is expanded, it is possible to arrive at a different conclusion. Although new, abstract modes of architectural design belong almost exclusively to the twentieth century, the styles and traditions that form the modern movement have evolved from the cumulative experience and experimentation of the preceding *two* centuries. In effect, *all* of the architecture of the twentieth century, irrespective of its outward modes of presentation, is an outgrowth of the romantic movement and its later nineteenth-century successors. The shallow, so-called traditional architecture of our own century is one apparent development from the eclectic traditions of the recent past. Equally, if less obviously, the more significant avant-garde movements, whether expressionist or rationalist in orientation, represent an expansion of tendencies discernible as far back as the mid-eighteenth century. One of these earlier tendencies was the picturesque, and its "revival" in the 1940's should be regarded as an attitude native to the new tradition, and not as something extraneous, the resuscitation of which would inevitably produce yet another rootless, hybrid, historical style.

In its eighteenth-century heyday, the picturesque was not a style in any of the customarily accepted senses of the word, but instead was a visual attitude, an aesthetic system borrowed from contemporary practices in literature and painting. When applied to architecture and the allied art of landscaping, it provided a stylistically neutral but emotionally stimulating frame of reference for the varied and almost simultaneous revivals of the late eighteenth century. Thus, the picturesque—considered as a distinctive kind of post-Baroque composing and massing of forms and as the arrestingly informal, natural siting of a building—became the means of reconciling the superficial diversity of architectural "styles" rampant at that time. In this sense, the renewed interest in the picturesque, encouraged by writers of the mid-1940's, allowed contemporary architecture to incorporate a significant facet of its own distinctive past with the mainstream of modernism, without thereby raising the spector of superficial stylistic revivalism. It should be remembered, however, that this movement came not from architects themselves, but from the journalistic fringes of their profession. The historically-minded critics of architecture made their voices heard once again, after a generation which had professed to outlaw the study of history. In effect, modern architecture during the 1920's and 1930's had tried frantically to

53. Sir Basil Spence. Cathedral of St. Michael. Coventry, completed 1961. Model.

53a. Harald Deilmann, Max von Hausen, Ortwin Rave, and Werner Ruhnau. Municipal Theater. Münster, 1954–56.

54. Le Corbusier. Project for the League of Nations. Geneva, 1927–28.

disown its venerable heritage, but now, after 1940, it rediscovered distinctive roots in an increasingly willful, occasionally pedantic fashion.

By 1945, the architecture of the International Style was under frequent attack for its austerely "functional" character. (Ironically, this very functionalism, originally supposed to have been one of its virtues, was largely fictitious.) Actually, it was the simple, scoured surfaces and the antiseptic, institution-like spaces that had fallen from favor. The architecture of the 1920's, with its commitment to an unadorned, astringent geometry, seemed totally out of phase with the rediscovered picturesque mode of soft surfaces and negligent massing. Furthermore, the much-advertised materialistic and self-generative formalism of the old machine aesthetic seemed entirely incompatible with the more homely virtues of the romantic aesthetic. On the other hand, the irregular layouts and the hovering, unstable geometry characteristic of such movements as De Stijl and of specific masterpieces as Gropius' Dessau Bauhaus (Figs. 13, 13a) and Mies's Barcelona Pavilion (Figs. 47, 48) owed an ultimate, if indirect, debt to the asymmetrical compositional principles of the eighteenth-century picturesque. As early as 1929 historians could write of the way in which the new architecture was carefully related to its natural surroundings. In mentioning Le Corbusier's 1927–28 League of Nations project (Fig. 54), Professor Hitchcock noted: "Uvedale Price, the great authority on the Picturesque, would have approved both terrace and ribbon windows. In a sense he recommended them more than a century ago when he suggested that houses might be 'picturesquely' designed solely with the idea of making the most of the circumambient view."[10] For one critic, then, the architecture of the twentieth century had never lost sight of its romantic origins, even during its most extreme and radical phase.

Therefore the subsequent modifications of the International Style introduced by Aalto and Wright, notably in Mairea (Fig. 36) and in Falling Water (Fig. 39), which led to the use of a greater variety of textures and freedom in the choice of materials, were not fundamentally a contrived revival of an irrelevant historical tradition, since that tradition had never completely vanished. Instead, these and later developments attempted to exploit in more emphatic ways compositional elements that had been latend in the modern movement all along. In such context, these works of the 1930's, and the subsequent new empiricism of the 1940's are not so much a reversal as they are a reasonably logical evolution beyond the pure forms and mercurial ideologies of the earlier, machine-age, International Style epoch. This organic line of development was not the only manifestation of a return to the early, romantic sources of the modern tradition. The new style evolved by Mies van der Rohe at

Illinois Institute of Technology, both in his master plan of 1939–40 (Fig. 49) and in sub-sequent designs for individual buildings, was, in its closed regularity, a return to a different, but complementary, facet of late eighteenth-century aesthetics, namely, the revival of the classic forms of ancient Greece. This development, generally identified by its somewhat contradictory title, romantic-classicism,[11] is a style, or collection of styles, that aspired to reach considerably beyond the limits of simple revivalism. Its immediate visual character was defined by a propensity for exacting formal contrasts and for relying upon an immaculate and untroubled expression of clear geometry. The use of pure geometric forms—cylinders, cubes, spheres, and pyramids, to name the most basic and frequent ones—went beyond the mere imitation of antique prototypes; it ventured as far as an abstract formalism in the works of Ledoux and Durand. In this way the ancient sources became little more than a pretext or a point of departure for the "new" architecture of 1800, resulting in a kind of purism that occasionally approximates the architectural character of the 1920's.[12] On the other hand, this tendency toward abstraction also led to a somewhat contradictory result, one which was altogether eclectic. This was true in the case of the early nineteenth-century German architect, Karl Friedrich von Schinkel, whose work, whether classic, Gothic, Renaissance, or rational in vocabulary, tends to have the same fundamental visual and compositional qualities of smooth surfaces, clear contours and openings, and sharply defined, autonomous geometric elements (Fig. 55).

Early in his career, Mies had been inspired by the rational and classicizing aspects of Schinkel's work.[13] Furthermore, his association with Peter Behrens during the years 1908–11 must have suggested the possibility of effecting a union between the newly emerging factory aesthetic (as seen in Behrens' work for the A.E.G.—the General Electric Company—in Berlin, Fig. 4) and these older tendencies (such a union actually was attempted with Behrens' German Embassy in St. Petersburg, 1911–12, Fig. 55a). Significantly, Behrens did not completely succeed in integrating these two strands of the modern tradition, either in his pioneering work before 1914 or in his more expressionist efforts of the 1920's. Such an achievement was no more in his power than was the possibility of a synthesis within the grasp of his contemporary, Olbrich, in the Darmstadt Art Colony (Fig. 23), where so many quasi-historical references had been loosely cast together. It was only in the 1920's that a compact, compressed formulation of a modern style, in which the various elements are not simply presented as a review or recapitulation but are welded together in an indissoluble whole, seems to have become feasible. The total, nearly universal solution that was provided by Mies in his ultimate style seems to have been attainable only at that moment when the International Style, having run its course, allowed him to develop beyond the unstable geometry of the Barcelona Pavilion. Having already sampled neo-classicism and the factory aesthetic, Mies, in the 1920's, absorbed the Anglo-American side of the romantic-picturesque tradition through a study of the early works of Wright,[14] and he discovered the radical principles of modern painting through contact with De Stijl. The Barcelona Pavilion, 1929 (Figs. 47, 48), represented a tentative synthesis of these factors, but with too much emphasis upon the latter two. It was not until the master plan of I.I.T., 1939–40 (Fig. 49), that the four elements found a stable, equal, universal harmony in the simple, but richly endowed, late style of Mies.

Ironically, Mies fully developed his ultimate principles at a time when his stark mode of expression was totally out of fashion. From the various forces of the modern tradition, both near and remote in time, he had extracted a super-personal statement, much as Wright was then doing with his organic architecture of the late 1930's. On the surface, Mies seemed to be out of step with the contemporary reassessment of the modern movement in the light of its picturesque antecedents, a development which was recognizable not just in the work of Wright, but also in that of Aalto, Gardella, Gropius, Breuer, Scandinavian architects as different as Gunnar Asplund and Sven Markelius, and Le Corbusier and his young Brazilian disciples.

55. Karl Friedrich von Schinkel. Altes Museum. Berlin, 1822–28.

55a. Peter Behrens. German Embassy. St. Petersburg, 1911–12.

This exploration of a new avenue, in which contemporary developments could be made to rejoin the main line of a tradition reaching back to the eighteenth century, led to a general misinterpretation of the importance and achievement of the International Style when viewed from the vantage point of the 1940's. It was not necessary, as it then seemed, to scrap the achievements of the 1920's in order to rediscover the past. The iconoclastic architecture of the interwar period, with its insistently futurist, mechanistic, anti-historical orientation, was as much a part of the two-century-old chain of developments as any other. Indeed, in spite of a negative attitude toward its heritage, the International Style had, itself, made a remarkably sweeping synthesis of diverse trends. It had forged an original and wholly unified style out of elements as dissimilar as romantic-classic Purism (its rational theories originating with Laugier) and the rational, mechanistic structuralism of the nineteenth-century railroad station and exhibition hall builders (its doctrine of structure coming from medievalists and archaeologists like Pugin and Viollet-le-Duc). To this amalgam was added the oracular moral homilies of Ruskin and of Victorian criticism in general, along with the socially alert sentiments of William Morris and the Arts and Crafts Movement. Before the resolute culmination of the International Style, this material must have seemed hopelessly self-contradictory; afterward, the seemingly incompatible elements turn out to be parallel rather than divergent paths leading in the same direction. No subsequent movement could for long overlook the immensity of this achievement.

A useful, if somewhat personal, indication of some of the new patterns of design and expression that appeared after the peak years of the International Style is furnished by a brief assessment of the work of the rejuvenated Wright, beginning with the S. C. Johnson Building, Racine, Wisconsin, 1936–39 (Figs. 56, 57), and ending with the initial design for the Guggenheim Museum, New York, 1943 (Fig. 63).[15] The Johnson Building, to which the harmonious research tower was not added until 1949, is an almost epic statement (if such were possible) of the *détente* of the 1930's. Indeed, it might be accurately described as representing a kind of counter-International Style, replacing the customary smooth, clear finish with a warm red brick, and tempering the sharp clarity of glass wall with the less austere tubular glass to produce translucent, rather than transparent, walls. In effect, features of the International Style were here replaced by elements of German Expressionism together with a more personal form-language. It is significant that many of the most characteristic houses from this phase of Wright's career are illustrated in Bruno Zevi's books: the Willey House,

56, 57. Frank Lloyd Wright. Laboratory Tower and Administration Building for S. C. Johnson & Son, Inc. Racine, Wisconsin, 1936–39 and 1949–50.

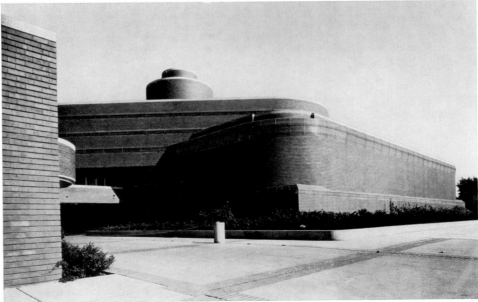

58. Frank Lloyd Wright. Lloyd Lewis House. Libertyville, Illinois, 1940.

59. Frank Lloyd Wright. Paul Hanna House. Palo Alto, California, 1937.

60. Frank Lloyd Wright. Ann Pfeiffer Chapel, Florida Southern College. Lakeland, Florida, 1938–59.

Minneapolis, Minnesota, 1934; Taliesin West, near Phoenix, Arizona, begun in 1938 (Fig. 42); and the Sturges House, Brentwood Heights, California, 1939 (all in the English edition of *Towards an Organic Architecture);* the Winkler-Goetsch House, Okemos, Michigan, 1939; and the Rose Pauson House, Phoenix, Arizona (added to the later *Storia dell'Architettura Moderna).* To this listing should be added the Paul Hanna House, Palo Alto, California, 1937 (Fig. 59), and the Lloyd Lewis House, Libertyville, Illinois, 1940 (Fig. 58). All of these buildings are illustrated in Henry-Russell Hitchcock's 1942 monograph, *In The Nature of Materials,* whose title provides one more distinctive phrase which, like organic architecture and new empiricism, characterizes much of the architecture of this epoch. Without exception these houses eschew the abstract stucco rendering, employed for a major portion of Falling Water in 1936, in favor of horizontal boarding, tawny brick, and often strikingly expressive rough stone masonry. At the same time the interlocking, hovering geometry of the 1920's is preserved, but in a more palpable, tactile form.

In the light of general contemporary developments, however, Wright's houses tell only a part of the story. This is true both in respect of his own personal creative accomplishment and in respect of the development of contemporary architecture throughout the world. Wright's extraordinary capacity at this period is best seen in Florida Southern College

61. Hadrian's Villa. Tivoli, 2nd century A.D. Site plan.

62. Frank Lloyd Wright. Florida Southern College. Lakeland, Florida, 1938–59. Site plan.

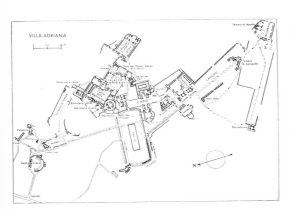

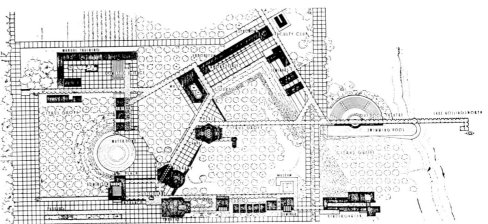

63. Frank Lloyd Wright. The Solomon R. Guggenheim Museum. New York. Initial project, 1943.

64. Frank Lloyd Wright. Midway Gardens, Restaurant. Chicago, 1914.

64a. Frank Lloyd Wright. Imperial Hotel. Tokyo, 1916–22. Plan.

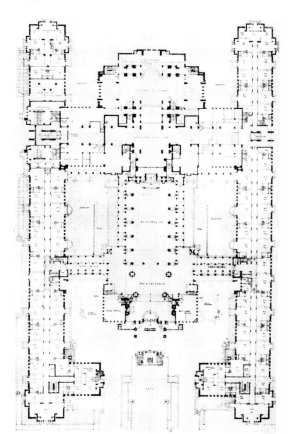

(Figs. 60, 62), Lakeland, Florida, a project planned in 1938, the construction of which was begun in 1940. This design was a plan for an academic campus as superficially free and unfettered as Mies's contemporary Illinois Institute of Technology plan was rigid and inflexible. Mies's I. I. T. design is, in effect, a checkerboard with identically proportioned elements linked to each other by duplication and repetition, creating a unity that is implicit rather than expressed. Wright, in the plan for Florida Southern, goes to an opposite extreme. There, a fluid integration of the varied elements, circular and polygonal in shape, is brought about by the continuous flow of sheltered walk-ways linking the several principal buildings. Its plan is one of the rare instances in contemporary architecture in which the sense of movement and total unity approaches in more than just a superficial way a distinctly baroque harmony, not only between the forms of the building themselves, but also in their relation to, and dominion over, nature. Curiously, Wright seems here to have passed beyond the eighteenth-century picturesque landscape and siting technique, with its undulating, irregular topography creating accidental, quasi-naturalistic effects, to discover, deliberately or accidentally, an earlier, even more dramatic planning technique, one which could, at the same time, contribute to the continued growth of his personal organic manner.

The Florida Southern layout, with its various diagonal axes meeting, intersecting, or terminating at the individual buildings, brings to mind the kinds of relationships between parts found in the plan of the second-century Hadrian's Villa (Fig. 61) at Tivoli.[16] This type of radiating axial scheme might also be thought of as a dismembered, asymmetrical translation of seventeenth-century baroque landscaping in the manner of Vaux-le-Vicomte or Versailles. If this is the case, then the freeing of the axial scheme from its original strict regularity, and the more ingenious, subtle integration of the buildings into the site, might represent an effort on Wright's part to arrange a reconciliation between seventeenth-century regularity and eighteenth-century picturesque irregularity. Even this synthesis, however, does not exhaust the referential possibilities contained in the Florida Southern plan. The whole series of dislocated, reflexive, axial, "exterior" corridors and the variously shaped buildings which they connect are superimposed upon a Durand-like checkerboard grid, which is expressed in the outlines of the pavement. The ultimate result is thus a tripartite amalgamation of three successive planning techniques to be found in the Late Baroque and early modern periods.

Furthermore, in contrast to the distilled simplicity of Mies's I. I. T., Florida Southern offers a more uninhibited means of drawing together many currents of the present and recent past, one which had its own kind of discipline, more supple but equally difficult to comprehend, either through perception alone or through historical analysis. At the same time, this historicizing in Wright's later work is a surprisingly consistent outgrowth of the planning schemes of his early period. The free, expansive outburst of Florida Southern is the heir of his more academically inspired layouts, like the Wolf Lake Amusement Park, 1895, Midway Gardens, Chicago, 1914 (Fig. 64), and the Imperial Hotel, Tokyo, 1916–1922 (Fig. 64a).[17] Florida Southern, a masterpiece of Wright's late style, sums up and revivifies elements both from his own past and from the tradition of modern architecture without, however, stooping to banal revival or imitation. While this scheme of things is suggestive of Le Corbusier's procedures with a building like the Villa Savoye (Figs. 27, 28, 30, 31, 33), it is unthinkable that Wright was emulating his younger European contemporary. Neither architect confessed publicly to this manner of utilizing the past.

Wright's manner—whether at Florida Southern, or in the plan of his own desert camp, Taliesin West, begun in 1938 (Fig. 42), or in the shape-conjuring of the first Guggenheim Museum project of 1943 (Fig. 63)—clearly represents an extreme statement of his intensely

65. George Howe. Thomas House. Fortune Rock, Mount Desert Island, Maine, 1939.

66–68. Harwell Hamilton Harris. Havens House. Berkeley, California, 1941. Plans of ground and upper floors, view.

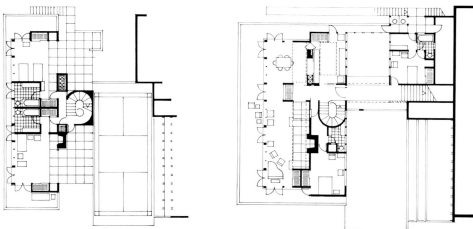

personal mode of expression. Nonetheless, its superficial side, a certain fluent, relaxed (though not casual) quality of composition, siting, and texture, was more in harmony with the stylistic leanings of other architects than was the tense, calculated austerity of Mies's contemporary steel, glass, and brick paraphrase of romantic and rational classicism. Wright's reconciliation of opposites seems to have taken place on a sensuous, perceptible level, while Mies's personal synthesis was inward, meditative, and intellectual; Wright's was extroverted and outgoing, Mies's turned in upon itself. The buildings of other contemporary architects understandably did not share in this rarefied creative synthesis, but instead dealt successfully, and often extremely well, with more immediate, practical problems relating to the furtherance of the modern idiom.

The general style of 1940–50 may have tended toward self-effacement and anonymity, but this was only another extreme position, in a way the complement of the personal baroque expressionism of Wright or the classicizing mannerism of Mies. In the middle, one finds a large and important group of architects who sought a stable normalcy within the framework of the modern movement but managed to avoid the various style problems present on the frontiers of architectural development.[18] Among the many fine houses designed at the beginning of this period, none is more representative than George Howe's Thomas House, Fortune Rock, Mount Desert Island, Maine, of 1939 (Fig. 65). In the projecting cantilever of living area and balcony over the water it is comparable to Wright's Falling Water, but in other important respects it is quite different. The structure is dramatized by the outward thrust of the rugged concrete supports in a way quite unlike the floating, hovering effect of Falling Water. In addition, Howe made use of a traditional clapboard siding and a pitched roof, so that the effect is more literally native and indigenous (without becoming anonymous) than Wright's invariably idiosyncratic domestic work of the period. At the same time, despite its traditional and rustic aspects, Howe's Fortune Rock house is firmly set in the new tradition of modern architecture; it represents no more of a withdrawal from the original positions of the avant-garde than most of the contemporary houses of Gropius and Breuer or the projects of Mies or Le Corbusier.

Other contemporary dwellings that illustrate a similar exploration of rough or naturalistic materials as a feature to modify the severe plainness of the International Style's first manner are common at this time. The work of William W. Wurster and of John Yeon on the West Coast of the United States in the late 1930's and early 1940's is of particular distinction. An especially noteworthy instance of this supposedly regional manner (whose stylistic implications were international at the time) is the Havens House, Berkeley, California, by Harwell Hamilton Harris, 1941 (Figs. 66–68).[19] Inspired by the precipitous site, the architect has thrust from the hillside a series of three superimposed cantilever forms, two of which form balconies. The structure is made to seem more daring and precarious by means of a two-story courtyard and entrance ramp which is set between the hillside and the outward thrust of cantilevered balconies and living spaces. Consequently, the floating, air-borne theme common to Fortune Rock, Falling Water, and the Villa Savoye is once again transformed in an original fashion. The success of this and similar themes in domestic architecture during the last few decades suggests that imaginative modern house design thrives when abnormal or, at least, distinctive sites are offered as a challenge to conventional notions of layout and form.

The evolutionary direction suggested by these two houses, one by Howe, the other by Harris, might be simply described as the introduction of natural and organic modifications into the restrictive severity of the original machine aesthetic. These modifications can also be seen in a house designed by Carl Koch at Snake Hill, Belmont, Massachusetts, 1940 (Fig. 69). Koch, a disciple of Gropius and Breuer, had also worked in Stockholm with Markelius. Again a steep hillside site inspired a vigorous, picturesque design on three levels, realized in native stone and unpainted vertical fir siding. The naturalistic quality was literally carried into the house by allowing a rock outcrop from the hillside to protrude

69. Carl Koch. House at Snake Hill, Belmont, Massachusetts, 1940.

70. Le Corbusier. Lannemezan house type for an engineer. Project, 1940.

71. Sven Markelius. Markelius House. Kevinge, near Stockholm, 1946.

72. Walter Gropius and Marcel Breuer. New Kensington Housing Estate. Near Pittsburgh, Pennsylvania, 1941.

72 a. Richard Neutra. Channel Heights Housing Estate. San Pedro, Los Angeles, California, 1943.

into the living room, a feature similar to Wright's treatment at Falling Water. In contrast to other houses of these prewar years, a strained, hybrid quality is happily absent, and the total result adds up to a robust offshoot of earlier modern efforts. Although veering away from a literal expression of the machine aesthetic, the course marked by the organic leanings of these three houses does not completely negate prior accomplishments. Instead, the implications of an earlier rationalism are present in these new growths, contributing in essential ways to the development of a more rugged, varied, naturalistic style.

In Europe there was a paucity of contemporary domestic design, a fact which makes other expressions of this tendency difficult to find. Le Corbusier's weekend house near Paris, 1935 (Fig. 45), with its cavern-like properties, is certainly a related predecessor, though perhaps not a direct influence on this rugged new domestic style. Far more vital to this point are some unbuilt Le Corbusier projects of 1940, the Lannemezan house types (Fig. 70), one for a mason, the other for an engineer. In these designs, the machine aesthetic discipline was modified, but not overwhelmed, by a wider choice of surface materials (rough stonework, concrete, and wood) in much the same way that the International Style had been deflected in contemporary domestic architecture in the U. S. A. Those few houses done in neutral countries of Europe during the 1940's, insofar as they have any pretensions to a modern mode of expression at all, scarcely measure up to the unbuilt projects of Le Corbusier or to the distinctive works built in the Western Hemisphere during those years. Sven Markelius' own house (Fig. 71) at Kevinge, near Stockholm, while of 1946, and hence, strictly speaking, postwar in date, illustrates this tendency, which was just becoming known as new empiricism. Although parallel in many ways to the more distinctive American designs, it is so bland and so lacking in any sort of personal touch that its homely virtues can easily pass unnoticed. It is a kind of modern architecture that does not carry a great deal of conviction chiefly because of an apparent diffidence or lack of any urgency to make a positive, forceful statement. Not even in the work of Alvar Aalto does one find so detached and negligent an attitude toward clarity of form or expression; in contrast to this house by Markelius, the works of the American architects of about 1940 seem positively doctrinaire in their modernism!

Much of the genial rusticity so apparent in the houses of this period is also found in large-scale construction, notably in war housing in the U. S. A., where war-induced shortages of materials caused architects to favor wood and other less essential materials. The best known of these housing projects, as well as one of the most ingratiating in aspect, is the New Kensington Housing, near Pittsburgh, Pennsylvania, 1941 (Fig. 72), by Gropius

73. William W. Wurster. Office Building for Schuckl Canning Company. Sunnyvale, California, 1942.

and Breuer. The unfinished vertical boarding, which had been used by the same architects in the Chamberlain House, Wayland, Massachusetts (Fig. 41), the previous year, was successfully employed in a group of two-story row house structures that were irregularly disposed on a rolling site. Other well-known designs in this genre include Richard Neutra's Channel Heights, San Pedro, Los Angeles, 1943 (Fig. 72a), and Carver Court, Coatsville, Pennsylvania, 1944, by George Howe, Oscar Stonorov, and Louis I. Kahn. Carver Court, late in date and probably constrained by more stringent wartime restriction than the others, is rather barren and harsh in aspect. In retrospect, however, the skimpiness of its detail and the severity of its clapboard exteriors have some of the vitality as well as some of the character of social responsibility, found in the visually different European public housing of fifteen years earlier.

Among the few large buildings constructed during the war, none is perhaps more startling or historically important as an indication of general architectural trends than the office building for the Schuckl Canning Company, Sunnyvale, California, 1942 (Fig. 73), by William W. Wurster.[20] Here, in a non-domestic program, the characteristics of the International Style—thin, smooth walls, strip windows, and flat roof terraces—are translated from the earlier media of steel, concrete, and stucco to an expression in wood with a display of elegance and sensitivity. Whether this building would have been built in exactly the same form had there been no restrictions on the use of materials is, of course, difficult to say. In any event, the vocabulary and precedent for this type of transliteration of the earlier machine-age style into something less smooth and abstract in surface and darker in color were already present in the domestic architecture of the day. Perhaps the Schuckl building should not be considered as anything more than the fortuitous use of a domestic style for a commercial structure—especially when large buildings were rarely built—but it nonetheless represents the tendencies of its day better than most.

Contemporary with the establishment of this aspect of modernism in the United States was the development of another offshoot of the new architecture in Brazil,[21] where the personal manner of Le Corbusier had already had a provocative effect upon several men, the most striking of whom was Oscar Niemeyer. At the same time, the work of Lúcio Costa, Affonso Eduardo Reidy, and the brothers Marcelo and Milton Roberto was reaching a similar level of distinction. Despite the war, this rapid growth of a new school was recognized abroad and much material was published during these years by *The Architectural Review,* simultaneously with the reinvestigation of the picturesque tradition. Among the most characteristic buildings designed in Brazil during the war years was a

74. Oscar Niemeyer. Yacht Club. Pampulha, 1942.

75. Oscar Niemeyer. Church of São Francisco. Pampulha, 1943.

76, 76a. Oscar Niemeyer. Kubitschek Weekend House. Pampulha, 1943. View and section.

77. Ignazio Gardella. House for a vintner. Castana, 1946.

78, 79. Marcel Breuer. Geller House. Lawrence, Long Island, New York, 1945. Floor plan and view.

group at Pampulha, where Oscar Niemeyer was given the opportunity to display his personal style in several different directions.[22] First, in 1942, came a Casino, a Yacht Club, and a Restaurant (Fig. 74), all of a recognizably abstract concrete and glass idiom. Nevertheless, they evidenced a permissiveness in the shaping and massing of forms that separated them from the more rational and classical works of their obvious source and inspiration, the recent projects of Le Corbusier.

The liberation of modern architecture's formal discipline that took place at that time in Brazil—a development paralleling, without exactly echoing, the somewhat corrosive effects of European and North American developments of the late 1930's and early 1940's— may also be viewed as a regionalist, indigenous trend, based upon the lyrical, curvilinear forms of Brazil's traditional colonial Baroque.[23] Such an emphasis upon native continuity in the development of a more supple, mature contemporary mode of expression shows certain similarities to the regionalist trend in the U. S. A., whether it be the New England manner of Howe or of Gropius and Breuer or the San Francisco Bay regionalism of Wurster and others. At the same time, these developments (echoed also in the Finnish modern architecture of Alvar Aalto) reflected the same trends of thought that produced the picturesque revival in the English magazines of the early 1940's. All of these superficially divergent trends represented a movement in the direction of achieving not a compromise, but at the very least a sense of rediscovering the roots and traditions from which twentieth-century architecture could be enriched.

Two even more influential designs were built by Niemeyer in 1943: the church of São Francisco at Pampulha (Fig. 75) and the house designed for Juscelino Kubitschek (Figs. 76, 76 a). The former, a concrete structure with parabolic vaults, is one of Niemeyer's best and most famous works; the characteristics of it were important factors in establishing his professional reputation. The Kubitschek House is also both imaginative and sensible. Its reverse-sloped mass is derived, as one might reasonably expect, from certain small Le Corbusier domestic projects of the 1930's. The rusticated ramps leading up to the entrance provide a pleasing echo to the pent forms of the roof, and underneath the reverse slope of the roof there is a palisaded "pediment," the silhouette of which is the inversion of a triangular gable. The somewhat forced and unnecessary rusticity of this "pediment" is at least a token gesture in the direction of contemporary European works such as those of Aalto or, indeed, of any related to the idea of new empiricism.

Interestingly enough, the reverse-sloped "butterfly" roof turns up in other types of architecture and the possibility of Brazilian influence in its development should not be ruled out. One such example is a house for a vintner (Fig. 77) built at Castana by Ignazio Gardella in 1946.[24] The Italian architect, however, only made use of the formal idea, and employed his native traditions for the details and other features of construction. Similarly, the "butterfly" roof silhouette dominated two of Marcel Breuer's houses of the 1940's, the Geller House (Figs. 78, 79), Lawrence, Long Island, New York, of 1945, and the Exhibition House erected in the garden of the Museum of Modern Art, New York, 1949.[25] Both of these houses made use of the wooden siding and other regional touches that were fast becoming an almost local idiom in New England and the Northeast at that period. In this sense, Breuer's work suggests a combination of certain Corbusian themes, taken either at first or second hand, with the post-Bauhaus type of dwelling that Gropius and he had been developing since their arrival in the U. S. A. in the late 1930's.

The extent of this apparently fruitful confluence of several strands of modern architecture seems to have had its most original expression in the first house that Breuer built for himself in New Canaan, Connecticut, 1947 (Fig. 80). Indeed, the sensitivity and ingenuity of this tensioned frame structure hovering above a recessed basement transcend the level of regional vernacular modernism without, however, ignoring the effectiveness of such features as natural wood siding. The result is a small house which develops the theme of an architectonic form visually liberated from the ground, a theme pioneered by Le Corbu-

80. Marcel Breuer. Breuer House I. New Canaan, Connecticut, 1947.

81. Paul Rudolph. Healy House. Sarasota, Florida, 1950.

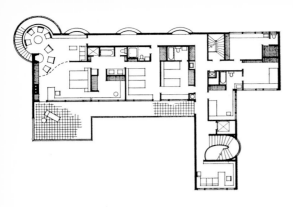

82, 83. Eric Mendelsohn. Russell House. San Francisco, 1952. Plan of second floor and view.

84, 85. Marcel Breuer. Breuer House II. New Canaan, Connecticut, 1951. Floor plan and view.

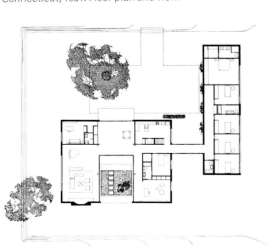

86, 87. Philip Johnson. Richard Hodgson House. New Canaan, Connecticut, 1951. Floor plan and view.

sier and Wright, as well as by Breuer's own master, Gropius, in the Dessau Bauhaus. At the same time, there is a clear, if perhaps fortuitous, re-emphasis of a picturesque or neo-picturesque attitude, indicating yet another possibility of synthesis and summation within the evolving pattern of modern architecture. For reasons that are still unclear, Breuer's 1947 house was one of the last in this general development of modern domestic architecture. About 1950, this type of house, which incorporated both picturesque and functional elements, was gradually replaced by a kind of domestic planning that was more regular in outline, conventional in the relation of its form to the ground, and even academic in its total effect. Before this shift became complete, one or two noteworthy offshoots of the older synthesis were built. Thus, some of the familiar characteristics of lightness and precarious balance were still present in certain houses by Paul Rudolph (built in partnership with Ralph S. Twitchell) of the late 1940's and early 1950's, although elements of the new formalism are simultaneously evident. For example, the Healy House, Sarasota, Florida, 1950 (Fig. 81), is a cottage of simple, rectilinear plan, elevated on stubby blocks; the exterior is mostly glazed, with louvers fitted for regulating the glare of sunlight. The most interesting feature of this house, however, is the fiberboard and plastic roof supported by suspended steel bars, which are, in turn, braced by diagonal rods along the sides of the house. The result is a tense, structurally expressive design of considerable originality which, although quite regular and closed in shape, has much of the spirit of unstable, lightly balanced forms that was characteristic of the period in modern architecture that was just coming to an end.

Another house belonging to this transitional moment in contemporary domestic design was the distinctive Russell House, San Francisco, 1952 (Figs. 82, 83), designed by one of the displaced veterans of twentieth-century architecture, Eric Mendelsohn.[26] As had often been the case with the great houses of the modern movement, a hillside site was again a determining factor. The result is a redwood mansion, a relatively ordered and closed form, largely liberated from the ground and with a round corner element projecting outward from the principal mass. Consequently, Mendelsohn, in the Russell House, looks in several directions. The first is a backward glance toward the adventurous, spectacular quality of the avant-garde of the 1920's, both expressionist and rationalist. At the same time, however, one finds a place for it within the frame of the San Francisco Bay regionalist mode, which had already stimulated the works of Wurster and of Harris in the early 1940's. Finally, in the careful regularity of its exteriors, Mendelsohn looks forward to the almost academic side of new architecture which blossomed in the 1950's.

The real inauguration of the new, formalizing domestic trends took place in two houses at New Canaan, Connecticut, in 1951: Breuer's second house (Figs. 84, 85), designed for himself; and the Richard Hodgson House (Figs. 86, 87, 229) designed by Philip Johnson.[27] In contrast with the detached character of his 1947 house, Breuer's second residence is firmly fixed on the ground. Although the most noticeable forms are of a sturdy, rough fieldstone, the handling of the wall planes, especially when seen in plan, resemble the Mies van der Rohe projects for a country house of 1923, which featured slab-like brick walls reaching outward, embracing the site as well as the interior spaces (Fig. 88). Breuer's second house is built around a court in an almost regular U-shaped plan, so that it seems more closed than the early Mies scheme. When it is viewed from certain angles, its regularity is especially striking, and a similiarity with the over-all pattern of Johnson's Hodgson House is revealed. Both are set directly upon the ground, neither above nor within it; both are U-shaped in plan, though Johnson's is the more regular and emphatic; and both have a side which offers a void (of glass) in the center flanked by blank masonry wall-planes. Consequently, both houses have a marked formal regularity and even monumentality, though in a personal way, while at the same time they pick up certain aspects of the modern movement's earlier traditions—aspects which are largely Miesian in derivation. In both houses, there is a sense of return and of an endeavor to recapture elements

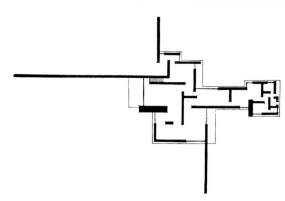

88. Ludwig Mies van der Rohe. Project for a brick country house. 1923. Floor plan.

89. Harwell Hamilton Harris. Ralph Johnson House. Los Angeles, 1951.

90. Eliel Saarinen. Railroad Station. Helsinki, designed 1904, constructed 1910–14.

91. Eliel Saarinen. School Building. Cranbrook, near Detroit, Michigan, 1925.

92. Eliel Saarinen. Project for Chicago Tribune Tower. 1922.

from the 1920's, joining these with a tendency to discard any neo-picturesque features. Such urges would seem not to be isolated. Indeed, they are complemented by other, more drastic, returns to still older aspects of the modern tradition. This seems to be the case in the contemporary work of Harwell Hamilton Harris, especially in the Ralph Johnson House, Los Angeles, 1951 (Fig. 89).[28] Here, instead of following up the distinctive personal characteristics of his earlier Havens House, Berkeley, 1941 (Figs. 66–68), Harris reached back to earlier twentieth-century regional modes of expression, and created an amalgam of the San Francisco architecture of Bernard Maybeck and the southern California style of Charles and Henry Greene.[29] The indigenous wood-frame style of Maybeck and both Greenes was contemporary and parallel with the early efforts of Wright and with the works of Hoffmann, Olbrich, Behrens, and other Europeans who had achieved distinction in modern architectural design before 1914.

This return to a pre-Expressionist or pre-International Style phase of design, seen in the work of Harris around 1950, exemplified a strong tendency in architecture of that day, and also found notable expression in the ultimate works of a Finnish architect, Eliel Saarinen, done at the same time.[30] Saarinen, born in 1873, belonged to the first generation of pioneers rather than to the generation (born in the 1880's or later) who inaugurated the International Style. He had gained considerable recognition with his 1904 competition design for the Helsinki Railroad Station, the construction of which was delayed until 1910–14 (Fig. 90). In some ways this railroad station design is more novel than the designs

of Olbrich and Hoffmann of the same period, though it does not go as far as the almost machine aesthetic designs then being produced by Behrens. Its novelty is somewhat tempered, however, by a conventional monumentality which asserts itself at the expense of the handsome generalized and even abstracted detailing. Saarinen's project for the Chicago Tribune Tower, 1922 (Fig. 92), which placed second to that by Howells and Hood, is more conventional neo-Gothic, and is disappointing, chiefly in the light of the excessive admiration to which it has been subjected in recent years. (One realizes that much of the praise is scarcely deserved when the Saarinen design is compared with the well-known Gropius and Meyer project for the same competition.) Saarinen subsequently came to the United States, and in the 1920's and 1930's was responsible for the design of a group of school buildings at Cranbrook, near Detroit, Michigan (Fig. 91). These buildings, coming during the culmination and decline of the International Style, in no way match the radical efforts of contemporary European architects nor do they measure up to the constant adventurousness of Wright. Instead, they represent a handsome, yet bland, compromise in which elements of modernistic detailing are mixed with other features which are of abstracted neo-classic leanings, or of a smoothed-over quasi-historical character, in the fashion of much Scandinavian twentieth-century architecture.

With this in mind, the re-emergence of Eliel Saarinen into the mainstream of contemporary developments in the 1940's is surprising and gratifying. In part, it can be ascribed to the association that he formed with his son Eero, to establish the partnership of Saarinen,

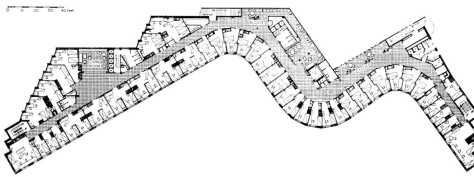

95, 96. Alvar Aalto. Senior Dormitory, Massachusetts Institute of Technology. Cambridge, Massachusetts, 1948. View and plan of a typical floor.

97, 98. Le Corbusier. Pavillon Suisse, Cité Universitaire. Paris, 1930–32. Plan of the ground floor and view.

Swanson, and Saarinen. Another factor contributing to the elder Saarinen's ultimate achievement can be attributed to the reintroduction and renewed vigor of tendencies that had been fashionable and significant in the first decade of the twentieth century. This almost cyclical pattern of evolutionary return in architectural taste helps account for the renewal of Eliel Saarinen in the years just before his death in 1950, and probably also explains the revived popularity of Wright during the last two decades of his career. The similarities between Saarinen's two recognized late masterpieces, the Tabernacle Church, Columbus, Indiana, 1940–42, and the Christ Lutheran Church in Minneapolis, Minnesota, 1949 (Figs. 93, 94), seem to indicate that the architect developed very little during that decade. The two churches are somewhat dryly romantic in spirit but, for the most part, they were handled with a gentle touch and designed with clear, simple shapes that owe a great deal to the geometry of the International Style. Both works are more emphatic in their formal inflections than many of the works which had characterized the *détente* of the 1930's or early 1940's and, despite the architect's Scandinavian origins, there is not the slightest trace of the aformalist new empiricism. Another design typical of Saarinen's last years was the Des Moines Art Center. Containing both galleries and studios, this structure is formed of low, rambling wings, whose picturesqueness is heightened by

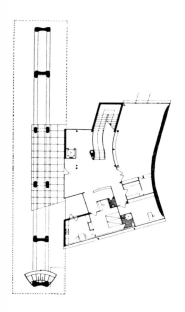

the sensitive stonework. Its long horizontals offer a homely echo not only of the International Style, but of one of its sources as well: the early prairie style houses of Frank Lloyd Wright.

Such architecture—neither especially reactionary nor avant-garde—is, despite a certain evasive, noncommittal quality, more than incidentally interesting. Indeed, there are several buildings of quality from the late 1940's that marked the end of an architectural recession and were, in effect, harbingers of a creative renaissance which was to become distinguishable around 1950. They precede by a few years the next development, which re-established the actual and symbolic leadership of two veterans of the 1920's, Mies and Le Corbusier. The edifice which stylistically and even ethnically is most closely related to the work of the elder Saarinen is Alvar Aalto's dormitory for M. I. T., Cambridge, Massachusetts, 1948 (Figs. 95, 96, 336 a). Of a jagged, saw-toothed, neo-expressionist character on one side (a character which functionally expresses the rising stairs), the dormitory gains its somewhat dramatic tone from the fact that its façade (facing the Charles River) is a continuous, undulating curve. The simplicity of the detailing is not without distinction, but the red brick of the exterior was somewhat unexpected, at least in the context of radical modernism as it was understood at the time. The serpentine mass seems to be a derivation,

99, 100. Marcel Breuer. Co-operative Dormitory, Vassar College. Poughkeepsie, New York, 1949–50. View, plans of ground and upper floors.

101, 102. Affonso Eduardo Reidy. Pedregulho Housing Estate. Rio de Janeiro, begun 1947. View and transverse section of the serpentine block.

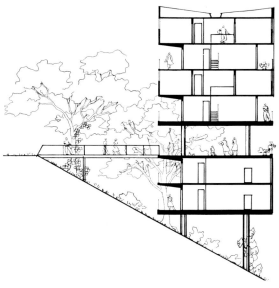

103. Robert H. Matthew, Sir J. Leslie Martin, Edwin Williams, and Peter Moro. Royal Festival Hall. London, 1951.

104, 105. Leo Calini, Massimo Castellazzi, Vasco Fadigati, Eugenio Montuori, Achille Pintonello, Annibale Vitellozzi. Termini Station. Rome, 1951. Exterior view and concourse.

voluntary or involuntary, from the much larger forms of Le Corbusier's 1930 plan for Algiers (Fig. 169), or from eighteenth-century picturesque row houses at Bath such as Lansdowne Crescent, 1794. Comparison can also be made with the curving wall of the service block of Le Corbusier's Swiss Pavilion, Paris, 1930–32 (Figs. 34, 97, 98), but there Le Corbusier seems to have employed curves for a more formal, sculpturesque reason, while Aalto's undulating form was justified by securing a view of the river for a greater number of rooms.[31]

A smaller but equally representative structure in this field is the Co-operative Dormitory at Vassar College, Poughkeepsie, New York, 1949-50 (Figs. 99, 100), by Marcel Breuer. In a building equivalent in scale and program to Le Corbusier's Swiss Pavilion of twenty years before, Breuer recaptured something of the style and ethos of the climactic moment of the International Style, as he had done in his 1947 house in New Canaan (Fig. 80). At the same time, an adjustment to the changing times was brought about in a certain relaxation of the composition and by the use of painted white brick instead of the more "pure," classic stucco or smoothfaced ashlar. The main body of the building is lifted from the ground on *pilotis,* in the fashion of Le Corbusier, although in Breuer's work one misses the willful, determined shaping of plastic form that is invariably present in the structures of his elder contemporary. Instead, there is a certain dry, forthright clarity that is more in the spirit of the Bauhaus than under the spell of the relatively subjective Purist tradition.

The nature of the distinction between these two currents flowing out of the International Style becomes manifest when Breuer's Vassar Dormitory is compared with a contemporary design by a Le Corbusier disciple, Affonso Eduardo Reidy's Pedregulho project (Figs. 101, 102), Rio de Janeiro, begun in 1947 although not finished until the mid-1950's.[32] A precipitous sloping terrain is dominated by a 853-foot-long, six-story serpentine slab. Elevated on *pilotis* in the Corbusian tradition, the second and third floors are separated by an open "street" level, thus detaching the upper two-thirds of the undulating slab from the base. The effect of solid above void rivals anything built then or earlier by Le Corbusier himself. On the lower, more level portion of the site are smaller apartment slabs and a freely composed series of structures forming a school. The small-scale articulation of this building established a sensitive contrast to the unbroken curving sweep of the slab which dominates from above. The result verges upon a somewhat arbitrary formalism which, while representing the same level of growth out of and away from the International Style seen in Breuer's Vassar Dormitory, also suggests the latent image-making potential of the original Purist aesthetic. At every stage of development, this approach is different from the more rational, sober approach of the Bauhaus group. In this way, the family variants within the original International Style were often preserved in the second generation.

Simultaneously, a number of structures in other countries also exploited one or another aspect of these parallel lines of development. In London, the Royal Festival Hall (Fig. 103), designed as the permanent contribution to the South Bank for the Exhibition of 1951 by Robert H. Matthew, Sir J. Leslie Martin, Edwin Williams, and Peter Moro, represents a particular moment in the development of modern architecture in England, years characterized as the end of the period of urgent reconstruction, or, to use the word of the hour, "austerity."[33] Although just as thoroughly indebted to the International Style as the buildings of Breuer and Reidy, the idiom used in Festival Hall is more eclectic. Instead of developing one distinct or idiosyncratic aspect of classic modernism, the hall's exterior, with its gaily picturesque façades (rendered in the proper abstract, nonhistorical way), suggests the spirit if not the letter of eclecticism. The whole building is so busy and active, its parts so distinctive, that the larger issues of its composition are confused and obscured. As a result, its importance as a symbolic new beginning for a second stage of English modern architecture is easily overlooked.

The Termini Station, Rome (Figs. 104, 105), is a similarly representative monument of this period.[34] Its main façade and ticket office were completed in 1951 by a team of architects headed by Eugenio Montuori. Utilizing a new and almost carefree design, these elements nonetheless harmonize well with the more ruthless, austere side wings, begun in a pure Fascist style in 1937. In the post-World War II portions of the station, the two not always well-integrated tendencies of recent Italian architecture, dramatic structuralism and arbitrary formalism, are juxtaposed with finesse (if not with perfect integration). The flat mass of the façade, with its strip windows, is almost as overwhelming and scaleless in conception as the earlier side wings, but this forced austerity forms the perfect backdrop for the sway-backed curve of the shed which forms an expressive entry and exit space. In addition to the contrast between rational and lyrical, this design also presents a picturesque touch appropriate to this period of contemporary design in which *architettura organica* was still one of the chief rallying cries. Some ruins of the ancient Servian wall were incorporated into the design of the entry, suggesting that the message of *The Architectural Review* with respect to the preservation of ruins had been taken up by the Italian architects, who were, however, dealing with ruins nearly two millennia more ancient! Such diverse and even contradictory tendencies suggest the strength of the latent eclectic leanings of modern architecture. Similar features can be seen in other Italian works of the period, notably in a series of Roman apartments by Luigi Moretti, 1947–50, one in the Via Bruno Buozzi and another in the Monteverdi quarter.[35] Both display a kind of picturesqueness in the irregular, rough textural details of the basements, a romantic quality heightened by the expressionist, almost surrealist shaping of the stucco-surfaced forms of the succeeding floors. At the same time, the recess of the basements and the orderly fenestration provide allusions to the modern tradition of twenty years before.

The contemporary works of Pier Luigi Nervi, structures which are simultaneously of architectonic as well as of technological significance, were less eclectic than the other Italian buildings of this period.[36] Because of Nervi's preoccupation with the constructive side of architecture, his works provided the most noteworthy extension of the rational aspect of the modern aesthetic in the period immediately after the war. Nervi's most daring and sensitive work is to be seen in the interiors of the Turin Exhibition Hall, 1948–49 (Fig. 106, 236), where thin precast concrete elements were assembled in a large barrel vault of corrugated section. This development, which tended to invest the forms of the building with a more pronounced expression of loads and directions of forces, was a change from the Purist attitude of the 1920's, in which the rational quality of the form often implied indiffer-

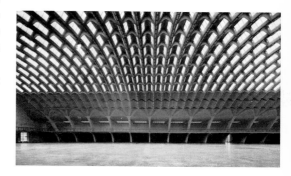

106. Pier Luigi Nervi. Exhibition Hall. Turin, 1948–49.

107. Auguste Perret. Buildings at the Place de l'Hôtel de Ville. Le Havre, begun 1947.

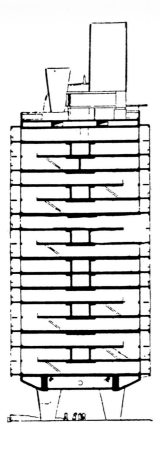

ence to the matter of structural expression. By 1950, however, the Purist-derived attitude was disappearing, and in its place there arose a greater interest in the characterization of a building by the expression or representation of its constructive element. In this respect, Nervi's structures point up a change which had been coming about for more than a decade in the works of Mies van der Rohe and Le Corbusier, changes which came to complete fruition in two monumental works of this period.

Le Corbusier's *Unité d'Habitation,* Marseilles, 1946–52 (Figs. 108–110), and Mies van der Rohe's Lake Shore Apartments, Chicago, 1949–51 (Figs. 111–113), are the two works which signaled the closing of the immediate postwar period and opened a new phase, the maturity of contemporary architecture. The stylistic uncertainties of the 1930's and 1940's were at last overcome, but the new beginning, although possessing qualities all its own, was a further development of the hopes and ideals of the 1920's. Indeed, with these two buildings, something on the order of a renaissance of the modern idiom was generated. To this pair of structures by Le Corbusier and Mies can be added, albeit with some hesitation, the ultimate work of Auguste Perret: the designs for reconstruction of the central quarter of Le Havre, begun in 1947 (Fig. 107). Perret's position is roughly parallel to that of Eliel Saarinen at the same moment in the U. S. A.; that is, he represents a generation older than that of the 1920's, one whose creative contribution was originally made before 1914. His work of the 1920's and 1930's, while not without distinction, was unimportant in the midst of the creative furor of that period, but his style, by a process of cyclic revolution and reversal, gained a renewed significance after a lapse of a quarter of a century. Perret's Le Havre reconstruction is thus, as one would suspect, ambiguous in its intentions and appearance. His characteristic style is best known as a manner expressive of the post-and-beam system of reinforced concrete framing, which he favored for nearly half a century. Its outward appearance, however, is equally indebted to the French nineteenth-century tradition of vernacular urban architecture, with its generally cautious academic detailing of façades in which regular rows of windows are linked together with relatively standardized decorative schemes.[37] Furthermore, Perret's late work is as traditional in its general composition as it is in detail. The buildings, although placed on rather open sites, are organized around a familiar pattern of streets and squares, and the various functions—governmental, commercial, and residential—are largely intermixed in a way familiar to the traditional French provincial centers as well as to that of Paris itself. If this new center of reconstructed Le Havre lacked a truly new concept, it was, nonetheless, a venturesome gesture. Before the war, the perfunctoriness of academic officialdom in France was outrageous and, even though he had received government commissions in the 1930's, Perret was still looked upon with some condescension from official quarters. This somewhat tentative work, in a compromise style, if not unrelated to one aspect of the *détente* of the 1930's, turned out to be the vanguard of a much more adventurous building constructed at about the same time by the man who had once been one of Perret's most ardent disciples: Le Corbusier.

Le Corbusier's *Unité d'Habitation* (Figs. 108–110), situated on the Boulevard Michelet in an outlying district of Marseilles, was commissioned by the Ministry of Reconstruction in 1946, and was finally finished six years later in spite of difficulties caused by inflation, unstable ministries, and opposition from a variety of entrenched conservative groups. In retrospect, it seems evident that this revolutionary statement of mass housing heralded a new and promising phase in the growth of modern architecture. It was designed to shelter more than 1,400 persons within one single, monumental, seventeen-story slab elevated on *pilotis*, with individual apartments offering a maximum of privacy and convenience. In the *Unité,* one could recognize a building which was the tangible realization of its architect's years of thought and experience with respect to the problems of the individual and his relation to an urban pattern of living. In intent and in appearance, this apartment structure was meant to be neither an isolated architectural experience nor an object solely for the ex-

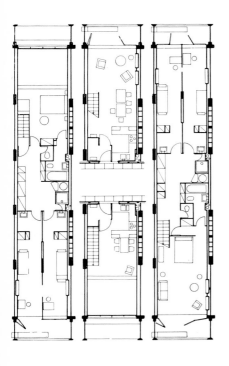

pression of a contemporary aesthetic, although the programmatic utilitarianism of the *Unité* in no way interfered with the creation of one of modern architecture's most powerful statements of pure form. With this building, it seemed as if the prewar machine aesthetic of immaculate forms had been reborn in a new medium of expression. Its rough-textured lack of finish may have been at odds with the appearance of the architecture of twenty years before, but its style nevertheless responded to a particular constructive medium (reinforced concrete) in a way that was consistent with the ideologies of early modernism. Curiously enough, this reawakening of the modern tradition, its emergence from the web of such crypto-modern deviations as new empiricism, was, in effect, only a partial fulfillment. The hopes for a new architecture were again left half-realized, in part because external appearances were once again taken to be more important than the various generative factors which brought them into being. The primary visual impact of the external appearance of the *Unité,* its striking shaping of abstract form and the creation of a lyrical concatenation of stimulating, suggestive shapes out of a supposedly refractory material—raw, unfinished concrete—is so profound that it tends to obscure the generative considerations which determined its forms. There is something inescapably, and perhaps inappropriately, spiritual about this secular building, a factor which again lessens an appreciation of its basic purpose as habitation. Certainly few public edifices or churches of this period have achieved this same state of formal transcendence. Hope for the replanning and redesigning of cities along the line and scale implicit in the Marseilles fragment (the *Unité* was, in fact, a pilot project for other apartment slabs on the same site which were never built) has not been well rewarded, and the few efforts in this direction, most of which took place in England in the last few years, have tended to be rather timid translations of the aims and ideals explicit in Le Corbusier's Marseilles projects. True, Le Corbusier has built, and designed, repetitions of his *Unité* elsewhere (Nantes, Berlin,

108–110. Le Corbusier. Unité d'Habitation. Marseilles, 1946–52. Transverse section, plans of three floors with duplex flats, and view.

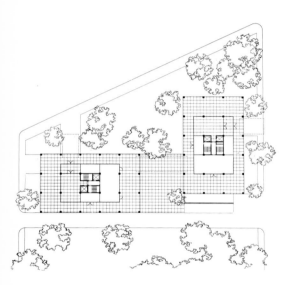

111–113. Ludwig Mies van der Rohe. Apartment Towers, 845–60 Lake Shore Drive. Chicago, 1949–51. Views and plan of the ground floor.

Briey-en-Forêt, and Meaux), but the point of view represented in these large-scale developments—the isolation of each dwelling unit, the provision for common services and facilities, as well as the scope and scale envisaged by Le Corbusier—has found little response in the work of other planners. Consequently, critics are perhaps too prone to view this major contribution to postwar building as a question of aesthetics and taste rather than as a matter of total architecture.

Ironically, Mies van der Rohe's Lake Shore Apartments, Chicago, 1951 (Figs. 111–113), the chief and conspicuous rival to the rough-textured concrete manner of Le Corbusier, are more susceptible to formalist interpretation than the *Unité*. The visual impression created by these apartment blocks is one of delicate precision in contrast with the forcefulness of Marseilles. A comparison of the Miesian with the Corbusian style of tall buildings, each of which uses a rectilinear structural grid to expressively determine form, seems to indicate that the modern tradition had split into two almost incompatible parts. The Miesian style of about 1950 appears to have little or no connection with the sinewy, robust concrete framing which was at the core of Le Corbusier's new idiom of raw concrete. Mies's clear, meticulous steel frame linearism, with its gem-like reflective surface of glass, seems to have more in common with the static closed forms of romantic classicism than with the restless, hovering, slab-like forms of the International Style. Furthermore, the Lake Shore Apartment towers are more purely a stylistic and constructive achievement, and have little importance in the development of new and more felicitous types of individual apartment layout. As such they are only incidentally related to the complex problems of large-scale residential planning.

This apparent divergence of intent and accomplishment on the part of Mies and Le Corbusier is all the more remarkable because earlier in their respective careers their personal contributions to the elaboration of a new aesthetic were originally complementary rather than contradictory. One should not be misled by the primary visual differences between these two postwar monuments into overlooking the important similarity of principle in their postwar styles. In contrast to their earlier work, both architects concentrated on a more determined expression of the building's structural skeleton. Indeed, the outward differences of style might plausibly be explained by the fact that buildings in concrete must necessarily have different characteristics from those in steel because of differences in the nature of the material. Each then demands a particular external character if the form is to reflect the structure with equal conviction and appropriateness in each instance. The programmatic and stylistic indecisiveness of so much of the architecture of the late 1930's and early 1940's, which had temporarily disorientated the modern movement, stimulated a counterreaction in buildings like the *Unité* and the Lake Shore Apartments.

To fully comprehend the development that was taking place around 1950, it is helpful to review the courses followed in the early careers of Mies and Le Corbusier. The *juvenilia* of each architect was quasi-academic in form and spirit, deriving for the most part from the less adventurous facets of their common master, Peter Behrens. After 1918, they developed in different directions, Mies under the influence of German Expressionism, Le Corbusier in the midst of the post-Cubist aesthetic of Parisian painters. By the mid-1920's, Le Corbusier's Purism had been realized in buildings of an extremely personal and uncompromising character; Mies's style was growing more slowly and deliberately, and never completely shed its romantic, academic heritage. By 1929, however, the year of the Villa Savoye (Figs. 27, 28, 30, 31, 33), and the Barcelona Pavilion (Figs. 47, 48), the revolutionary characteristics of the two architects revealed themselves as coequal and parallel, if not exactly identical. Both were aiming at new spatial experiences through visually provocative buildings that comprised gravity-defying, seemingly impalpable, weightless forms. They shared a common unconventionality with respect to the ambiguous way in which the interior spaces and volumes of the structure were defined, so that the exact point of closure, usually accomplished through a glazed surface, was a matter of surprise and uncertainty. In a personal

way, each architect created a distinctive fission and fusion which upset and then destroyed the habitual notions of solid and void, form and space, with respect to conventional architectural composition. Their stylistic growth and maturity having come into phase for a second time, their modes then drifted apart during the 1930's, as each explored various paths of development, but they again developed a tangential accord in their even more personal and individual styles of the 1950's. This phenomenon is clearly seen in a comparision of the Lake Shore Apartments with the Marseilles *Unité*.

The basic geometric form, along with the impersonal, but structurally expressive, metal contours and crystalline glass surfaces of Mies's Lake Shore Apartments is the outgrowth of a very different world of style from that which informs the individualized shapes and robust, accidentally textured, concrete surfaces of Le Corbusier's *Unité*. In effect, the pristine, hermetically sealed glass box is quite unrelated to the open, breathing wall of the concrete cliff dwelling, but these differences are differences of presentation, they are variations of key or mode or instrumentation within the realm of possibilities opened by the original modern movement a quarter of a century earlier. Both buildings are parallel outgrowths of the earlier, and more obviously collateral, works of their respective architects. True, Mies regularized his once-complex compositional schemes, whereas Le Corbusier's development moved from the very simple, self-contained (and, upon occasion, hermetically sealed) forms of the 1920's toward the complex diversity of plastically modeled images and shapes so evident in his work since 1945.

By the beginning of the 1950's, there had been much important work produced by architects other than those who had been closely associated with the early triumph of modernism; the names of Aalto, Nervi, Gardella, Niemeyer, Reidy, Howe, and Wurster come to mind almost as readily as the names of those who made their first contribution to twentieth-century architecture at an even earlier date: Wright, Perret, and Eliel Saarinen. Despite this body of diverse work, however, it required only a single well-publicized construction each by Mies and by Le Corbusier to reaffirm their position of eminence. Their work, more than that of the intermediary generation, was the springboard for the next phase of contemporary architectural development. It was destined to be a period of growth and development along several paths, both personal and collective. In pondering the new architecture of the 1950's, the personal contributions of the elder generation, in particular of Wright, Gropius, Mies, and Le Corbusier—however atypical they may seem—ought properly to be the next concern.

# Chapter III
# Wright, Gropius, Mies van der Rohe, and Le Corbusier:
# Their "Late" Styles

The prevalent architectural climate after 1945 was one of caution and restraint rather than enthusiasm and spontaneous invention. This hesitant atmosphere was as much attributable to a state of spiritual and intellectual shock as to the material havoc wrought by the combat of 1939–45 and the ensuing superhuman dimensions of the reconstruction task. A reluctance to rush into the planning of a bold, radically different world and environment was as characteristic of the nations that had been spared large-scale war destruction and the degradation of defeat as it was of those that had suffered the greatest physical damage. This benumbed state of affairs is in marked contrast to the utopian, even flamboyant, responses given by an earlier generation following the conclusion of the World War I holocaust. Thus, the architectural developments which occurred just after World War II did not constitute a fundamental revolution in design equal to that which crystallized in Europe after 1918.

While a renewal and refocusing of the modern tradition became evident in the work of Le Corbusier and in the work of Mies and his followers around 1950—when the work of these two masters finally burst from its intermediate phase—this was by no means a notably, youthful, or revolutionary development.[1] Only later, toward the middle of the 1950's, would the personal contribution of a new, younger generation become discernible. The new, highly stylized buildings and projects, which became more numerous by the late 1950's, seemed to liberate the modern movement from the excesses of a hero-worship that had gripped much excellent design for a decade, but their appearance seems belated. Furthermore, certain rigid, massive, almost scholastic characteristics prominent in these new buildings certainly belied the brash, futuristic spirit that had so thoroughly enlivened much of the avant-garde architecture of the 1920's. The older architects, participants in the original modern movement, were immediately capable of further development, while their younger contemporaries understandably tended to remain dazzled by the earlier achievements—considerably beyond a normal period of apprenticeship. Consequently, these older masters dominated the creative activity of the 1950's in two different ways: first, through their prior achievements, which provided grist for the younger men; and second, through their new work, which once again established their right to occupy the creative vanguard. Moreover, Wright, Mies and Le Corbusier now evolved individual styles that were somewhat detached from many of the immediate material concerns for new techniques, new social and economic configurations, and instead were largely subjective. In creating a manner of their old age, each moved toward the exploration of an increasingly private, sublimated, transcendental style. Old thought patterns dating back to the years of their youth and apprenticeship, by which these men habitually approached the problem of extracting a design from a set of particular material and environmental circumstances, became more and more a matter of instinct, and less and less one of conscious, rational analysis. The result was a drift toward either highly simplified or complexly differentiated forms, a tendency customary in "late" works of distinguished artists. Admiration of these ripened personal styles by younger architects was rarely accompanied by comprehension of the motivations lying behind the mannerisms—least of all of the historical-biographic process by which personal experience and old age modifies and individualizes the workings of mature creative genius. Even had they been fully understood, it does not necessarily follow that procedures valid for a Mies or a Le Corbusier on the basis of a three- or four-decade period of experiment, reflection, and refinement were well-advised models for other architects whose background and training had been shaped by very different forces.

The output of Wright's last two decades, during which all sorts of unexpected evocations of past and future thrust themselves to the surface, can be compared profitably with the striving, searching, experimental character of Borromini's last years.[2] Of Wright's final works, the Guggenheim Museum, New York City, a design of 1943 which was not built until 1957–59 (Figs. 63, 114–116), is the best known, and, in spite of much hostile criticism from even the friendliest of sources, remains probably the most enduringly significant and typical. The very fact that Wright's stanchest supporters were among those disillusioned with the outcome, is perhaps the most eloquent proof that the works of a genius's old age cannot be estimated exclusively, or even chiefly, through the criteria that were appropriate for earlier endeavors.[3] This building is many things, perhaps least of all a museum; but in a makeshift way it functions in its museum capacity chiefly because there are so many other distractions and because the public had already become adjusted to the idea of makeshift museums. Many have felt that Wright built this great space to serve as a cenotaph for himself as a creative individual, if not precisely for the ideals that he and his architecture earlier represented.

The outer shell and inner surfaces, in their smooth, trim fashion recall the abstract, impalpable, weight-denying exteriors of International Style buildings, despite the ineptness with which traces of the rather sloppy formwork were left in the otherwise non-rational pile-up of curving and undulating shapes. However impulsive and organic these shapes may be, the diffident, textureless way in which they were realized seems to form an unexpected bond with that part of the modern movement toward which Wright had been vocally hostile in the past. The project drawings for the Guggenheim Museum, as well as its famous model, would seem to bear out the fact that this smooth, unvaried, nontactile form was pretty much what Wright had in mind. He was concerned primarily with the creation of a unique interior space, one that not only would be thrust upon the entering spectator in the clearest and most unencumbered fashion but, at the same time, would also determine the exterior mass. Wright was not always his own best guide and apologist, but in this case his statements elucidate his intentions:

"Here for the first time architecture appears plastic, one floor flowing into another (more like sculpture) instead of the usual superimposition of stratified layers cutting and butting into each other by way of post and beam construction.

The whole building, cast in concrete, is more like an egg shell—in form a great simplicity—rather than like a crisscross structure. The light concrete flesh is rendered strong enough everywhere to do its work by embedded filaments of steel either separate or in mesh. The structural calculations are thus those of the cantilever and continuity rather than the post and beam. The net result of such construction is a greater repose, the atmosphere of the quiet unbroken wave: no meeting of the eye with abrupt changes of form. All is as one and as near indestructible as it is possible for science to make a building."[4]

A parallel edifice could not, needless to say, be built in any material other than poured concrete; in this instance it is significant that, unlike his experiment with the use of concrete in the Oak Park Unity Church of 1906 (Fig. 117), Wright was not trying to find a logical form of *expression* to fit the potentialities of the material. Instead, he had the form in mind first, and it was the flexibility of the concrete structural method that actually served and facilitated the realization of his concept—a romantic dream which could not have found architectonic embodiment without twentieth-century technology, regardless of the poorly executed details marring the building. Under these circumstances, Wright's architecture of the 1940's and 1950's rejoins the tradition of the International Style in a fashion infinitely

114. Frank Lloyd Wright. The Solomon R. Guggenheim Museum. New York, 1957–59.

115, 116, 116a. Frank Lloyd Wright. The Solomon R. Guggenheim Museum. New York, 1957–59. Interior view, detail of the dome, and section.

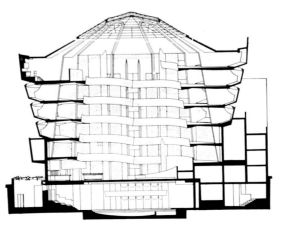

more profound and meditative than was the case in the more obviously influenced Falling Water. It has to be emphasized that this was not a casual, happenstance gesture, but a necessary reconciliation with the European masters against whom Wright had so often thundered, a step that was necessary if his ultimate thoughts and visions were to find an adequate and satisfactory means of expression.

Wright's entire career seems to be made up of a sequence of revolts and turnings-away from specific situations or fixed accomplishments. Yet, at the same time, a thread of continuity links each of his separate phases. Wright's Oak Park career was a reaction against the platitudes of suburban Queen Anne and colonial revivals, but those two offshoots of eclecticism themselves provided the nourishment and raw material for his reaction. Similarly, the Los Angeles period of 1917–24 was a reaction against his own first maturity, but it was substantially and obviously bolstered by the cumulative experience of his earlier houses. The series of reactions continued until, toward the end, the accumulated weight of his heritage must have been overwhelming. Now that Wright's career is terminated, it is possible to realize that in its ultimate stages the images could be released from so rich and complex an accumulation only by drastic and superficially contradictory gestures. Under these circumstances it is trivial, yet obligatory, to enumerate the lines of descent that culminated in the Guggenheim Museum, not because they are in themselves of great individual import, but rather because they suggest the degree of continual reintegration which came about in the major late designs by Wright.

The basic form of the Guggenheim Museum, with its continuous, outward-expanding helical ramp, is, at its most remote, a Mesopotamian ziggurat turned upside down. The application of this ancient form to a museum might seem to be due to the influence of Le Corbusier, whose *Mundaneum* project of 1929 (Fig. 118) is an ancestor not only of Wright's particular inversion, but also of his own project for a Museum of Contemporary Arts in Paris (designed for Christian Zervos in 1931), which subsequently formed the basis for his museums (of the 1950's) in Ahmedabad and Tokyo. In Wright's own work, however, the ziggurat form had already appeared as early as 1925, but, of course, to serve a different program, in the Gordon Strong planetarium project. Thus, the source of the Guggenheim Museum is clearly not unilateral.

That there should be this curious reciprocal relationship between the planetarium project of 1925 and the museum project of 1943 brings this series of cumulative associations back even further, to the romantic-classic architecture of the French Revolution. The cenotaph-like quality of the Guggenheim, noted by many critics, recalls the many monuments in the form of dramatically illuminated spheres or globes that appeared in the imaginary schemes of eighteenth-century French architects.[5] For example, Boullée's project of 1784 for a cenotaph dedicated to the memory of Sir Isaac Newton is a colossal hollow sphere which, on the interior of its shell, contains a representation of the cosmos (Fig. 119). Like Wright's Guggenheim project, Boullée's Newton Memorial is the kind of visionary project that disdainfully ignored the habitual methods by which architectural forms were made to conform, in one way or another, with the constructional facilities at hand. Indeed, it would be difficult to decide which of the two designs is more arbitrary in the demands that it makes upon the art of building. In the light of the generally rational and materialistic orientation of modern architecture, this startling formalism would seem totally unjustified; and in large measure it is. This assumption might even be fortified with Wright's personal polemic, which points in several parallel lines toward the development of new architectural techniques, but in conjunction with certain romantic contradictions. The importance of the Guggenheim Museum, and of other works from the last two decades of Wright's lifetime, resides not so much in a development of new directions pointing toward the future as in the way in which these forced and arbitrary monuments provide a resumé of both the architecture of the early twentieth century and the entire romantic movement reaching back to the mid-eighteenth century. It is not altogether unlikely that these late works in-

117. Frank Lloyd Wright. Unity Church. Oak Park, Illinois, 1906.

118. Le Corbusier. Mundaneum project. 1929.

119. Etienne-Louis Boullée. Cenotaph for Sir Isaac Newton. 1784. Project.

120, 121. Frank Lloyd Wright. David Lloyd Wright House. Phoenix, Arizona, 1950. Exterior view, plans of ground and upper floors.

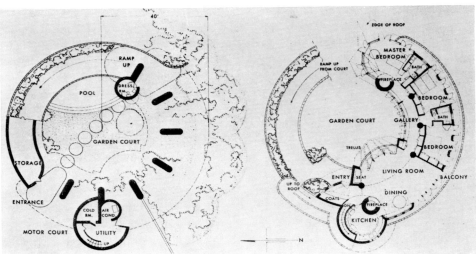

dicate the culmination—even, perhaps, the end—of a long, fruitful period in architecture. As has been suggested earlier, the Guggenheim Museum is not an arbitrary and capricious development within the whole of Wright's *œuvre*. The theme of the spiral ramp—or better, the theme of "one great space on a continuous floor" realized through the formal and structural device of the unfolding, theoretically endless, spiral ramp—is prevalent in other designs of his last years. In domestic architecture, the best-known example is the David Lloyd Wright House, Phoenix (Figs. 120, 121), which was designed somewhat earlier than its 1950 construction date. As he had with the Guggenheim's textureless unvaried surface, the elder Wright employed another standard architectural formula of the 1920's, this time the house on stilts, which he had denounced time and again in his writings. The inclining circular plan, which begins at the bottom as a garden ramp and culminates, half way

through its circumference, in two counter-circular areas forming living room and work space, embraces a round courtyard on the ground level. This in turn is sheltered, but not isolated, from the desert beyond by the *pilotis* which support the body of the house. At the entrance to the house proper, at the top of the first incline, a second, narrower ramp leads up to a roof garden. Although imitation, as such, is not present, the paradigm of the Villa Savoye has nonetheless been invoked once again, but on an ideational rather than a formalistic level. In contrast to the abstract, "meaningless" surfaces of the Guggenheim Museum, Wright here made a great show of texture and linear pattern with the concrete block. The shape is constantly and significantly inflected by stepping the courses out or in, to create a molded, plastic effect, and the sweeping movement of the spirals is underscored by having the courses incline along the same slope as the ramps themselves.

The antithesis to this spiral "hanging" garden in Wright's later work is the 1948 Herbert Jacobs House (Fig. 122), Middleton, Wisconsin (the second house for this client), which is similar to Le Corbusier's weekend house of 1935 (Fig. 45), if only because its partly subterranean situation also generates a quality of mystery. The site of the second Jacobs House is atop a bald, wind-swept hill, with the forms of the house half-interred by what seems to be an artificial mound, a form so general and primeval as to successfully evoke memories of North American Indian burial places as well as of the tumuli of ancient Etruria. Even more important than these suggestive, if perhaps fortuitous, analogies with various remote traditions is the way in which Wright, in this as in other works of the period, renews his earliest contacts with the late nineteenth-century American domestic tradition. In this respect, the frontier-like Jacobs House of 1948 is a highly stylized response to the rugged New England houses of H. H. Richardson, notably the R. T. Paine House, Waltham, Massachusetts, 1884.[6] The physical sense of permanence and security, which the actual form and siting of the Jacobs House suggests, is duplicated and reinforced by the building's stylistic role as the perpetuator of late nineteenth-century romantic and organic traditions.

In an analogous way, the Unitarian Church (Fig. 124), Madison, Wisconsin, projected in 1947, also re-established a link with the Anglo-American tradition which had originally

122. Frank Lloyd Wright. Herbert Jacobs House II. Middleton, Wisconsin, 1948.

sponsored Wright's debut sixty years before. True, the rising slope of the auditorium roof (culminating in a great outward sweep over the lectern and manifesting itself on the exterior in the prow-like wedge of glass and stone) might almost be a belated architectural realization of the early Cubist vocabulary seen in paintings by Picasso and Braque about 1910. In contrast to this suggestion of a European influence, however, there is an even stronger sense of indigenous tradition. The church's exterior form, with its broad expanse of pitched roof and conspicuous display of rough stonework, joins it to the same Richardsonian or Queen Anne tradition from which the second Jacobs House evolved. It is, then, all the more significant that Wright's presumed first independent design, dating from 1887, was also a Unitarian church (Fig. 123) (for Sioux City, Iowa), the general form of which bears a curious resemblance to his later masterpiece. The early church project is literally suburban Queen Anne in style, with all the conventional features indicated in stone, shingles, and leaded glass. Such echoes of the past make Wright's second recapturing of the spirit, if not the letter, of this late nineteenth-century picturesque mode doubly noteworthy. A strain of unabashed nationalism and particularism thus threads its way through the *œuvre* of Wright, bursting through the surface from time to time in designs such as these. It is a natural and altogether expected strain, and contrasts with his belated fling at the more international, cosmopolitan, even urban kind of expression which appeared most notably in the Guggenheim Museum.

It has often been remarked that, in his late years, Wright allowed the arc and curved forms, or combinations thereof, to dominate his most imaginative works. Equally prominent, however, were the prow-shaped forms. These were a result of his preoccupation with the reflex diagonal, which grew out of the use of 30°–60° angle relationships in the axes of house plans designed on a hexagonal module. At the same time, Wright continued to turn out works based on themes found in his almost classic Oak Park period of the early 1900's, and the 1955 Harold C. Price House in Phoenix (Figs. 125, 126) is one of the best late examples of the prairie-style heritage in planning and layout. Composed of a series of shifting and sliding slab-covered spaces, dislocated on parallel planes around a central focus, this house is obviously derived from an archetypal source, the Ward Willitts House, Highland Park, Illinois, 1902. In re-using his old theme, however, Wright's searching mind discovered a new way to establish the floating slab above the building's volume. The open atrium of the Price House (the classical reference speaks for itself), with a fountain under the *impluvium,* is roofed with a hovering, lightly perched slab elevated on metal supports above the reverse-tapered piers. It is yet another unique response by Wright to the desert environment of Arizona, an environment that is not completely unrelated to the midwestern prairie situation. It is interesting to contrast this house with the earlier David Lloyd Wright House, with

123. Frank Lloyd Wright. Unitarian Church. Sioux City, Iowa, 1887. Project.

124. Frank Lloyd Wright. Unitarian Church. Madison, Wisconsin, 1947.

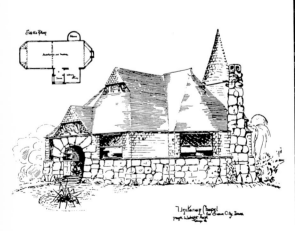

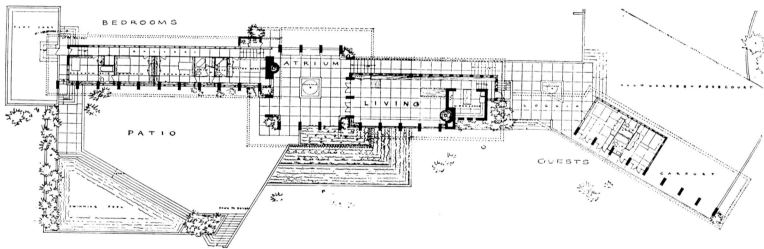

the prewar Pauson House, or with Taliesin West itself, in order to see how Wright's response to a topographical situation never tended toward the evolution of platitudinous, stereotyped solutions. For Wright, a situation was a challenge to which he responded by trying to exhaust a whole range of possible answers; it did not stimulate him to search for *the* definitive response, a goal which has tended to attract Mies van der Rohe in the works of his entire mature career.

Despite his overwhelmingly romantic sensibility, Wright had always been inclined to recognize the role of technology in architecture, to an even greater extent than many architects who have made an unjustifiable fetish of "technological expression" in their designs. As early as 1903, Wright stated that the machine was a great substitute for tools, and he repeated it in 1930 and again in 1953.[7] His reaction to the Futurist-derived Purist epithet, "the house is a machine for living," was assimilative rather than negative, and was represented by a willingness to accept the statement as a point of departure for something else. One of the tragedies of Wright's career was the fact that only a relatively small number of his large-scale projects of structural challenge, especially skyscrapers, were actually

125, 126. Frank Lloyd Wright. Harold C. Price House. Phoenix, Arizona, 1955. View and floor plan.

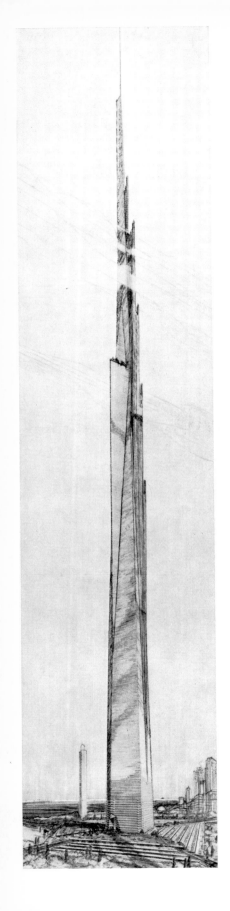

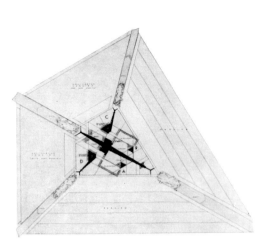

built. Wright prepared several designs for works of this sort, culminating in the 1956 Mile-High Illinois project (Figs. 127, 128), a work of imagination and daring which, had it appeared fifty or one hundred years earlier, would have attracted much attention and controversy. As it was, however, it came at a time when caution, skepticism, and even conservatism were rampant in modern architectural circles.

The Mile-High Illinois was, of course, a dinosaur out of its element, a belated development of structural and aesthetic principles that had been utilized by Gustave Eiffel in his tower for the Paris Exposition of 1889. Wright's monster, regrettably, belonged to an extinct species—no one in the 1950's was especially impressed by the expression of height as a distinctive quality or value—even though this skyscraper was yet another of Wright's appropriations of the Cubist aesthetic some fifty years after its first formulation. Nor did it matter that this 528-floor project was an indirect outgrowth of another work of his youth, the romantically conceived windmill tower built in 1896 on his family farm at Spring Green, Wisconsin (Fig. 129), which was affectionately named "Romeo and Juliet" out of consideration for the dichotomous nature of its form and structure. The whole notion of reconceiving the scale of tall urban buildings and of rethinking their structural systems along nonrectilinear bases, both embodied by the Mile-High Illinois, was not taken seriously in the 1950's, for modern architecture had by then turned its back upon exploration in order to concentrate upon the perfection of stereotypes. It is curiously consistent with the polyphasic character of Wright's late career that he, the former critic of cities as social and architectural entities, should have paradoxically provided one of the few visionary proposals of the post-World War II period for the reintensification of man's urban habitat. Significantly, Louis Kahn, alone among Wright's younger contemporaries, has been the only other architect to evolve similarly provocative towers.[8] As for the question of unusually tall buildings, it was some time after Wright's death before architects again interested themselves in the problem.

One of the very last of Wright's monumental projects, which was only recently completed, is the Marin County Center, California (Figs. 130, 131), a 1959 design that closes out the epic cycle of his career. The low-sprung arches of the long wings that seem to grow out of the flanking hills evoke in succession images of Richardson's rugged, monumental arcuated style, of the sublime colossi of romantic-classicism, and of the ultimate progenitor of both: those great engineering structures of ancient Rome such as the Pont du Gard (Fig. 132).

The low, flat dome crowning the prow-like element of the Marin County Center forms, in effect, the man-made replacement for the actual brow of the hill which was bulldozed away to make room for the building's climax. It, too, provides epic evocations: the dome of the Hadrianic Pantheon (Fig. 133) together with its innumerable successors, from Jefferson's Library at the University of Virginia down to those of the 1893 Columbian Exposition in Chicago, that academic backdrop for Wright's beginnings. With an almost frightening completeness, Wright is able to synthesize everything in this final design. It is the result of the accumulated experience of nearly three-quarters of a century of creation (seventy-two years to be exact, 1887–1959), a span of time which made possible not only the reiterated establishment of his own private aesthetic, but the spontaneous and free ingestion of his rivals' and opponents' contribution as well.

Compared with the ultimate statements of Wright's genius, the best of which reach far beyond the level of mere bravura and virtuosity, the later works of Walter Gropius are something of a puzzle.[9] Generally, they have not been accorded the enthusiastic reception that has been reserved for those of Wright, Mies, and Le Corbusier. In their hesitancy, restraint, and self-effacement, they provide a peculiar contrast both to Gropius' own distinctive contribution to the creation of the International Style and to the even more heightened individualism of both elder and younger architects in the 1950's. Gropius' postwar works,

130, 131. Frank Lloyd Wright. Civic Center. Marin County, San Rafael, California, 1959–61.

Page 72:

127, 128. Frank Lloyd Wright. Mile-High Illinois. 1956. Project. Elevation and plan of the base with parking lot.

129. Frank Lloyd Wright. "Romeo and Juliet" Windmill. Spring Green, Wisconsin, 1896.

132. Pont du Gard, near Nîmes, 1st century A. D.

133. Pantheon. Rome, 120–26 A. D.

134–136. The Architects' Collaborative. Harvard Graduate Center. Cambridge, Massachusetts, 1949–50. Views and site plan.

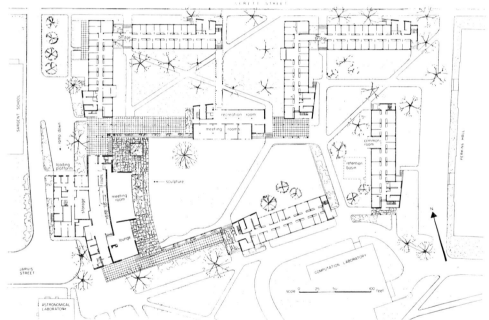

from the Harvard Graduate Center (Figs. 134–136) to the current work-in-progress, the Baghdad University project, have a disinterested, anonymous quality which can fairly be understood as a slackening of personal creative urge rather than any loss of control over design quality. Part of the difficulty of assessing these late works arises from the fact that, since the end of the war, Gropius has worked with The Architects' Collaborative, a group of younger, American-trained architects. Without doubt, at least a part of the character of his late works is due to the fact that he has thus developed in partnership with designers of another generation, who, although they may have shared many of his interests and views, nonetheless have not shared the experience of his active European career from the time of his entry into Peter Behrens' office in 1907, through his Bauhaus years until his arrival in the U.S.A. in 1937.

The desire to provide his associates in The Architects' Collaborative with some knowledge of this background, however secondhand that experience would necessarily have had to

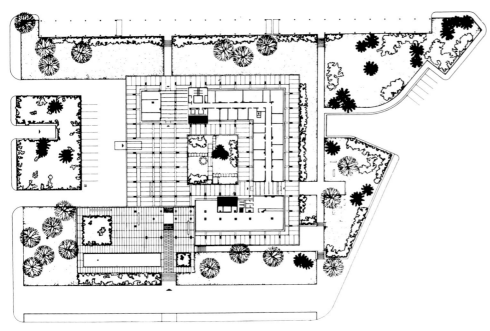

137–139. The Architects' Collaborative. U. S. Embassy. Athens, 1961. Exterior view, interior courtyard, and ground floor plan.

be, accounts for the somewhat retrogressive character of the layout and design of the Harvard Graduate Center, Cambridge, Massachusetts, 1949–50. On a wedge-shaped site, there are a group of dormitory blocks, some isolated but others interconnected by narrow wings in the manner of the Dessau Bauhaus itself. Relief from the sameness of scale and rectilinearity is provided by the ample, curved mass of the commons building. The effect of these buildings, rendered in buff-colored brick, conjures up the style, if not the total spirit, of the mid-1920's. When compared with the Bauhaus buildings (Figs. 13, 13a) themselves, however, there is something sterile and fossilized in the way the various elements of the Harvard design seem to have been too deliberately considered; and this does not compare favorably with the more adventurous designs characteristic of Gropius a quarter century earlier. Furthermore, a comparison of his Harvard buildings with the more novel designs that Mies was providing at the same period for I.I.T. (Figs. 49–51, 143, 144, 151, 152) suggests that Gropius was trying, in an almost sentimental way, to preserve the stylistic externals of his earlier work.

140–142. The Architects' Collaborative. University of Baghdad. Project of 1960.

The work of the former Bauhaus director that has appeared in the later 1950's is even more difficult to interpret. Notable among these designs are his plan for the University of Baghdad (Figs. 140–142), and his American Embassy (Figs. 137–139), Athens, completed in 1961. Both works were designed under the aegis of The Architects' Collaborative and, although Gropius was specified as the partner-in-charge, neither seems to have any essential contact with his personal style and predilections. Indeed, the rather eclectic results tend to resemble much of the recent architecture of the younger generation. One feels that the sources for the various features of these new Gropius designs are not merely extraneous to his personal manner, but are pastiches of the work of derivative second- and third-generation disciples. For instance, in the various parts of the Baghdad plan, there are traces of the influence of such architects as Niemeyer or Carlos Villanueva, or of Harrison and Abramovitz. One looks in vain for traces of the more familiar Gropius, or even of his own contemporaries. Nevertheless, we must admit that these recent Gropius designs manage to rise above the level of their putative sources (but just barely), and the Athens Embassy undoubtedly transcends the shallow formalism of one of its predecessors in this genre, Stone's highly touted but already rather passé New Delhi Embassy of 1957 (Fig. 288). Despite the sturdy, frank qualities that the Athens Embassy reveals in its construction, however, there is nothing in the design to indicate a personal imprint, or to suggest that this building results from a long and important career in modern architecture. Similarly, the Baghdad project seems to be a rather accidental offshoot, cautious in the safeness and familiarity of its eclectic modern vocabulary. It lacks the imprint of specific place, time, and creative personality in a way that necessarily sets it on a lower level of importance and value than the characteristic late works of Wright, Mies van der Rohe, and Le Corbusier. That Gropius has tended to put himself forward in the role of teacher and leader of younger contemporary architects is a factor that has often been used to explain the impersonal character of his recent work; but this is not a particularly satisfactory justification. Whatever the causes, the fact remains that of the major architectural figures of the twentieth century, only Gropius has somehow failed to develop a consequential and individual late style. Instead, he has drifted into a vernacular modern style of distinction but not of historical significance.

Mies van der Rohe's development during the 1950's was not superficially spectacular either.[10] It was in the nature of his achievement with the master plan for the I.I.T. campus, 1939–40 (discussed in earlier chapters) (Fig. 49) that it provide a closed frame of reference within which his later work would develop, but beyond which it would not go. This remarkable and profitable stabilization of style can be appreciated especially in two small parts of the I.I.T. campus that are of almost Brunelleschian conciseness: the Boiler Plant of 1950 and the Chapel of 1952 (Figs. 143, 144). That two such dissimilar programs could stimulate solutions so remarkably alike in shape and detail, as well as in stylistic consistency, has been a matter of considerable controversy. For many, it has been difficult, if not impossible, to accept so harsh and industrialized a style as a mode fitting and appropriate to an ecclesiastical program. It is the nature of contemporary architecture, however, and especially of that branch of which Mies is the most extreme and even poetic representative, to establish absolutes in an abstract, rather than a programmatic, context; thus, such critical considerations as those related to fitness of form or expression of character often tend to beg the question. If there is an unmistakable industrial quality to the I.I.T. Chapel, there is concurrently a domestic, residential quality to Wright's Unitarian Church in Madison (Fig. 124). On this basis, it would be possible, though not necessarily profitable, to argue that Wright's design is no more appropriate to, or expressive of, a religious situation than is that of Mies. The suggestive attributes are present in each building because they happen to be basic elements in the architectural vocabulary of their respective creators, not for any circumstantial reasons. Mies's style remains steady and unswerving no matter what the ultimate destination of the building may be; in a less extreme way, the same is true of Wright's style. Volume and structure are considered and expressed by Mies in a poised, tense relationship that establishes a precarious balance between classical articulation and baroque integration. Having arrived at this ordering principle, Mies has done no more for each individual building than create slightly different proportional, textural, or coloristic harmonies within a fixed and established system.

His achievement in transforming the unstable contemporary architectural idiom into something fixed and absolute is an intellectual and creative feat of the first magnitude. In effect, Mies has provided what seems to be a universal solution to the problem of exterior form

143. Ludwig Mies van der Rohe. Chapel, Illinois Institute of Technology. Chicago, 1952.

144. Ludwig Mies van der Rohe. Boiler Plant, Illinois Institute of Technology. Chicago, 1950.

and interior space, a solution which, in its all-encompassing simplicity, seems within the means of any other architect to apply to almost any circumstance or program. Despite this universality, it remains as personal a synthesis of the many conflicting factors of the contemporary situation as that achieved by Wright. Mies's "formula" of glass, metal, and brick proved itself easily transmittable to temperaments as diverse as Philip Johnson, Gordon Bunshaft, Eero Saarinen, and Alison and Peter Smithson, all of whom borrowed aspects of this vocabulary in their works of the late 1940's and early 1950's. Yet the unique historical process by which Mies arrived at his terse, all-encompassing style was not repeated by these younger architects, for, understandably, they were more concerned with the package than with its contents. Once again, the outward style of a contemporary architect's work— its visual features—was mistaken for the entirety of its communicable message.

The blending of romantic, mechanistic, and academic features in Mies's late style has been commented on before. Related to this synthesis is the emergence of what might be characterized as the temple-like image of his new buildings. First of all, in the matter of keen adjustments of detail, Mies has approximated one crucial aspect of the Attic Doric style of the mid-fifth century B.C., at least so far as is possible with modern materials and techniques. Significantly, these adjustments are never carried to the point of exact uniformity or of sterile perfection. The Farnsworth House, Plano, Illinois, 1946–50 (Figs. 145, 146), is a fine example of this, for formal regularity is introduced only to be subsequently modified into an unbalanced symmetry rather than coldly academic harmony. The frame of the house is formed of two slabs supported by eight white steel "I"-beams arranged in regular fashion, with four facing each of the long sides. Three equal bays are created between steel columns, but the classicizing image is somewhat clouded since the end-columns are not at the corners. Instead, the slab projects beyond the last column in a cantilever which is one-fourth the length of the major bays. The problematic, uncertain character of this structural relationship is further stressed by the dislocation toward one end of the slab of the glass box which constitutes the interior. In this way, an entrance portico is formed at one end, its length equivalent to one full bay, and it is open across the entire width of the house. In order to avoid the suggestion of a temple or megaron-type of entry, however, the steps descend from one side rather than from the end, leading to an open deck slab rather than directly to the ground. The result is outwardly serene, yet full of latent tension; it is inescapably mannerist in the way in which it draws such an extremely logical structure and design to the brink of irrationality.

145, 146. Ludwig Mies van der Rohe. Farnsworth House. Plano, Illinois, 1946–50. Floor plan and view.

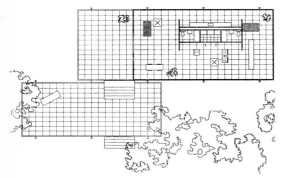

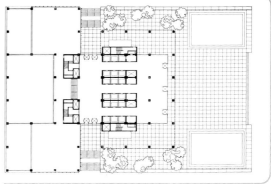

Some of these same qualities are present in the Seagram Building (Figs. 147–149), New York, 1955–58 (designed in temporary collaboration with Philip Johnson), although in a notably less striking way. The uniformity of the Park Avenue tower is, for example, contradicted by the group of lower, block-like masses which are juxtaposed to its base at the rear, toward Lexington Avenue. The stark, uncompromising handling of the principal entrance space, with its exposed bronze piers and overhanging slab, seems to be a kind of refusal to dress up or academicize a severe, rational solution, one that is distinctly lacking in expressive charm. Crown Hall, the largest and most imposing of Mies's buildings executed at I.I.T., 1955, to serve as the School of Architecture, presents another formulation of Mies's astute, understated mannerism (Figs. 151, 152). Regular, symmetrical, and almost academic in its outward shape, with an axial entrance, it achieves a free, uninterrupted interior space through the use of four giant steel girders above the roof. Supporting these girders are the four principal vertical members of the façade, the regular spacing of which invokes the paradigm of the Farnsworth House. At the same time, Crown Hall's monumental scale is accounted for by the inclusion of a secondary bay system within its major supports. As in the Farnsworth House, the major columns of Crown Hall are not placed at corners; instead the glazed volume projects beyond, creating, in a more prosaic and symmetrical way, a mannered effect of dislocation. When such niceties of thought and effect are appreciated in Mies's

147–149. Ludwig Mies van der Rohe and Philip Johnson. Seagram Building. New York, 1955–58. Exterior views and plan of the ground floor.

150. Ludwig Mies van der Rohe. Promontory Apartments. Chicago, 1949.

mature designs, it becomes obvious that despite the relative ease with which others have imitated his style, it has been virtually impossible for anyone to recreate the totality of his art. Nevertheless, the detachment and lofty isolation of this late style, which avoids the pitfalls of lifeless academicism that lie just beyond the balanced elastic tension he has created, is neither so pristine nor unique that the sources of its inspiration are completely concealed. The influences of such dissimilar figures as Schinkel, Wright, and Le Corbusier are present, in one form or another, in the genesis of his designs, whether in the slabs of deck or roof, or in the peristyles of steel colonades. Of course, Mies has also absorbed other stimuli. The one tentative, and hence unsatisfactory, building of his American career—the Promontory Apartments (Fig. 150), Chicago, 1949—bears, in the rhythm of its fenestration and expressed structural cage, the unmistakable influence of the earlier Chicago School of tall building design exemplified by such Louis Sullivan works as the façade of the Gage Building, 1898–99. On the other hand, the temple-like image came to the fore in the 1958 project for a Bacardi Office Building, Santiago de Cuba (Fig. 153). Here the roof "slab" was to be supported by eight detached columns, two along each side; and as at Crown Hall and Farnsworth House, there were none at the corners. The singularity of Mies's distilled and mellowed style is even more apparent in the Bacardi office in Mexico City (Fig. 154), completed in 1961, a building less spectacular in structure than the unexecuted Santiago de Cuba project. A recessed basement portal leads to a spacious, austere entrance lobby stretching the full height of the building, a galleried room which is symmetrically flanked by stairs. The glazed *piano nobile* is supported by four rows of six steel "I"-columns, with the outer rows serving as the industrial age "order" of the exterior. (Again, there are no columns at the corners.) The subsidiary "order" is composed of smaller "I"-mullions welded to the metal surface, and these redivide the five major bays of the façade into five secondary elements. The effect of the interior is, quite simply, majestic.

The very permanence of the Miesian idiom now sets him apart from his younger disciples, notably, Philip Johnson. Johnson, in his 1957–60 Proctor Institute (Fig. 155), Utica, New York (finished a year before Mies's Mexico City building), created a space of similar proportion and dignity, but one in which elegance ceased to be a matter of almost mathematical austerity and instead became a question of subtle visual effect. Thus, the important element of the stair became a delicately perfect thing in contrast to the more matter-of-fact detailing of Mies. Through a comparison of these buildings, it becomes clear that, by the late 1950's a gulf was opening which was inexorably separating Mies and his work from the everchanging mainstream. The similarity of his new isolation to that which pertained in the

151, 152. Ludwig Mies van der Rohe. Crown Hall, Illinois Institute of Technology. Chicago, 1952–56. Floor plan and view.

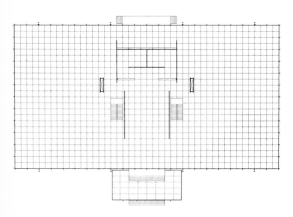

153. Ludwig Mies van der Rohe. Project for a Bacardi Office Building. Santiago de Cuba, 1958. Model.

154. Ludwig Mies van der Rohe. Bacardi Office Building. Mexico City, 1961.

155. Philip Johnson. Museum of Art, Munson-Williams-Proctor Institute. Utica, New York, 1957–60.

late 1930's and early 1940's is obvious. Nor have Mies's new projects for an office tower in Baltimore, Maryland, completed in 1962, or for a Federal Center in Chicago, completed in 1964, or an office for Krupp, near Essen, Germany, completed in 1964, in any way altered a picture which took shape nearly a generation ago.

In the light of these buildings, it is clear that Mies's need to arrive at a new synthesis in the most recent phase of his career was not of the same order as that of Wright. The concentration of his efforts into a single, all-pervading mode of expression, and the gradual immuration within that mode of those few but significant extraneous influences that had worked upon its painstaking evolution, in effect made a further effort at synthesis quite unnecessary. Mies's reconciliation with the architecture of the past, and especially with the Schinkelesque aspect of romantic-classicism, is thus less spectacular and more predicatable than Wright's continual response to historical stimuli. During his early career, Mies was more profoundly attached to this understated neo-classic aesthetic than any other of his contemporaries, so that even when influenced by the most anti-classic of modern tendencies, Mies always retained a very real trace of that regularizing and stabilizing point of view. This was the case in the 1929 Barcelona Pavilion (Figs. 47, 48), where the almost invisible columnar supports, lost as they were in an ambiguous space defined by a set of illusively shifting and sliding wall planes, nonetheless provided a tenuous suggestion of the temple-like image that became more explicit in his late work. Of all twentieth-century architects, Mies has developed the most unitary and single-minded manner and, as a result, his need for reintegration with the flow of history has been negligible. Perhaps this came about because Mies was, and is, the only instinctively conservative architect of genius who has always worked in the characteristic modes of expression of our century.

In a somewhat different fashion, the buildings designed and erected by Le Corbusier since the early 1950's also represent a stage of fulfillment predicated upon his earlier accomplishments, but activated by an unending search.[11] Even more than the ultimate works of Wright, they represent probings that cut through the accumulated efforts and debris of the past. In these buildings, notably at Ronchamp (Figs. 158, 161, 163–166), La Tourette (Figs. 170–175), and Chandigarh (Figs. 176–185), as well as in others scattered across the globe from France to India, the forces of tradition, innovation, and regeneration which were at work (in particular and individual ways) in the late designs of Mies and of Wright are once more in evidence. These buildings are perhaps the most broadly representative, as well as the most profound, group of monuments to emerge in the course of the twentieth century. Creatively, they are uninhibited: lusty, rich, the product of an imagination released from the fetters of prosaic, everyday restrictions, yet an imagination whose outpourings are never out of touch with the broad universal base of established modernism. In this way the most seemingly surrealistic formal inventions take on a reality that is both sensible and convincing; and the most ordinary of sources or needs can become the springboard for the most lyrical of creations.

The direction of this fulfillment was already revealed in the transmutation of the machine aesthetic in the Marseilles *Unité d'Habitation,* 1946–52 (Figs. 108–110), especially in the shapes of the *pilotis,* the broken surfaces caused by the *brises-soleils,* and the startling forms of the concrete-scape on the roof terrace (Figs. 46, 157). There the genius of Gaudí, as manifested in the roof forms of the 1905 Casa Milá, Barcelona (Fig. 156), seems to re-emerge, transformed by the Cartesian, almost Cézannesque, discipline of Le Corbusier.[12] This enrichment of Le Corbusier's style occurred without any fundamental retreat or turning away from the aims and forms expressed two decades earlier. Indeed, the austere discipline of Purism itself insured that his subsequent growth would be measured and regulated, no matter what spirit the forms themselves might acquire in the process of development.

The hilltop pilgrimage chapel of Notre-Dame-du-Haut, Ronchamp, 1950–54 (Figs. 158, 161, 163–166), grows out of this lyrical sense of order; and the dialogue that its alternately coiling and unfurling masses conducts with the crest of the ridges on the distant horizon is no

156. Antonio Gaudí. Casa Milá. Barcelona, 1905–10. Detail of the roof.

157. Le Corbusier. Unité d'Habitation. Marseilles, 1946–52. Detail of the roof.

sudden recantation on the part of a Gallic rationalist turned suddenly and inexplicably mystic.[13] Far from it. While Ronchamp represents the furthest point on a road towards subjective formalism—a point from which his very last designs were receding—its shapes are not aberrant or quixotic, but are, instead, the outgrowth of one special, if not frequently appreciated, aspect of his original machine style Purism. The form of the Ronchamp chapel displays an involvement with land forms, a concern that was anticipated in those mound-like concrete forms on the Marseilles roof which imitate the shapes of the distant mountains just barely visible beyond the high parapet. If, in the 1950's, Le Corbusier seemed bent upon echoing the forceful masses of earth and rock that surrounded his sites—where in the 1920's his buildings had been static objects set in contrast to a passive, tranquil land-scape, as was the case with the Villa Savoye (Figs. 27, 28, 30, 31, 33)—this change of sentiment and emotional response represented an enrichment of possibility, not the rejection of an old attitude. The earlier, more docile, yet willful concern for an expressive relationship between building and landscape logically preceded the later tendency in which the chapel at Ronchamp and the Assembly Building at Chandigarh strive to compete as equals with the superhuman visual forces of the landscape. Indeed, these expressive and dramatic elements in the landscape would remain inert and unremarkable without the presence of just these very buildings. As a young architect and polemicist, Le Corbusier had written of Michelangelo's apse at St. Peter's in the following terms: "To give forth emanations, storm, gentle breezes on plain and sea, to raise mighty alps with the pebbles that go to form the walls of men's houses, this is to succeed in a symphony of relationships."[14] Today, a generation later, these remarks seem especially appropriate, but with respect to the author-architect's own buildings.

To appreciate Le Corbusier's unique vitality, one has only to think of the protective environmental relationship between structure and site typical of the late buildings by Wright. More specifically, one ought to recall the way in which the powerful, massive forms of the

158. Le Corbusier. Notre-Dame-du-Haut. Ronchamp, 1950–54. Exterior altar.

second Herbert Jacobs House (Fig. 122) or the Marin County Center (Figs. 130, 131) are submerged, half-buried, within the dominating contours of their sheltering hills or mounds. Whereas Wright finally came to identify himself and his buildings in the most literal fashion with the terrain upon which—or rather into which—they are placed, Le Corbusier never relinquishes his role as the activator of forces, the creator of pulsating forms which by their very presence galvanizes the latent energy of the site. The forces released in this confrontation between man and nature are analogous to the conflicting tensions in the buildings of Michelangelo or to the recurring explosions set off by the turbulent forms of Borromini. Yet, Le Corbusier's buildings possess a vocabulary and syntax all their own, and their formal resolution is as characteristic of twentieth-century style as the earlier solutions were of the High Renaissance or of the Baroque.

Two houses of the early 1950's can give a fair index of the range of Le Corbusier's work at that time, while indicating his flexible response to differing situations. These are, first, the Jaoul Houses, Neuilly-sur-Seine, 1952–56 (Figs. 44, 159), and second, the Shodan House (Fig. 160), at Ahmedabad (India), designed and built over the same four-year period. The former, with its tile vaults, was an outgrowth of the 1935 weekend retreat near Paris (Fig. 45), whereas the Shodan House picks up, and reinterprets at thirty years distance, many of the themes of his houses built during the heyday of Purism.

His practice of re-using earlier motifs is often hidden behind outwardly novel features. The external form of *brut* concrete characteristic in his work since 1945 has seemed, to many of the most observant and veteran critics, to be largely an about-face from the sleek, impalpable, shell-like appearance of his buildings of the 1920's. Indeed, the intellectual clarity and the exactness of expression that were so important a part of his earlier manner —so important, in fact, that they then seemed to be the very crux of his style—today seem quite foreign to the primitivistic, cultivatedly archaistic manner of his later work, beginning with the Marseilles *Unité* of 1946–52. Yet continued study and increased familiarity with his total *œuvre* tends to reveal persistencies of theme and of basic shape.

Unique among the great and near-great architects of the twentieth century, Le Corbusier is a noted painter and has even designed projects that have been turned into sculpture. His painting has had historical significance only during one period, the Purist apogee of 1918–24, however, and the rest of his work, sensitive to the various movements since Purism, has usually followed other currents at intervals of ten to fifteen years with a surprisingly uncertain taste. Although the painting done by Le Corbusier since about 1924 has been of personal rather than general significance, it nonetheless put him in intimate contact with the various forces operating in another, and frequently more vital, art form. Perhaps most important, these contacts occurred at a time when other architects were often at a loss for visual stimuli. Consequently, Le Corbusier as an architect had less need of the specific, yet self-contradictory, historicizing that seemed requisite for Wright in the 1950's because he, Le Corbusier, had been in more intimate and continuous contact with the totality of the contemporary revolution in the arts. Of course, his activity as a painter (Fig. 162) does not completely account for the remarkably individual imprint of Le Corbusier's forms or for the compelling accent which has always been present, regardless of specific differences in momentary style. Yet, it is clear that the genesis of his buildings' shapes are akin to creative processes in painting and sculpture, even though his forms easily withstand scrutiny from a purely architectural point of view as well. A rich fund of historical allusions, largely from classic and pre-classic Mediterranean sources, entered his work at an early stage, so that his particular synthesis was already well established, in the Villa Savoye, by 1929 (Figs. 27, 28, 30, 31, 33); this was at least partially brought about through the catalytic agency of modern painting. Subsequent stimuli from the past were mostly minor, and his continuing repertoire of ideas adapted from the past, stemming as it does from early studies, has become more thoroughly integrated with the passing of time.

Ronchamp, with its almost complete avoidance of right angles and straight lines, is

159. Le Corbusier. Jaoul Houses. Neuilly-sur-Seine, 1952–56.

160. Le Corbusier. Shodan House. Ahmedabad, 1952–56.

161. Le Corbusier. Notre-Dame-du-Haut. Ronchamp, 1950–54. Exterior pulpit.

162. Le Corbusier. Still Life. Oil on canvas, 39″ × 32″. 1926.

superficially his most anti-mechanistic work, but a work that was, nevertheless, largely based upon earlier experiences. Yet the clarity and exactness with which the form has been rendered is inescapable. The mottled gray of the rough concrete shell overhead contrasts with the whitewashed gunite surface of the concealed-rubble walls, and the whole is carefully enlivened with touches of color at the door and in the glass of the funnel-like window apertures. Transcending individual details, the whole building becomes an epic experience of architectonic form which has not been duplicated by any other architect of our time. Certainly, each work by Le Corbusier is an event of more than local and individual significance. Here, in fact, there is a passionate, even sentimental, effort to translate the visual and accoustical properties of the landscape (a dome-shaped hill set in the midst of a plain, which is, in turn, completely surrounded by an outer ring of hills) into the forms of an ecclesiastical architecture that will possess a space of ineffable character (l'espace indicible).[15] This striving for an indescribable, unforeseen spatial quality is perhaps not too far removed from the aim of Wright, expressed in connection with the Guggenheim: "Not ... a cellular composition of compartments, but one where all is one great space on a continuous floor." Concomitantly, Le Corbusier's Villa Savoye had approached this continuous, ineffable (indicible) character through its patent ambiguities and paradoxes, particularly through its conceptual blending of interior and exterior. A similarly elusive, paradoxical, sometimes implausible aspect is present in Ronchamp in a variety of ways. The undulating walls of the exterior help generate eddies and whirlpools of space that draw the pilgrim up to and around the form of the building. The entrance that is habitually used (the others being for special ceremonial occasions only) is somewhat disguised through its being located at the far side of the building, thus becoming an incidental feature in a continuously shaped form. The novelty of this form is so pronounced that many familiar architectonic elements, such as a "principal façade," are made virtually unrecognizable. Having gained the rather obscure entrance, one is surrounded and psychically submerged by the interior counterpart of the undulating exterior walls. These mold and shape a space on the interior which, by its contractions and expansions, sets up further imaginary visual currents to engulf the eye and body in a unique and exhilarating experience. Even the floor is irregular, following the natural contour of the gently sloping ground on the crown of the hill and thereby providing an echo of the rising curved form of the concrete shell overhead.

Ronchamp also creates a critical problem in terms of its "appropriateness," since its form is no more specifically churchly in character than those of Mies in the Chapel of I.I.T. (Fig. 143) and Wright in the Madison Unitarian Church (Fig. 124). Certainly, the strange, almost exotic form of Ronchamp possesses an ethereal, spiritualizing quality—indeed, this is a part of the ineffable, mysterious quality of its space. Furthermore, the indelible impression of cavernous other-worldliness is quite distinct and more inexplicable than the spirituality inherent in the rather surreal forms of the Marseilles roof or in the ambiguous Cubist geometry of the Villa Savoye. Indeed, Ronchamp seems almost specifically pagan rather than Christian. This is, of course, only natural coming from an architect who has been continually fascinated by the Helladic and Hellenic traditions, and their subsequent offshoots, while remaining largely indifferent to the Gothic. However, there is an element present in the handling of the forms at Ronchamp which also suggests, even creates an illusion of prehistoric megaliths.[16] The very presence of this feature carries the imagery of Le Corbusier's monument back beyond archaic Doric or Mycenaean precedents to the scattered remains of the Bronze Age. (Even the seemingly less archaistic Villa Savoye can be regarded in terms of a prehistoric Swiss lake-dwelling, thus indicating that the imprint of prehistory on Le Corbusier is far from new.) Standing in front of the prow of Ronchamp, just below the brow of the hill and the artificial mound left to "landscape" the site, the spectator or pilgrim sees the integral forms of the spreading walls and the great bulging concrete canopy not as the conventionally articulated façade and portal of a Christian church, but instead as the piled-up rocks of a freestanding megalithic tomb. Once inside, he is faced with an even more inescapable suggestion of a megalithic gallery grave— specifically, one like that at Bagneux, near Saumur (Fig. 168), with its stone-roofed spaces some nine feet high. The irregular openings in the west wall of Ronchamp suggest the imprecise way in which the various upright stones of the neolithic gallery grave are joined together, thus admitting irregular splashes of light. Even more striking, however, is the way in which the apparently huge, monolithic burden of the sagging concrete roof comes to rest upon the slanted walls, leaving a slim crevice through which light pours, again suggesting the effect produced on the interior of the gallery grave because of the irregular meeting of the horizontal and vertical megaliths.

Despite this preoccupation with a pseudo-neolithic "constructivism," Le Corbusier con-

165, 166. Le Corbusier. Notre-Dame-du-Haut. Ronchamp, 1950–54. Interior view and perspective.

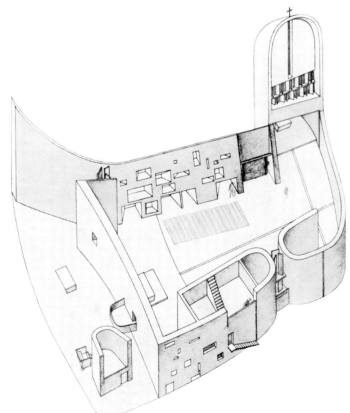

Page 89:

167. Drawing of Hadrian's Villa, Tivoli, by Le Corbusier, 1910.

168. Megalithic grave. Bagneux, near Saumur, 2nd millenium B. C.

169. Le Corbusier. Project for the reconstruction of Algiers. 1930.

tinued to find inspiration in specific details of Roman architecture. In the three small side chapels at Ronchamp, the system of celestial lighting is drawn through the funnel-like tower forms, suggested, he tells us, by the inner recesses of the Serapeion at Hadrian's Villa, Tivoli (Fig. 167).[17] However, the most significant anticipations are to be found in the architect's own past: the inescapable analogy of its prow with a similar acute-angled form on the service tower of the Swiss Pavilion, 1930–32 (Figs. 97, 98); or the fashion in which the undulating, swaying, curved forms of its plan, complete with its partly concealed cul-de-sac side chapels, draw their inspiration from the layout of the curved slab forms found in the 1930 project for reconstructing the city of Algiers (Fig. 169), the transfer from the colossal urban format to the diminutive ecclesiastical program effected by turning the interlocking curved shapes of the earlier scheme "inside out." In these several ways, the Chapel at Ronchamp occupies a special place in Le Corbusier's postwar work, imposing one remembered image upon another to create a building of unusual psychic and symbolic richness, but integrating the various images with more suppleness and maturity than was possible a quarter-century before. There is a consequent loss of the old sense of stress and mannerist compression; the spirit of the forms has become opulent, expansive, even baroque, even though rendered in the language of rough concrete and gunite. In contrast to Mies's style, which becomes progessively more mannerist (in an aristocratic sense) through a compression of conflicting tendencies into a single mold, there is an opposite sense of expansion and release in the later work of Le Corbusier, so that its original mannerist qualities of inversion and complexity of overlapping images and references are largely dissipated.

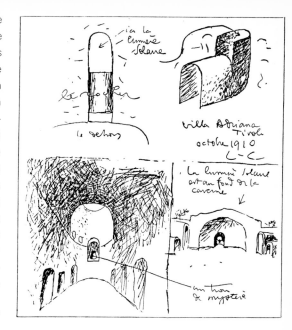

It is something of a shock to turn suddenly from the exuberant forms of Ronchamp to the more dour, static impression produced by the 1957–60 chapel and monastery of La Tourette (Figs. 170–175) at Eveux-sur-l'Arbresle, a few miles from Lyon.[18] Part of the difference, however, is readily explained by the nature of the program, that of a hermitage which is, in effect, in total opposition to the pilgrimage program of Ronchamp. Ronchamp is designed to be seen from a considerable distance, to be a visual magnet inexorably leading the pilgrim on to his goal. On the other hand, La Tourette is isolated, secluded, largely hidden; it nestles into the wooded slope of a hill instead of occupying the summit. The downhill façade of La Tourette, comprising, on the top stories, the *brises-soleils* of the small, individual monk's cells, offers a superb view of the surrounding countryside, even though the building itself is not a conspicuous object in that landscape. Once again, this contrasts with the situation at Ronchamp, where the crown of the hill is so broad and flat, and its perimeter so thickly wooded, that the view from the top is focused mostly upon the horizon, and not upon the total landscape at the foot of the rise.

In effect, the church of La Tourette is the monastery's only public space. The undulating surfaces of Ronchamp are rejected in favor of a roughly foursquare form, and, at first glance, the chapel seems to be a perfectly ordinary rectilinear cube. Only gradually do the slight slope to the walls and the decline in the roof become noticeable. Such variations suggest, ambiguously, a degree of refinement together with a perplexing, disturbing crudity. This effect is complicated by the awkward, ungainly concrete stilts that support much of the superstructure on the downhill side of the building; their dry, bony character is quite different from the more robustly handled *pilotis* of the Marseilles *Unité*. The sumptuousness of form, so characteristic not only of Marseilles and of Ronchamp, but also of the earliest Chandigarh buildings, the High Court of 1952–56, here seems to have been displaced by a new key or mode; the inspiration seems implicity monastic, and indeed, specifically Cistercian. (Le Corbusier in 1956 had written a moving preface to a book of photographs of the twelfth-century priory of Le Thoronnet.[19]) Even the Cistercian's customary rejection of a large bell tower as an inappropriately worldly vanity and its replacement by a small, open belfry is followed at La Tourette. The interior court, formed by the U-shaped monastery set against the south wall of the church, is perhaps the most perplexing feature

of the entire building. Instead of a cloister surrounded by an arcade, Le Corbusier has designed here a series of enclosed ramps that cross back and forth in the center of the open space, connecting the different levels and wings of the monastery. For the most part, these are raised above the level of the ground and thus produce an effect not too far removed from the Futurist and Constructivist traditions of a generation ago. At the same time, the court is an arena in which are placed forms such as the pyramidal oratory, the stark geometry of which suggests the angular vocabulary of romantic-classicism rather than the more Cézannesque effects of cylinders and of abstract mountain forms that were present a decade earlier in Marseilles and contributed much to the effulgent shaping of Ronchamp.

This leanness of proportion in supporting members and a certain awkward angularity in over-all geometry seems to have appeared for the first time in some of the details for the *Unité d'Habitation* of Nantes-Rezé, 1952–57, where tough, wedge-shaped slabs (Fig. 1) replaced the sturdier sculpturesque *pilotis* of the earlier Marseilles *Unité*. Whereas Le Corbusier's structural underpinnings of Marseilles display a pliant geometry that is at once Cézannesque and reminiscent of archaic Doric—forms that invariably imply an active animistic interplay of forces—those in the newer *Unité* at Nantes possess a rigidity and spareness that anticipated the ungainliness of La Tourette.

It is in the three major government buildings at Chandigarh (Figs. 176–185), the new capital of the Punjab in India, a program begun in 1950 and constructed over a decade, from the early 1950's to the early 1960's, that the evolution of Le Corbusier's late style is most thoroughly revealed.[20] Partly because of the vastness of the site and the size of the buildings, a relaxed, expansive quality pervades the whole ensemble. For the first time in his career, Le Corbusier did not feel a need to cram a multitude of ideas into a single, modestly proportioned structure. In addition, he was at last offered the challenge of an official governmental program, with all its endless variety of demands, after a lifetime of rejected and ignored projects. Chandigarh is, in spite of many unique features, the fulfillment of these unrealized aspirations.[21] To a considerable degree, Le Corbusier, with the construction of these buildings, took a gigantic step toward healing the breach that has existed during the entire twentieth century between the avant-garde and official patronage.

Situated at the juncture between a vast, monotonous plain and a long range of hills, Chandigarh is a site which affords an opportunity for a colossal tug of war between the shapes of man and those of nature. One approaches the group of interrelated buildings from the new city (built on the plain) by way of a long boulevard. Pointing toward

170–172. Le Corbusier. Monastery of La Tourette. Eveux, near Lyon, 1957–60. Exterior view of the "light-funnels" and interior views of the church.

173–175. Le Corbusier. Monastery of La Tourette. Eveux,
near Lyon, 1957–60. Exterior view, interior court, and plan
of the two upper floors.

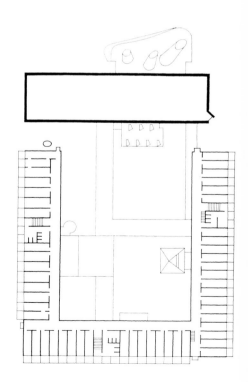

176. Le Corbusier. Chandigarh, begun 1950. Site plan, showing Capitol group at top center, situated between the city and the mountains to the north.

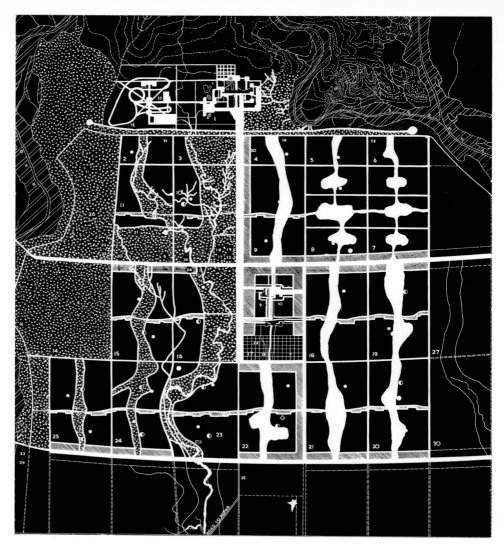

the low mountains in the distance, the axis of this boulevard bisects the site, leaving the High Court of Justice as the visual climax on the right, and the larger and more recent group comprised of the Secretariat and Assembly on the left. Although the approaches are reasonably direct, the first view of each of the forms is made both stately and exciting through the interposition of an artificial landscape of mounds and hillocks, deliberate yet fortuitous-seeming elements which partly conceal the buildings until the visitor has drawn close to them. In this way, the presence of such monumental forms gains the element of surprise. The man-made earth forms also provide variety for the broad terraces, complete with traditional reflecting pools, upon which the buildings are placed. Furthermore, they are situated in such a way as to provide an echo of the contours of the distant hills, causing the buildings to seem compressed between the forms of real nature on the one hand and of contrived nature on the other. The vast distances that really exist on the site are in this fashion telescoped, and the whole becomes more visually coherent; indeed the abstract organization of this real landscape provides one with a sense of discipline and contraction that is akin to many of Cézanne's views of Mont Sainte-Victoire.

The High Court (Figs. 178–180), first projected in May, 1951, and constructed from a somewhat revised scheme during 1952–56, reflects the sumptuous modeling of the chapel at Ronchamp. The idea of a canopy-like structure that encloses in a single gesture both the interior and the veranda-like exterior spaces of the building appeared in the first project, but the arcades, which in that scheme defined the individual court chambers on the exterior, were rejected in favor of a mammoth, syncopated *brise-soleil*. The breezeway formed at the top of the building, underneath the undulating concrete canopy, opens into a huge portico and open-air *salle des pas perdus* at one end of the façade, which faces the Secretariat and Assembly across two large basins of water. The portico gains its ponderous monumentality from three massive piers, the starkness of which is given a challenging vibrancy through the use of a bold, Légeresque color scheme; from right to left, the piers are painted red, yellow, and green. (This detail was intended from the start, but was not added to the building until 1962 for lack of funds.) Behind the portico rise ramps leading to the building's upper floors; these dramatic causeways shuttle back and forth with a spatial excitement that cannot help but evoke the effects of Piranesi's *Carceri*.[22] Novel as it is, Le Corbusier's High Court also manages to conjure up the traditional pomp and dignity inherent in those official nineteenth-century European styles considered appropriate for law courts and palaces of justice, without for a moment stooping to the redundant bathos of lavish eclecticism. Miraculously, Le Corbusier's design effortlessly rises above the twin

177. Le Corbusier. Chandigarh, begun 1950. Model of the Capitol. From left to right: the Secretariat, the Assembly, the Governor's Palace (not executed), and the High Court are arranged in an arc around a vast central space designed with terraces, reflecting pools, and sunken gardens. The access roads leading from the city (at the bottom) to the individual buildings are below the principle ground level, thereby concealing most vehicle traffic from the spectators contemplating this architectural drama.

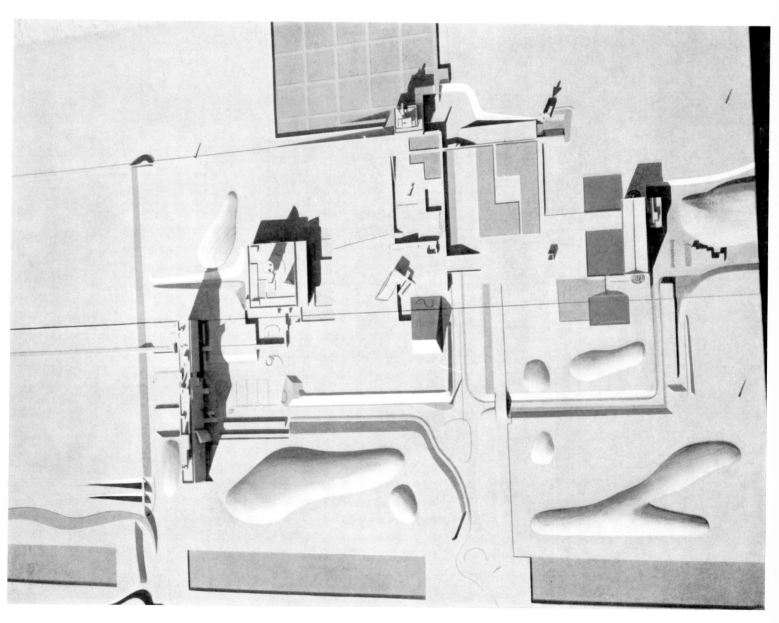

pitfalls of official punctiliousness and tasteless, overtly demonstrative form-mongering (so common a fault in the architecture of the mid-twentieth century). In doing so, it arrives at a solution that is majestic and vital, appropriate and personal all at once.

The Secretariat (Fig. 181), completed in 1958, stands on the threshold of Le Corbusier's drier, less opulent, post-Ronchamp manner—a manner evident in projects like La Tourette and the Assembly building at Chandigarh (the latter finished only in 1962) and constituting, in effect, a second "late" style. Functionally remarkable in its size and bureaucratic all-inclusiveness, it contains a number of notable features. These relieve a certain monotony inherent in the building's long façade, one function of which is to form a backdrop and continuation for the lower, but more powerfully inflected, silhouette of the Assembly, especially as seen from the esplanade in front of the High Court, more than a quarter of a mile away. The offices of the ministers are constructed as double-story spaces, and this fact plays a role in modifying the exterior treatment of the *brises-soleils* at a point to the right of the long façade's center line. Vertical circulation is handled by means of ramps, as in the High Court, but here there are two ramps, one on each of the long sides of the building. Furthermore, they are contained in huge, silo-like concrete towers which provide a dark, closed-in spatial sensation in contrast to the openness of the ramps and causeways of the High Court. This kind of contrast established between different buildings, in which various effects are produced by related forms and functional situations, is one of the delights of the entire ensemble at Chandigarh. Indeed, it is the kind of effect that could only be produced by the rare, perceptive architect who sees every detail in the context of the whole, and, moreover, in terms of his own creative past, a past which is understood in terms of those visual sensations and provocations that have incited each unique event.

178, 179. Le Corbusier. High Court. Chandigarh, 1952–56.

It is true that every major architect comes, at the summit of his career, to the creation of a building which represents much of his prior experience, but none has attained quite the intensity of accumulation and transcendence that is found at Chandigarh. It is not a matter of simple recapitulation, of covering the same ground once more, nor even of rejuvenation. The accumulated experience and wisdom of a lifetime are here manifested, not merely by an accumulation of remembered images and forms, but by the total conquest of an epic, superhuman site by a group of monumental buildings which nonetheless maintain scale and proportion with the dimensions of the human figure.

For the present, the Assembly building constructed from 1959–62, is the climax of the entire complex (Figs. 182–185). Approaching the site from the main access road, the visitor first sees the out-thrust curving slab of its portico on his left, but the brow of the terrace upon which the building is placed obscures his view of the lower portions. The easiest and most rational approach to the building is on its minor side, facing the parking esplanade in front of the Secretariat, and it is by this route that visitors and legislators normally enter the building. In this way, the principal entrance portico acts as a ceremonial, almost theatrical, backdrop to the huge space, more than a quarter-mile square, that is bounded on the opposite side by the High Court. (It will be completed by a structure, once designated as the Governor's Palace, but now projected as a Museum, that will be set beyond the present buildings toward the hills.) When completed, this great space will be further activated by a series of ramps, mounds, and trenches, added to the reflecting basins which are already in place.

The most revealing view of the Assembly is gained from the roof terrace of the Secretariat, a disarmingly obvious fact that serves to emphasize the rich pattern of interrelationships present among these buildings. Indeed, the Secretariat's roof terrace (another hanging garden or "castle in the air" on the order of that created a decade earlier at the Marseilles *Unité*) provides the culmination to the entire exterior ensemble, in part by the fantasy of its own forms, but, more significantly, by the sweeping, over-all view of the entire group and its landscape of flat plain, adjacent hills, and distant mountains. From this vantage point, the interplay of forces that were slowly and tantalizingly revealed to the spectator as he approached the government center from the city are finally revealed as a totality. The exterior form of the Assembly, with the hourglass-shaped form of the large chamber (a form literally derived from industrial cooling towers) and the tetrahedron skylight of its smaller chamber, succinctly indicates the sum of its varied spaces, spaces that frequently are bewildering when experienced from the interior itself.

180. Le Corbusier. High Court. Chandigarh, 1952–56. Ramps.

181. Le Corbusier. Secretariat. Chandigarh, completed 1958.

182. Le Corbusier. Assembly Building. Chandigarh, 1959–62. Façade facing parking esplanade as seen from an intermediate story of Secretariat.

182a. Jantar Mantar Observatory. New Delhi, 18th century.

There can be little doubt that the interiors of the Assembly are the most sublime created in our day. While the shapes of the two meeting halls can be readily and swiftly comprehended, the various subsidiary spaces—foyers, ramps, and causeways, culminating in the vast black-ceilinged, three-story space that Le Corbusier has baptized the "forum"—provide, in their never-ending elaboration, a character that is vaguely Kafka-like, yet not explicitly hostile. Indeed, all of the abstract forces operating here, the raw texture and color of the concrete, the blood-red color of certain painted areas, and the threatening dark of other areas, should properly add up to a daemonic, cacophonous interior in which man as an individual is vulnerable and at the mercy of hostile forces. Yet the effect which is subjectively perceived immediately upon entry, and is gradually sustained through increasing familiarity, is both breathtaking and physically satisfying. The darkness is an immeasurable relief from the brilliant light outside. Such spatial confinement as exists is a contrast to the boundless, yet equally active, landscape from which one has just come. If it were a space opening directly off a city street, or closed plaza, the dark, indoor forum of the Assembly would, perhaps, be oppressive in many of its effects, and hard to justify. But, as the climax to so much of what has gone before, it is a stroke of genius. Here, Le Corbusier has outdone

himself both in size and invention. The interweaving patterns of circulation are handled with the vigor and functionalist self-righteousness of 1920's Constructivism. Yet the result, especially in the vast columned space of the forum itself, might reasonably provoke the spectator to ask himself if this is, perhaps, akin to what it was like some 2,500 years ago in the great audience chamber of Persepolis, the Hall of the Hundred Columns. There is, of course, nothing like a hundred columns in this vast open room created by Le Corbusier, and the brutal concrete effects of twentieth-century architecture are a world removed from the bejeweled opulence of the Achaemenian Empire. Nonetheless, it seems reasonable to think that the terraces and buildings of Chandigarh, together with its original spatial effects, are as close as the architecture of our own day will ever come to such vanished Asiatic splendors as those once found on the plateaus, both natural and man-made, of southern Persia.

To the question of whether Le Corbusier submitted, consciously or unconsciously, to specific Indian influences while designing the monuments of Chandigarh, the response must be in part, evasive. Obviously, these buildings are European in style, since they belong to the mainstream of a new tradition begun and developed in Europe. Furthermore, the archi-

183. Le Corbusier. Assembly Building. Chandigarh,1959–62. Entrance Portico facing terrace and façade of High Court.

184. Le Corbusier. Secretariat and Assembly Building. Chandigarh, 1958 and 1959–62.

185. Le Corbusier. Assembly Building. Chandigarh, 1959–62. Foyer.

tectural language of Chandigarh's capital buildings is specifically the personal one of its architect. Nevertheless, these forms and spaces generally respond to the exceptional demands of the torrid, humid climate of the Indian subcontinent. Above and beyond such environmental factors, there are certain provocative similarities between these buildings for a new India and specific monuments of its distinctive historical traditions. While these similarities are something more than sheer coincidence, it would be preposterous to claim them as literal prototypes.

In this respect, various features of Chandigarh, especially those concerned with the integration of individual buildings into the entire site, are in accord with a specific example of Mogul architecture, the sixteenth-century palace-villa of Fatehpur Sikri, where several levels of terraces and platforms provide a context for the siting of large and small structures. There is no question here of Le Corbusier having lifted individual details or specific features; instead, the resemblance is more suggestive and subtle. In a different but equally puzzling way, the sculpturesque roof forms of the Assembly evoke certain of the shapes found in several little-understood "observatories," like New Delhi's Jantar Mantar (Fig. 182a), built by an eighteenth-century maharaja to indulge his scientific curiosity. The novel forms and surrounding mystery of these buildings are a striking anticipation of Le Corbusier's formal personal vocabulary. However, since Le Corbusier's use of roof terraces populated with unusual, almost surrealistic forms goes back to earlier European examples of his work, this specific resemblance is not a crucial one in accounting for his unique inventions. Indeed, all the historical references in his late work tend to be even more generalized than before, and his memory enriched with subsequent encounters. Consequently, it is even more difficult to identify specific sources; indeed, resemblances with the past in this work are more a matter of poetic reference as they are of direct, simple influence.

Equally revealing is a comparison of the government buildings at Chandigarh with those built a half-century before by Sir Edward Lutyens and Sir Herbert Baker for the viceregal capital in New Delhi itself. There, in buildings that are among the grandest triumphs of a now outmoded eclecticism, exist elements of a native tradition of ornament blended with, indeed dominated by, the compositional formula of European academicism. Certain of the elements and much of the program of Le Corbusier's architecture at Chandigarh are al-

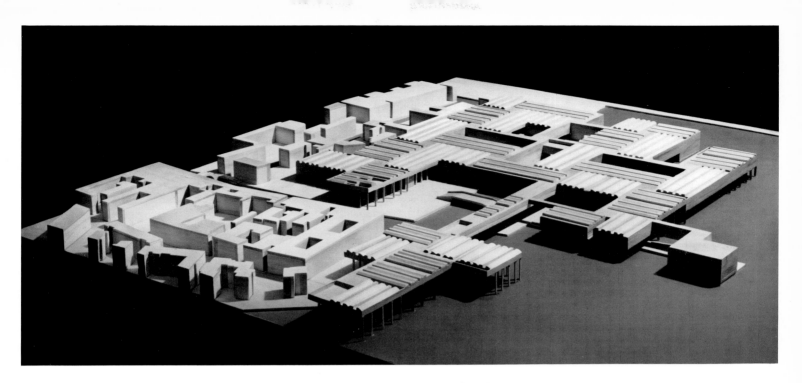

ready present here. What separates these two efforts by an unsurmountable gulf is the degree and intensity of the integration, and the creative genius that allows Le Corbusier's buildings to rise above the somewhat pedantic limitations of the earlier ones. It was a difference that had already been seen in the contrast between Le Corbusier's early works like the Villa Savoye, and the more tentative modern works of an earlier generation represented by Olbrich, Hoffmann, and Behrens.

The Assembly at Chandigarh was the most spectacular of Le Corbusier's achievements among those completed in the years just before his death in 1965. However, in the final months of his life, he worked intensively at several new projects, two of which merit special attention. The first was for a chapel at Firminy (Fig. 187), whose conical tower is a provocative descendant of the one found atop the Chandigarh Assembly. The second was for a new hospital in Venice (Fig. 186), whose basic concept is as remarkable for its originality vis-à-vis the previous work of its architect as it is faithful to the spirit and tradition of its intended location. In both cases the ideas revealed by the forms are personal, visionary, and—on paper at least—somewhat enigmatic. For this reason, as well as for the fact that the "personality" of Le Corbusier's buildings often have depended upon his close personal supervision, one cannot look forward to their possible construction without a certain apprehension. Consequently, in one sense, the cycle of Le Corbusier's work has been abruptly terminated by his death, a death that, on the evidence of his continued inventiveness, cannot help but deprive contemporary design of countless germinal ideas—forms that must now go forever unrecorded.

In a way, Le Corbusier was the despair of his younger contemporaries, given that his imagination was invariably one jump ahead of their ability to absorb the results of his relentless search for form. Whereas Wright seemed, at the end of his life, to have recorded all that he possessed in his heart and mind, that his work was in effect "complete" at the moment of his death, Le Corbusier's career remains unfinished; certain of his final visions destined to remain as unrealized hopes, or, as with Mozart's *Requiem,* as concepts of genius terminated by the less certain hands of able disciples. In the evolution of their late styles, both Wright and Mies, each in their own ways, sought to round out, to make definitive, ideas that had come to them much earlier. Le Corbusier, on the contrary, seemed, in his final

186. Le Corbusier. Second project for a hospital in Venice, 1965. Model.

187. Le Corbusier. Project for the church of Saint-Pierre. Firminy-Vert, 1964. Model.

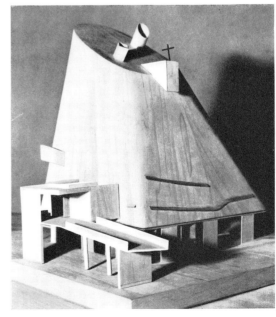

187a. Le Corbusier. "The open hand." Sketch for a monument at Chandigarh. In the distance, the High Court at the left; the Assembly at the right.

works, to be invariably on the threshold of some new discovery. No other architect created so much anticipation, even suspense among his admirers. His works remained unpredictable. For some he was a gadfly, for some a misanthrope, for others a dreamer. But above all else, he was simply an architect.

This account of the late careers of four elder architects of the mid-twentieth century, whatever its fascination, gives only a part of the total picture of recent building. At every stage of development, other designers were detaching one or another aspect from this immense catalogue of achievement, or were reacting against some facet of established orthodox modernism. Time and again, throughout the decade of the 1950's, determined individual efforts to create new forms and spaces were forthcoming. The subsequent chapters will document this often-dramatic adventure.

# Chapter IV
## The Early 1950's: Variations on Familiar Themes

The modern architects of the heroic period were a small band who, in spite of occasionally fierce rivalries, maintained a remarkably united front in the face of public and professional opposition.[1] Until the late 1930's, their scene of action was exclusively in Western and Central Europe, with only an occasional and isolated response from further afield. Beginning in the period just before World War II, however, modernism took root in North and South America as a consequence of normal and inevitable growth, although this growth was certainly encouraged by the hostile reaction against modern architecture under the dictatorial regimes of Germany, Italy, and Russia. Rather more than a decade later, this geographical expansion was complemented—indeed, its promise was fulfilled—by the adoption of the modern design idiom throughout the previously hostile profession. By expanding the creative and productive base of contemporary architecture, the once violent opposition was not so much annihilated as assimilated. Consequently, elements of superficial or routine design production were subversively introduced into the once radical, idealistic new architecture. To this broad professional recognition—one which was indeed fraught with a certain amount of duplicity—were added the heady, unfamiliar elements of popular acceptance and even enthusiasm. An audience for the new architecture was at last assured, and, even more important, a clientele composed not only of individuals, but also of corporate and institutional patrons, sought to avail itself of the changing pattern of design. Modernism descended from the Olympian heights of an elite avant-garde to become a universal art. As will be seen, these were mixed blessings.[2]

To nurture this social and material success of modern architecture during the early 1950's there were several strata of serious, capable designers, as well as the inevitable opportunists. Indeed, the creative recrudescence of Wright, Mies, and Le Corbusier (discussed in the previous chapter), while contributing to the somewhat superficial triumph of modernism, conversely was sustained and encouraged by unprecedented popular adulation. The sympathetic interest in contemporary modes of construction also favored the appearance of a host of fresh talents. Some of these emerging architects had earned a measure of success as early as the 1930's, but for the most part, this group is properly identified as the generation of the 1950's. Collectively, their work and their attitudes are much more difficult to characterize than those of the old International Style, and their buildings consequently more varied in style.

Outwardly, they were more individualistic in their exploitations of form, though most, from the serious to the superficial, from the disciplined to the inventive, were gripped by similar sentiments with respect to the changing times and to the recent past; and all were prey to similar doubts and misunderstandings concerning the new tradition.

Crusading zeal was no longer a potent force giving urgency and immediacy to the outward forms of this new architecture. One of the lasting—and, in part, debilitating—effects of the postwar neo-picturesque tendency was the questioning and dismissal of many rationalizing dogmas that had prevailed in the 1920's. Heedless of the historical injustice they were committing, many prominent architects of the 1950's were inclined to reject the substance of the socio-mechanistic culture of early modern architecture, even though they paid lip service to certain of its outward stylish forms. Consequently, although they continued to employ the inherited vocabulary of modernism—indeed, it is perhaps possible to speak of a "revival" of the International Style, at least on a level of taste, around 1950—the original sense of the forms was greatly diluted, when it was not transformed altogether. This exteriorizing tendency, best revealed in the American commercial architecture of the period (where the glass and metal building of Skidmore, Owings and Merrill had become a universally recognized paragon), led to an increasing accentuation of superficial formalism, which culminated in the late 1950's and early 1960's. Indeed, a continuing preoccupation with the package, at the expense of the content, of the building resulted in much of the chic but trivial "originality" so characteristic of the early 1960's.

The current and recurring divorce between architectural design and the myriad realities of our incessantly changing contemporary life remain a basic dilemma all through the development of modern architecture.[3] True, the 1920's had made a noble and nearly successful effort to heal this wound, but its success was in a small series of buildings, domestic and institutional, which were designed for the delectation of an intelligentsia possessing specialized tastes and interests. Consequently, this style had little hope of popular success, at least in its unadulterated form. One of the first manifestations of the reopening of this fissure was seen in the ideological uneasiness of the immediately post-World War II period, with its rejection of the Futurist, utopian, and mechanistic implications of the International Style, and its concomitant retreat to the shelter of a picturesque past. Subsequently, the creative efforts of the early 1950's, led by the renaissance of Mies and Le Corbusier, and fortified by men such as Johnson, Rudolph, Saarinen, and Kahn, seemed incapable of discovering a common theoretical basis to channel and discipline continuing efforts, and, most important, to sustain the organic development of a mature modern style. Instead, their relevant theoretical utterances, like their buildings, seem to fly off in a variety of different, only half-related directions. In many respects, the buildings of that epoch in spite of many virtues, tended to accentuate an already considerable isolation both from contemporary life and from creative developments in other fields.

Where thirty and forty years ago, architects once found sustenance and encouragement among the revolutionary achievements of Cubism and subsequent artistic movements, today there is but little common ground for exchange between architects and painters. The situation bears a certain resemblance to that which pertained through much of the nineteenth century, when the radical movements in painting, notably Romanticism and Impressionism, had little to offer in the way of technique or style that could have been even remotely suitable to the needs of architectural design. Painting today, with its emphasis upon the immediate expressive primacy of media, and upon certain shock techniques either with respect to the media itself or to certain unexpected elements of content, is too bound up with its own introverted preoccupations to provide any general themes susceptible of architectural adaptation. Nothing could be further removed from the situation forty years ago when the revolutions of Cubism, Futurism, and De Stijl provided new ideas about space and volume that were readily (if belatedly) adapted to building techniques. In the case of Futurism, architects even found an emotionally charged vision of an ideal city of tomorrow, a concept organized upon the theme of constant movement, transformation, and flux, which reinforced the new ideas of dynamic spatial interaction. To a considerable extent, much of the glib, oversimplified quality characteristic of so much architectural design of the past decade, of building after building of an epigrammatic succinctness, can be attributed to the disappearance of a common ground of exchange between architecture and the other plastic arts.

There is, however, an even more revealing explanation of this crisis of the 1950's. A growing study of the past in its multifarious aspects by many thoughtful architects, a tendency that had revealed itself by the mid-1940's, was constantly filling the void created by an absence of new theory and aesthetics. This shift from aggressive doctrinal polemic to passive, if somewhat furtive, historical contemplation led to the creation of designs that were in large measure textual exegeses upon aspects of historical or even modern style. The chief stimulus to this recent historicizing tendency is found, surprisingly, in Mies's early (and never abandoned) taste for the forms and rhythms of Germanic romantic-classicism, rather than in the more richly suggestive allusions synthesized by Wright and Le Corbusier. But the overt, widespread historicism of the 1950's and 1960's was not inspired solely by the desire to discover the matrix of a contemporary style discipline. Instead, the resources of the past were increasingly used for their stimulating representational suggestiveness; and the postwar, neo-picturesque was the first manifestation of this tendency. The subsequent reaction against the natural and the rustic, which came to the fore in the early 1950's as a revival of the International Style in American commercial architecture and, later, as the New Brutalism of English journalistic thought, was itself a notably contradictory development. It manifested admiration for the machine aesthetic in its conspicuous use of metal and glass, but at the same time it sought out a refined, academic, almost Palladian regularity of plan and elevation as the prime means of order and discipline.[4] These tendencies towards regularity were only a preparation for the massive resurgence of eclecticism as a working method, a resurgence which has, perhaps more because of accident than deliberation, characterized many superficially typical buildings of the late 1950's and early 1960's.

Isolated from other areas of creative activity, thrown back upon such resources and stimuli as could be derived from a not always discriminating (not always perceptive, either) study of history, architects have seen the scope of their activity restricted by still other forces. More and more building is being done without the active participation of genuine architects. In the field of planning, notably of suburban development and urban renewal, the architect frequently has found himself in a subordinate role, hindered in his efforts to gain acceptance of his ideas and ultimately prevented from expressing his creative ego in even the most minor, superficial ways. This degradation of architectural creativity, reflected in so much of today's building, has been brought on by certain wants and failures in the

188. Oscar Niemeyer. Presidential Palace. Brasília, 1959

189. Lúcio Costa. Plan of Brasília, 1956.

 1 Plaza of the Three Powers
 2 Ministries
 3 Cathedral
 4 Cultural center
 5 Bank and business district
 6 Amusement quarter
 7 Hotels
 8 Broadcasting tower
 9 Stadium
10 Race course
11 Main square
12 Government printing office and newspaper quarter
13 Observatory
14 Barracks
15 Botanical garden
16 Storage houses and industry
17 Station
18 Market halls and stockyards
19 Cemetery
20 Zoological garden
21 Airport
22 Embassies
23 Golf club
24 Presidential Palace
25 Brasília Palace Hotel
26 University campus
27 Residential district
28 Housing district
29 Yacht club
30 Artificial lake

profession itself, notably its emphasis upon a staff organization that separates the process of design from the acts of negotiating the job and dealing with the client. It is clear that under such circumstances, creativity can neither prosper nor assert its virtues. It is tragic and sobering to realize that, in this period of unprecedented construction, it is rare for an architect of stature to be called upon for the design of massive projects. There are but two instances: Le Corbusier at Chandigarh (Figs. 176–185); and Costa and Niemeyer at Brasília (Figs. 188–192).

Indeed, Brasília, with its noble aspirations marred by a vaguenes and uncertainty of form, shortcomings that become inescapable when its major buildings are compared to those at Chandigarh, vividly exemplifies the numerous problems encountered by the individual architects of the post-International Style generation when they sought either to recreate the concepts of their elders or to find a place for their own ideas in the shadow of these *anciens*. True, many of the ill-considered aspects of Brasília were the consequence of haste, of a need to commit the nation to the fact as well as to the principle of a new, remotely located federal capital before elections and political manoeuvring squelched the entire project. However, the ultrasimple forms for the major government buildings, and, in particular, the dome and saucer of the legislative chambers, are fundamentally banal, and lack real monumentality. Part of this problem concerns the architect's failure to suggest scale either through the application of textures or details (however meager) or through contrasting the size of related or juxtaposed buildings. The core of the difficulty at Brasília is to be found in the very nature of Niemeyer's personal manner of design. Heavily influenced by the drawings, and particularly by the sketches of Le Corbusier, he possesses the knack of turning out dramatic projects of a rich, inventive sort. Unfortunately, he tends to let the process of building-creation rest with the sketch. The elaboration and ultimate construction of his projects do not result in any genuine development of the basic idea. Instead, the concept is embalmed, the impulsive spontaneity of the sketch is lost, and the actual building will often look more like a clever photograph of a model than like a real construction. In addition, the vast spaces separating the various official buildings at Brasília are inescapably monotonous, thus highlighting the superficiality of the architectural concept,

190. Oscar Niemeyer. Senate, Secretariat, and Assembly Building. Brasília, 1960.

191. Oscar Niemeyer. High Court. Brasília, 1960.

192. Oscar Niemeyer. Presidential Palace. Brasília, 1959.

whereas at Chandigarh Le Corbusier skillfully employed artificial landforms to shelter his buildings and give them an additional scale-reference. Niemeyer's failure—one typical of many architects of good will of his generation—has been to mistake the initial *esquisse* for the complex totality of a completed building, with the result that his work is not only derivative but anemic in spite of its originality and the verve of the basic concept.

Laboring under all sorts of material and emotional difficulties, there was a tendency for architects working in the early 1950's to find themselves in the grip of a "siege" mentality. They held fast to certain formalistic aspects of the new architecture at the expense of those less visible inner motivations which had triggered the revolution in design during the 1920's. Where stucco had once served as an effectively neutral constructive surface for most advanced architects of the International Style during its initial phase, by the 1930's an interest in materials per se gradually developed. By the 1950's such plain, unaccented surfaces as had been eagerly sought for a quarter-century earlier were no longer acceptable in an age more concerned with appearances than with principles. Le Corbusier's new *béton brut* (Fig. 193) and Mies's pale brick, tinted glass, and black steel (Fig. 194) were the new surface media employed by architects who earlier had been somewhat less concerned with the expressive textures of their constructed forms. Younger architects did not hesitate to borrow these, or to employ other surfaces of their own devising. The various new personal idioms that emerged during the 1950's, becoming and more idiosyncratic towards the end of the decade, were largely founded upon a deliberate quest for new kinds of metal, stone, or synthetic surfaces.

Curiously, the new individuality in architectural design in the 1950's, especially as centered in the United States, was not apparent from the work executed early in the decade. Indeed, before 1955 or 1956 a certain uniformity seemed to be the dominant feature, one which we today recognize as illusive but which was then given a certain reality by the dominance of "glass box" commercial architecture. Sameness was obtained through the persistent technological and stylistic refinement of the universally utilized glass curtain wall, which could be employed with equal facility in tall urban towers or in low, spreading rural offices, laboratories, or schools. Indeed, this sameness did not preclude numerous designs of considerable quality. The high level of American commercial architecture was very different from the over-all result of the contemporary postwar reconstruction movement in Europe, where mass housing was a more pressing requirement than commercial design. There, in innumerable government and municipally financed projects, a bleak, barracks-like uniformity is sadly prevalent, except for the scattered *Unités* of Le Corbusier at Mar-

193. Le Corbusier. Unité d'Habitation. Marseilles, 1946–52. Detail of columns.

194. Ludwig Mies van der Rohe. Alumni Memorial Hall, Illinois Institute of Technology. Chicago, 1945–46. Detail of the façade.

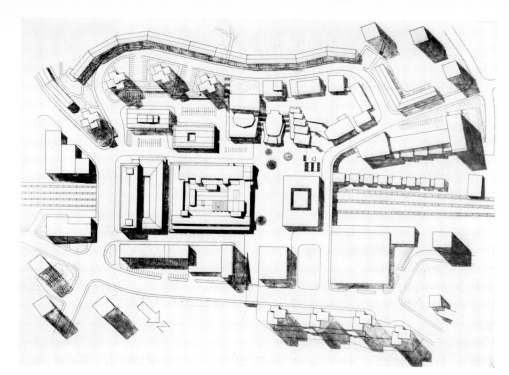

seilles (Figs. 108–110), Nantes-Rezé, and Berlin, or in the carefully considered (sometimes overly fussy) housing satellites of neutral Sweden, notably at Vällingby (Figs. 195, 196). Apart from German designs of the late 1950's, there are no European refinements of typical assembly-line American work, where a care in detailing and in the creation of attractive envelopes made the somewhat anonymous glass vernacular of the 1950's one of the most memorable features of the decade. Nevertheless, it was destined to become the cradle for new departures in the works of Saarinen, Kahn, Johnson, and, in England, in the efforts of the parents of New Brutalism, Alison and Peter Smithson, that would emerge by 1960.

In this context, Lever House (Figs. 199–201), New York, designed by Gordon Bunshaft of Skidmore, Owings and Merrill, and finished in 1952, possesses an archetypal importance.[5] In appearance and in genesis, it manages to be simultaneously distinctive and anonymous: the work of an individual functioning within a large organization; and a building of modern style, yet one acceptable to the cautious tastes of a major corporation's directors and executives. It succeeded both as a work of art and as an image of prestige advertising. Even more, it was the basis for an entire "school," a trend in commercial architecture which reached fever peak in the mid-1950's, belatedly spread to Europe at a point when its popularity was ebbing in America, and now, in the 1960's, is currently being replaced by a new and more massive style of office tower design.

Although the outer surfaces of Lever House were uniformly of glass, much of this glass was necessarily opaque, because the functioning of the interior spaces called for, in effect, ribbon windows rather than complete glass walls. This feature, however, was not developed for purposes of distinctive or logical expression, since the taste of the moment demanded uniformity rather than contrast. Such simplification was not only in contrast to the variegated brick and tubular glass sheath of Wright's Johnson Wax tower (Figs. 56, 57), completed in 1950, but it was even more at odds with such glass-walled buildings of the 1920's as the Van Nelle Factory, Rotterdam, 1927 (Fig. 197), designed by Mart Stam for the firm of Brinkman and van der Vlugt, or Gropius' renowned Bauhaus (Figs. 13, 13a) itself. In the earlier masterpieces of the style of the 1920's—simultaneously Cubist and functional—the massing reflected the taste of the day for complex, even unstable, geometric interplays, for

197. Johannes Andreas Brinkman and L. C. van der Vlugt. Van Nelle Tobacco Factory. Rotterdam, 1927.

198. Skidmore, Owings & Merrill. Pepsi-Cola Building. New York, 1958–59.

vivid contrasts between opaque and transparent surfaces. In the International Style revival of the early 1950's, however, we are confronted with a series of forms in which such contrasts have been either rejected or diluted beyond recognition. While the Lever House preserves a sense of contrast in the opposition of its twenty-four-story vertical tower to the horizontal slab above the open street level, even this token gesture toward the more dynamic compositional practices of the 1920's disappears in the subsequent Skidmore, Owings and Merrill *œuvre*. Even in this building, their first major glass-walled structure, the firm concealed the irregular machinery and water tower shapes on the building's roof behind a regular glazed surface, thus allowing regularity to dominate the very point where time-hallowed New York skyscraper tradition called for tapering and diminution, and where the International Style tradition would have called for functional expression.

Of course, the source for the diluted machine imagism of Skidmore, Owings and Merrill is the late manner of Mies rather than the more distant heroic period of the International Style. The movement and flux of the International Style had already been filtered and purged of its transitory qualities to the point where it simultaneously possessed classic monumentality in its static modular regularity, as well as a reduced, apparently efficient, vernacular simplicity by virtue of its seeming absence of detail. In Lever House, the architect seems to have stressed the latter aspect of the Miesian idiom, for its surfaces are almost devoid of rhythmic accent (though in the best of their subsequent commercial towers the designers of Skidmore, Owings and Merrill are more classically Miesian in their fervid adoption of his crisp linear vocabulary). In this respect, the firm—unlike many lesser ones—has not fallen to the thoughtless exploitation of the once-idolized mode in a superficial spirit. Nonetheless, even the most adept followers of Mies have tended to borrow the simple regularity of the master's surfaces while remaining largely insensible to his pure and classic sense of rhythmic accentuation and of proportion, whether in details or in over-all shape.

In one respect, it is an oversimplification to discuss at great length just one of the many large buildings designed by this prosperous firm. Part of the importance of Skidmore, Owings and Merrill and the cause of its deserved position far above most other corporate architectural operations, is that it has consistently maintained a remarkable standard of quality in large, efficient buildings. Not even by hewing to an extremely narrow range of creative possibility has the firm diminished the respectability or basically sound quality of its designs. The chief criticism—or perhaps frustration—produced by the process of refining the details and proportions of the building's outer shell is that the designers have tended to submerge behind the surface of the design numerous aspects of internal planning and arrangement. Indeed, such factors as circulation, ventilation, and lighting, thanks to the now universal employment of standarized mechanical and electrical equipment, no longer seem to offer a challenge with respect to purely architectural planning and design. Because of these new technological conditions, architects are provided with yet another reason for concentrating upon the outward image. Understandably, the Miesian models so frequently chosen at that time were ideally suited to accommodate such a species of design, whereas the methodology of Le Corbusier or of the Bauhaus group involved perplexing rational and emotional concerns with both program and site that, in the 1950's, could be put aside due to technological standardization.

The process used by Skidmore, Owings and Merrill to refine the idiom which they adopted as their corporate signature, and which their widely admired designers, notably Gordon Bunshaft and Walter Netsch, succeeded in perfecting, can be appreciated when Lever House is compared with the more recent Pepsi-Cola building (Fig. 198), finished in 1959. (The comparison is conveniently made since both are handily located within a few blocks of each other on New York's Park Avenue.) Though the surface and silhouette of Lever House are of an effete, brittle regularity, a ghost of the interlocking Constructivist-De Stijl geometry remains in the hovering effect created between its contrasting major elements.

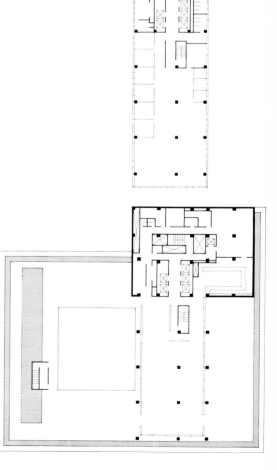

199–201. Skidmore, Owings & Merrill. Lever House. New York, 1951–52. View, typical floor plan, and plan of second floor.

These lingering memories are excluded in the single raised rectilinear volume of the Pepsi-Cola building, where the only contrasting accents are in the delicate detailing of the window sills and mullions. Nothing less than an exquisite silvery glass jewel box, this most restrained and perfect of all commercial buildings by Skidmore, Owings and Merrill is, nonetheless, architecturally bankrupt; it is, paradoxically, a stylistic dead end, a cul-de-sac from which the taste-makers of the firm have sought to escape in some of their most recent designs, especially the Banque Lambert, Brussels, 1958–62 (Figs. 206, 300), or the Rare Book Library, Yale University, 1962–64 (Fig. 205). These new buildings remain arbitrarily simple in outline, while presenting a new aspect of tactile monumentality in reaction against nearly half a century of increasing transparence and fragility.

Before the exhaustion of the crystalline phase of their work, Skidmore, Owings and Merrill demonstrated how their polished manner could be adapted to fit a rural site. This happened first in the Connecticut General Life Insurance Building, at Bloomfield, Connecticut, 1954–57, and was later developed on an even larger scale in the sublime, mountainous site of the Air Force Academy (Fig. 204), Colorado Springs, a project of 1954 by Walter Netsch, constructed from 1956–62. Against all reasonable predictions to the contrary, the firm's refined style managed to stand up to the rugged natural forms that loom up behind the terraces and platforms upon which the various low buildings are placed. In New York itself (the original home of the style which nonetheless is as characteristic of Chicago, Los Angeles, or Dallas as it is of New York), the larger commissions designed by Skidmore, Owings and Merrill in the late 1950's, the Union Carbide Building, 1957–60 (Fig. 202), and the Chase Manhattan Bank offices, 1957–61 (Fig. 203), are immediately comparable in shape and scale to Mies van der Rohe's great brazen lady, the Seagram Building, 1955–58 (Figs. 147–149), itself rather a latecomer to the new Park Avenue scene.[6] Both the Union Carbide and the Chase Manhattan buildings comprise larger volumes than the Seagram, filling their sites more completely (though Chase Manhattan does have a terraced plaza), and hence cannot be viewed so advantageously. Predictably, however, it is in the handling and ultimate refinement of detail that Mies's all-encompassing superiority is most evident. The elder master has produced a sharp, crisp effect in his continuous mullions (formed of I-beams), providing, as it were, a railroad track to the sky. Across this surface, light is received and reflected with ever-changing touches of chiaroscuro which affect the linear accents of the sheer vertical tower. The mullions of the Skidmore, Owings and Merrill buildings, simpler and more rectilinear in profile, cannot provide this vital, enlivening accent to the sheath of glass and metal. In addition, since the "glass walls" are lighter than that of the Seagram Building, they are prone to be excessively reflective and glare-inducing.

Many of the qualities already established in the Skidmore, Owings and Merrill designs of the early 1950's are also found in several designs by a more personal, idiosyncratic architect, Eero Saarinen (1910–61).[7] While the progression of his works is a remarkably accurate bellwether of the tastes and preoccupations of that decade, his style is far from being merely typical of its day, largely because of a conceptual adventurousness which was often achieved at the expense of polish and refinement. In most respects, his mature works, beginning with the General Motors Technical Center (Figs. 207–209), Warren, Michigan, 1948–56 (designed in partnership with his father Eliel, who died in 1950), are more representative of the varied *creative* urges of the period than are the more uniform products of larger corporate offices. Indeed, instead of reflecting a simple preoccupation with but one strain of the modernist tradition, Eero Saarinen's General Motors complex suggests a notably rich heritage.

General Motors had first requested a project for its proposed technical center in 1945. The design provided by the Saarinens at that time was a peculiar effort to achieve a streamlined effect, rather in the manner of the bulbous automobile design of the late 1930's and the 1940's; it seems to have stemmed from a muddled and misguided desire to produce an image appropriate to the client and his product. No action was taken on this proposal, but

Page 110:

202. Skidmore, Owings & Merrill. Union Carbide Building. New York, 1957–60.

203. Skidmore, Owings & Merrill. Chase Manhattan Bank. New York, 1957–61.

204. Skidmore, Owings & Merrill. U. S. Air Force Academy. Colorado Springs, 1956–62.

205. Skidmore, Owings & Merrill. Beinecke Rare Book and Manuscript Library, Yale University. New Haven, Connecticut, 1962–64.

206. Skidmore, Owings & Merrill. Banque Lambert. Brussels, 1958–62.

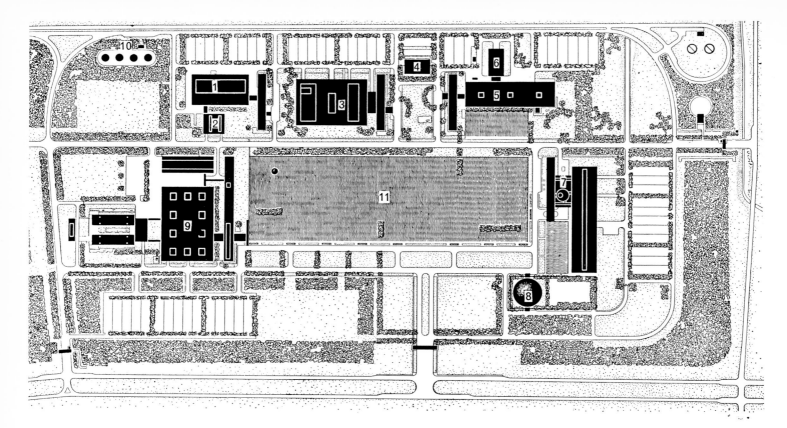

207. Eero Saarinen & Associates. General Motors Technical Center. Warren, Michigan, 1948–56. Site plan.
1  Service section, with offices and workshops
2  Generating station
3  Process development section, with offices and workshops
4  Restaurant
5  Engineering section, with offices and workshops
6  Engine testing center
7  Styling section, with offices and workshops
8  Auditorium
9  Research section, with offices, workshops, and laboratories
10  Tank depot
11  Artificial lake

in 1948–49 a revised scheme was requested. The huge, twenty-two acre central lagoon was preserved from the old scheme, but its shape was regularized and the individual buildings were made distinctively independent as well as simplified and rectilinear in shape. Furthermore, the transitory and superficially stylish aspects of the 1945 design were eliminated. The result was so infinitely superior to the initial scheme that its new clarification must, in considerable measure, be due to outside influences, notably Mies's then new I.I.T. campus (Figs. 49–51), as well as the greater role played by Eero, the younger Saarinen. The debt to Mies is apparent both in the restrained detailing of the buildings and in the over-all plan. The final project included a tall office slab placed to one side of the mammoth lagoon, thus adding a high, dominant, anti-classic accent to the Saarinen complex. The horizontal serenity of the Technical Center today is, in part, the accidental consequence of the fact that this building was discarded at the last moment, its intended vertical accent replaced only with a series of fountains and a water tower.

Eero Saarinen stoutly maintained that his final, rationalized, and somewhat Miesian scheme was inspired by automotive know-how: "General Motors is a metalworking industry; it is a mass production industry. All these things should ... be expressed in the architecture of its Technical Center.... The design is based upon steel—the metal of the automobile. Like the automobile itself, the buildings are essentially put together, as on an assembly line, out of mass-produced units. And down to the smallest detail, we tried to give the architecture the precise, well-made look which is a proud characteristic of industrial America."[8] This statement is subject to criticism on the grounds that it is highly doubtful that the products of industrial America characteristically manifest a well-made look, except in the most restricted, specialized instances. Certainly, for the past thirty years, mass-produced American automobiles have not been characterized by elegant design—in fact, their design ridicules the aesthetic of machine technology. To have assumed that the positive virtues of his G. M. buildings would in some way reflect the client and his wares was somehow sadly naïve, as the relationship is purely imaginary. But even if G. M. cars were the result of such design refinements as can be seen in its buildings, would the architect then be justified in deriving his design philosophy from the program in this fashion? Should factories look like the products they turn out? Should corporation offices resemble the products that their staff markets? Or should school buildings literally express the pedagogic ideas of their principals and teachers? What, indeed, is the rightful role of expression in architecture?

In the accepted jargon of the historian, we speak of the way in which the Cathedral of Chartres expresses—indeed manifests in an intense, archetypal way—the quality of life in the thirteenth-century community or the symbolic methodology of contemporary theology. We have discovered, some four hundred and fifty years after that era, that the palace, gardens, and city of Versailles express a concept of political absolutism typical of its day. Each of these manifestations of architectural form express something relevant and unique about the time, but the architects of Chartres did not arrive at its design by consciously trying to emulate "the spirit of the time," any more than did their Versailles counterparts. In a similar fashion, are we presently justified in speaking of Le Corbusier's Marseilles *Unité d'Habitation* as if it expressed the age—our age—in the same all-embracing way that Chartres and Versailles did theirs? Certainly, the *Unité* represents certain aspects of our new technology, and it is a marvelously explicit realization of one architect's beliefs concerning the solution of the contemporary housing crisis and of the future reorganization of our cities, but Le Corbusier did not arrive at the design of the *Unité* simply by endeavoring to express the character of either his program or his age in a literal, representational way. Nor did he try to characterize visually the nature of the Church and its role in twentieth-century life with the provocative and expressive shapes of Ronchamp. There is, indeed, a *content* to these buildings put there by the architect, but it concerns specifics of program and site, not vaporous notions of the spirit of the epoch. No architect, today or in the past, has ever been able to deliberately express his period, his time, in the conscious design of specific works. This kind of synthetic vision is denied to the creative imagination today, just as it was beyond the grasp of the architects of Chartres or Versailles. The result of the creative process, the finished building, *may* subsequently turnt out to be a sufficiently universal form, and *may* thereby express certain generalized, abstract qualities of its period to others, but

208. Eero Saarinen & Associates. General Motors Technical Center. Warren, Michigan, 1948–56. Engine testing center.

209. Eero Saarinen & Associates. General Motors Technical Center. Warren, Michigan, 1948–56. Engineering section, with offices and workshops.

this subsequently revealed character is a part of interpretation, and has never been a part of the programmatic content of the building that is worked out by the architect, or between the architect and his client in the process of design.

Yet that is exactly what Eero Saarinen time and again stated as his intentions: "I am a child of my period. I am enthusiastic about the three common principles of modern architecture: function, structure, and being a part of our time. . . . The third principle—the awareness of the thinking and technology of our time—is for me an ever-present challenge. I want always to search out the new possibilities in new materials of our time and to give them their proper place in architectural design."[9] All these matters, which Saarinen here claims as his personal philosophy, are exactly those things that no serious architect has ever been able to escape, even if he so willed it. If it is both typical and creative, a building will express the aspirations of its period, not because of what the architect *did* but because of what he *was*. In effect, the architect of General Motors fell into the trap of thinking of architecture primarily as a representational art, of thinking that somehow the buildings' contents should inevitably shape the outward image in some literally expressive, distinctive way: "The external form of my work varies greatly. But inside the solution of every problem there are underlying principles that hold it together and join each building I have done to every other one."[10] This complete faith in the *period* and in the particular *task* is a most curious, almost literary reading of the old functional doctrine which held that a building's external form was to be an accurate reflection of interior spatial need; but this doctrine made no point of deliberately expressing by means of external shape or detail the specific nature of the activities transpiring within. Saarinen's attitude seems to be the result of a most curious mingling of functional thought with Hegelian determinism, Ruskinian morality, and the eighteenth-century's *architecture parlante*.

Not only does Saarinen's theory, which he invoked not merely for the G. M. complex but for all of his other designs, fail to withstand careful analysis, but—and a more serious criticism—it is an inappropriate measuring rod for discussion of his buildings themselves. Despite their dubious philosophic substructure, these buildings, at their best, are among the most imposing works of the 1950's. Fortunately, they possess historical roots in the modern tradition—roots which exist even though Saarinen did not specifically recognize them—as well as contacts with the new developments found in the works of other creative architects in the 1950's. If G. M. fails (fortunately!) to fulfill its architect's purpose, to express automotive design and technology, it succeeds as architecture. Perhaps Eero Saarinen was innocent of stylistic preconceptions, and perhaps not—in the ultimate historical analysis it does not really matter. He was, however, brought up to be an architect, and from earliest childhood, he was encouraged to draw and to develop his powers of observation. He was a self-conscious and ambitious architect: "The only architecture that interests me is architecture as a fine art. That is what I want to pursue. I hope that some of my buildings will have lasting truths. I admit frankly I would like a place in architectural history."[11] Eero Saarinen's powers as well as his limitations are set down within and between the lines of that statement. The flaw in such an attitude is perhaps best recognized by the Corbusian invocation: "Architecture is the masterly, correct, and magnificent play of masses brought together in light."[12] To think of "architecture as a fine art" is to think as an academician or a historian of architecture, not as a vital architect. Thus, General Motors Technical Center is important as a major expansion of the Miesian idiom rather than as a realization of its architect's shaky ideals. It is a special and personal deviation from the main line of industrial-classicism espoused by Skidmore, Owings and Merrill or by Philip Johnson, and the modifications that it introduced were based upon Saarinen's special roots in the tradition of early modernism.

The short independent career of Eero Saarinen cannot be fully understood without reference to the longer and equally varied career of his father, Eliel, whose work goes back to 1900.[13] The elder Saarinen achieved his first international recognition with the Finnish Pavilion at the Paris Exposition of that year (Fig. 210), and followed it with the rambling, eclectic, modernist design for the Helsinki Railroad Station (Fig. 211) the competition for which he won in 1904. The qualities present both in the surface forms of this building and in its underlying spirit have much in common with Eliel Saarinen's subsequent work of the 1920's and 1930's at Cranbrook, following his emigration to the United States. The language of forms is derivative, but has been given a marked personal touch. This individuality, however, is subtle rather than sharply accentuated, the compositions deriving their discipline and coherence from a regular attention to detail, texture, and fenestration in the façades, and not from bold, spirited rhythmic accents. Eliel Saarinen's was always a lightly orchestrated *mezzo forte* architecture, using, for the most part, the thematic material of others. The exteriors feature rambling façades, the rhythms and proportions of which tend

210. Herman Gesellius, Armas Lindgren, and Eliel Saarinen. Finnish Pavilion at the Paris Exposition of 1900.

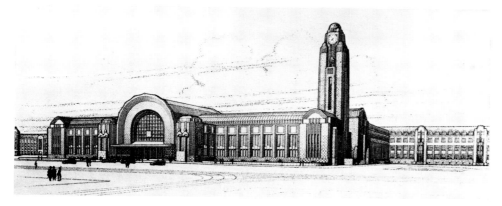

211. Eliel Saarinen. Project for the Helsinki Railroad Station, 1904.

115

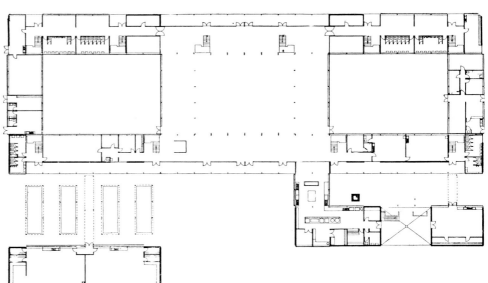

212–215. Alison and Peter Smithson. Hunstanton Secondary Modern School. Norfolk, 1950–54. General view, ground floor plan, court, and interior view.

to change or modulate at corners. These rambling, discursive façades prevent the creation of a pronounced effect of isolated mass, of volume set in space, as it has often been created by Frank Lloyd Wright, Mies van der Rohe, Le Corbusier, or for that matter, Philip Johnson, or Louis Kahn.

Remarkably enough, it is this rambling, strung-out quality in the plan and in the several elevations of General Motors that distinguishes it from the more volumetric forms and measured, stately rhythms of Mies's I. I. T., and keeps it within the traditional Saarinen design orbit. Saarinen's curtain walls for G. M. are, without doubt, a major achievement in the industrial fabrication of complete wall components, and their use is accounted for in the façade designs. In Saarinen's hands, however, the curtain wall design no longer respects the tense balance and cerebral discipline of Mies's I. I. T. units, where the structure and infill of glass and brick maintain a strict balance between parts. Instead, the long walls of glass and porcelain are contrasted with the short end-walls of brightly colored glazed brick to emphasize the sheath at the expense of structure, to underscore the almost limitless

continuity of planar surface at the expense of the exact rhythmic definition of volumes set in space. Eero Saarinen's liberation of the Miesian discipline from its frankly neo-classic matrix would probably not have been possible had the tendency toward rambling, non-volumetric façade compositions not existed in his father's work. Furthermore, it was this very opportunity of liberation that gave Eero Saarinen a head start in the pioneering of new tendencies in the mid-1950's, at a time when others were still enmeshed in the consequences of their devoted study of Miesian forms. In the design of the Auditorium and Chapel at M.I.T. in Cambridge, Massachusetts, 1953–56 (Figs. 230–233), the first, though tentative, consequences of this new possibility became visible. Consideration of these buildings, however, must be taken up in a later chapter, for they lie beyond the early 1950's, our present concern.

In addition to these, and other, American developments, still further exploitations of the handily codified Miesian idiom were possible. The only significant one to occur outside the United States, however, was the distinctive school (Figs. 212–215) built at Hunstanton,

Norfolk, by two intellectually articulate British designers, Alison and Peter Smithson. First published in 1954 by *The Architectural Review*, it was hailed by Philip Johnson as a notable instance of "not only radical but good Mies." Successful even in the most formal of its façades, it was singled out by that magazine's editors as a radical triumph on the order of Butterfield's century-old landmark of ecclesiastical architecture, the Church of All Saints, Margaret Street, a building which effectively inaugurated and codified the budding High Victorian architecture of the 1850's.[14] The Smithsons' very fine school does nothing of the sort, except on a purely local level. In fact, it is a very derivative design, in spite of the architects' claims, made through an editorial spokesman, that theirs is "a radicalism which owes nothing to precedent, and everything to the inner mechanisms of the Modern Movement." The architects imposed certain arbitrary conditions upon themselves which determined the outcome of the design. Chief among these were the concentration of the plan about a central space and two flanking courtyards, in order to achieve legibility without stooping to academic circulation schemes, and the decision to utilize maximum glazing, which in turn made the steel frame mandatory.

One doubts that Hunstanton would have existed in its particular form without the prior codification of Mies. Saarinen, a less cerebral designer than the Smithsons, may have been in some measure innocent of direct, willful borrowing at General Motors, but his English contemporaries knew only too well what they were taking from recent tradition, and, even further, what they were rejecting. Indeed, their apologia, with its effort to demonstrate the independent, rational singularity of their design, only seems to prove the opposite. Such verbal acrobatics are, of course, part of a predictable pattern within the modern movement. No architect can perhaps ever be wholly free of significant borrowings, yet the myth of modernism holds tenaciously to the supremacy of heroic, isolated, unfettered creation as its one unimpeachable criterion, valuing this even above technocratic orthodoxy.

To maintain, as Johnson does, that at Hunstanton the Smithsons were Miesian is not to denigrate in any fashion the building's individuality. Its steel frame is not of Mies's classic proportions, but instead is based upon structural calculations that were especially appropriate for the types of steel available. Rather than the orthodox regularity of Mies's separate and unique volumes at I.I.T., the Smithsons brought the whole together, and when certain features would not fit the form they were allowed to protrude. The resulting little shapes which are seen against the big one do not bespeak picturesque permissiveness, but possess instead a certain bold, raw quality that was perhaps latent, but most certainly undeveloped, in Mies's campus. This rugged, brutal articulation points out the rapid development of a tendency to move away from the pristine, imperturbable formalism of American industrial-classicism, whether it was that of the big firms or of the more individualistic designers like Johnson or Eero Saarinen.

The Smithsons' achievement at Hunstanton was swiftly followed by the crystallization of their approach under the banner of New Brutalism, and then by the rejection of the measured formal regularity of the school scheme. This they replaced by a kind of "anti-design," apparent in their project for the Sheffield University Extension, 1955 (Fig. 216), which their critic-defender, Reyner Banham, proclaimed (a bit hopefully) to be the "furthest development of New Brutalist architecture toward the completely aformal, antigeometric yet systematic compositional methods exemplified in painting by Pollock and Burri."[15] True, the plan and shapes in the Sheffield scheme, presented in harsh, starkly plain sketches, showed an ensemble of three buildings of almost random shape tied together by irregularly placed catwalks and stair ramps. The ensemble remained unpicturesque only because the design stopped short of detailed prettification and the masses were not willfully shaped and punctuated to accentuate, and thereby systematize, irregularity. The result does, indeed, offer a tenuous parallel to the methods of Jackson Pollock or Mathieu, but one feels that the issue here was a bit forced. In the Hunstanton School, the architects had successfully argued for using the constructive materials exactly in the finish that they possessed upon arrival on the building site; but this is not so much neo-Dada or *trouvaillisme* as it is the revival of certain Bauhaus attitudes that had been clearly articulated by Moholy-Nagy a generation earlier.

As *The Architectural Review* had noted in 1954, the appellation New Brutalist was invoked to describe this particular attachment to materials in their original or in their rough-manufactured state. As such, it stands in distinct contrast to the more calculated precisionism of the American architectural current, which, beginning with the curtain-wall simplicity of Saarinen and Skidmore, Owings and Merrill, ultimately developed into the punctured screen-wall clichés of Edward Stone and the forced, hothouse elegance of Minoru Yamasaki. In December, 1955, perhaps because of the limited number of designs produced by the Smithsons, Reyner Banham essayed a full discussion of New Brutalism.

Exorcising the ghosts of both new empiricism and the more recent new humanism, Banham launched his discussion with a mixture of sarcasm and insight.[16] Going on to embrace the aesthetic of Pollock, Paolozzi, and others, mingling the not exactly equivalent notions of *le béton brut* (Le Corbusier) with *art brut* (Jean Dubuffet), Banham then presented the idea in its *urform*, as the outgrowth of a 1953 house design by Alison Smithson, in which the structure was to be altogether exposed, with a complete absence of both interior and exterior finish. In spite of the admittedly facetious origin of the phrase New Brutalism,[17] Banham was able to marshal an extraordinary array of material to give substance to the bare idea. "Admittedly this emphasis upon basic structure is important, even if it is not the whole story, and what has caused Hunstanton to lodge in the public's gullet is the fact that it is almost unique among modern buildings in being made of what it appears to be made of. Whatever has been said about honest use of materials, most modern buildings *appear* to be made of whitewash or patent glazing, even when they are made of concrete or steel. Hunstanton *appears* to be made of glass, brick, steel, and concrete, and is in fact made of glass, brick, steel, and concrete. Water and electricity do not come out of unexplained holes in the wall, but are delivered to the point of use by visible pipes and manifest conduits."[18]

It would seem that Ruskin's hundred-year-old Lamp of Truth had been dusted off and invested with the iconography and secular paraphernalia of the machine aesthetic. Banham might well have added that the Marseilles *Unité* and the buildings of I.I.T. were really what they seemed, even though they did not make a fetish of pipes and conduits. He does, subsequently, admit Marseilles to the Brutalist canon, in lonely splendor with Hunstanton, while rejecting out of hand (though, upon reflection, with good cause), General Motors. Indeed, it is interesting to realize that if the criteria established by the Smithsons at Hunstanton were most rigidly and literally applied, among the few other buildings of the 1950's that might indisputably fall within the definition of New Brutalist would be Philip Johnson's Glass House (Figs. 223–227), and Le Corbusier's brick, concrete, and wood Jaoul Houses, Neuilly, 1952–56 (Figs. 44, 159), dwellings as different as day and night! Most other contenders, notably Le Corbusier's seemingly Brutalist Ronchamp (significantly published as the frontispiece of the December, 1955, *The Architectural Review,* contiguous with Banham's presentation of New Brutalist doctrine), are in one way or another flawed in principle if not in outward appearance. For instance, Ronchamp's rubble walls were smeared with gunite and subsequently white-washed, thus hiding much of the truth of its construction (Figs. 163–166).

Banham draws upon one other major construction to round out his picture: Louis Kahn's just completed addition to the Yale University Art Gallery, New Haven, Connecticut, 1952–54 (Figs. 218–220). "Here is a building which is uncompromisingly frank about its materials, which is inconceivable apart from its boldly exhibited structural method which—being a concrete space frame—is as revolutionary and unconventional as the use of the Plastic Theory in stressing Hunstanton's steel H-frames. Furthermore, the plan is very formal in the disposition of its main elements, and makes a kind of symmetry about two clearly de-

216. Alison and Peter Smithson. Project for the Sheffield University extension, 1955.

fined axes at right angles to each other." Thus the author invokes not only Brutalism's persistent factualism of structure and material, but also its equal devotion to "formal legibility of plan." Somewhat petulantly, he then goes on to discuss some presumed shortcomings of the Yale Gallery, commenting (astounding as it seems) upon the "arty" detailing! Furthermore, he finds the entrances at odds with the cross-axial planning which he proposes to have discovered there, and questions, under the circumstances, "why bother with an axial plan anyhow?" In fact, the cross-axial plan is hinged upon the vertical circulation and service cores of Kahn's Gallery in such a way as to make it an imaginary, rather than a truly visible, phenomenon.

The flaw in orthodox Brutalist thought is its exclusivity, which seeks intellectual satisfaction in tight codifications of principle that are somewhat less than realistic. Even though it seems unnecessarily fanatic, however, the contribution of Banham and the Smithsons has been to renew interest in the discussion of some of the most important basic issues of the modern tradition; and to revive these at a time when superficial external brilliance was becoming the most generally admired virtue of the profession's intelligentsia. In doing so, they have put us all on our mettle.

Banham's remarks on Kahn's Gallery, ill-considered though they were in certain details, were significant as a rare early recognition of the importance of this American-trained designer who, abruptly, late in life, caught fire with the creation of a series of unusually formed, widely discussed projects and buildings. From the vantage point of the early 1960's, it requires no great feat of perception and insight to recognize Louis Kahn as one of the creative giants of twentieth-century architecture; but in the mid-1950's it required some risk and much courage.[19] This writer witnessed the day-to-day growth of Kahn's Yale Gallery,[20] his first significant building. It was possible to watch the floor-ceiling structure of tetrahedron-webbed slabs emerge from their metal forms, to see the whole encased in a somewhat crudely articulated Miesian envelope of glass, metal, and brick, and, only gradually, to appreciate the logic that willed a rich, chiaroscuresque form for the interior, but a dry, shadowless wall for the exterior. (This experience was subsequently enriched by witnessing the last stages of construction of Le Corbusier's Jaoul Houses (Figs. 44, 159), in the winter of 1954–55 and, somewhat later, of Kahn's Richards Medical Research Building, Philadelphia, in 1959–60 (Figs. 371–373).

Like Hunstanton (Figs. 212–215), indeed, like Lever House (Figs. 199–201) and General Motors (Figs. 207–209), Kahn's Gallery was one more expansion of the seemingly closed Miesian aesthetic. The open spaces of the Yale Gallery were not so much cross-axial as universal, in the open, undefined, continuous, Miesian sense of the word, a space that was realized, for example, in Crown Hall at I.I.T. (Fig. 217). Kahn later moved on to more programmatically determined and detailed spaces, but at the moment of designing the Yale Gallery he was just beginning to find his way. The program was not merely demanding in the variety of services and functions required, but it was, in addition, equivocal, for the four floors and basement would have to provide temporary studios, offices, and classrooms, until the completion of yet another building. (This building happens to be Paul Rudolph's adjacent Art Center, Figs. 365–368, 370, itself of considerable consequence at a later time). Of course, the space occupied by these temporary "functions" would later be used for expanding the gallery area. Kahn's solution was the construction of a kind of warehouse, with uniform vast spaces, largely unbroken by structural columns, whose evolving functions would be recognized by movable partitions. In the process of working out the design, Kahn found that the crux of the matter was in the slab which formed both flooor and ceiling, as its tensile quality determined the wide separation of vertical support. Having established the structural challenge, Kahn then proceeded to realize it in the form of a tetrahedron, which, in his view, could have been constructed in a much lighter, more elegant shape than the one his engineer insisted upon. Thus, the entire spatial effect is governed by the sole permanent interior feature, the slab of tetrahedrons; the building is a vast un-

217. Ludwig Mies van der Rohe. Crown Hall, Illinois Institute of Technology. Chicago, 1952–56.

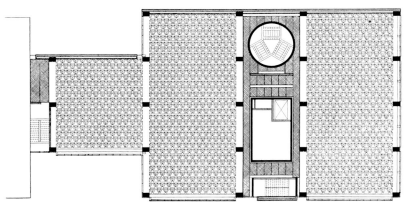

filled, five-layered sandwich of concrete webbing. The exterior offers an envelope of Miesian serenity, which, upon reflection, turns out to have been the only reasonable possibility at the time and under the limiting circumstances. The street façade is almost entirely of tan brick, but, over the entrance, which is set back and at right angles to the major segment of the façade, there is a continuous glass strip embracing the floors above ground. Here the spectator has a first glimpse of the structure and controlling feature of the building's interior. Approaching the Yale Gallery from its courtyard façade, the spectator sees a largely unbroken glass wall which allows the spaces to be visible from without, with the result that the only basic unchangeable fact of the building's space and structure is quickly manifest. Of course Kahn progressed immeasurably beyond the tentative personal features of this building, leaving behind first the Miesian aspect of universal space and smooth exterior surfaces, and then the accidental, but nonetheless significant, parallels with the New Brutalists of the mid-1950's and their self-sacrificing, determined (if as yet not especially productive) efforts to recapture and go beyond the rationalism and factualism of the old machine aesthetic. Kahn's ultimate accomplishment, which from the moment of completion of the Yale Gallery required still another four or five years of patient effort, was to find a method of determining significant form in which creativity seemed to operate simultaneously upon a subjective as well as upon a consciously rational process of deductive logic. The Yale Gallery, his first notable building, was, like the Lever House (Figs. 199–201) or Pepsi-Cola Building (Fig. 198), like Saarinen's General Motors (Figs. 207–209), or like Philip Johnson's 1947–49 Glass House (Figs. 223–227), an effort marking a transition from that Miesian fixation, the International Style revival of the early 1950's, to the new phase of largely formal determinism which seems to be dominating the architectural scene of the 1960's.

Philip Johnson is, of course, the best known and most thoroughgoing of the disciples of Mies, an admirer since 1930, and his first biographer.[21] His first house of 1942–43 in Cambridge, Massachusetts, was a reduced version of the German master's "court house" projects of the 1930's. His second, the Farney House, Sagaponack, Long Island, 1946 (Figs. 221, 222), with its vertical board siding and articulate plan separating living from sleeping areas, was more in the Harvard tradition of Breuer and of Gropius, who had been his masters in the early 1940's. With the design and construction of his own residence in New Canaan, Connecticut, the Glass House, 1947–49 (Figs. 223–227), the Miesian element definitively reasserts itself. The idea for the Glass House came from Mies's Farnsworth House project of 1946, which, interestingly, was not constructed until 1950 (Figs. 145, 146). Johnson did not adopt the iconography of the machine era for his glass, metal, and brick residence, but only the outward trappings. If it is possible to associate his frank handling of the material and structural elements of this house with some of the subsequently crystallized ideals of New Brutalism, Johnson himself would probably depreciate the importance of that relationship as accidental. Indeed, he published a thorough catalogue of the conscious sources for this house and its intended evocations.[22] These range from the revolutionary neo-classic designs of Schinkel and Ledoux to the post-Cubist compositions of Malevich and van Doesburg; from Choisy's diagrammatic analysis of building relationships on the Acropolis to Le Corbusier's 1930 plan for an agrarian community. For the first time since the day of Viollet-le-Duc, an architect frankly proclaimed that the making of a contemporary style proceeded from a study of the past as well as from a consideration of the physiognomy of one's own times. The result of all this consciousness is a small, simple structure, the shape, placement, and interior dispositions of which are historically mesmerizing. All of the buildings discussed in this chapter have been in one way or another largely retrospective, but never in quite so systematic and encyclopedic a fashion.

In addition to providing a kind of historical résumé of the modern tradition and certain of its classical antecedents, Johnson's Glass House (which must be seen in harmonic compositional relationship with its companions, the brick Guest House of 1953, Fig. 228, with its novel domical interior, and the arcuated precast concrete Pavilion in the artificial "lake,"

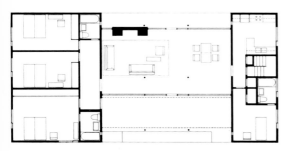

221, 222. Philip Johnson. Farney House. Sagaponack, Long Island, 1946. View and floor plan.

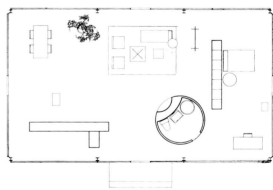

223–225. Philip Johnson. Johnson House, Glass House.
New Canaan, Connecticut, 1947–49. Exterior and interior
views, floor plan.

226, 227. Philip Johnson. Johnson House. New Canaan, Connecticut, 1947–49. Site plan and view of the Glass House with Guest House.

1961–62) offers one of the clearest harbingers of the increasingly strict formal tendencies that became manifest by 1960. Johnson's glass cube does not hover above the ground between concrete and steel slabs in the fashion of the Farnsworth House, which, in this respect, was one of the last significant examples of the unstable geometry that had dominated the architecture of the first half of the twentieth century, from Wright's prairie houses onwards. Instead, it is placed directly upon a brick platform which rests squarely on the ground. Consequently, because the interior is no longer isolated above the ground, interior and exterior spaces are more completely related. Furthermore, the visual impression of the structural frame is de-emphasized by replacing the clear, classic white of the Farnsworth House with black, thus creating a more neutral effect in combination with the chameleon-like qualities of the glass walls.

The interior of Johnson's house offers us one of the rare domestic realizations of Mies's universal space. The only object that fills the interior from floor to ceiling-slab is the circular brick service core. Spaces are defined by the placement of the furniture (almost exclusively Miesian), low cabinet units, and the works of art (notably a version of Poussin's *Funeral of Phocion*, Nadelman's life-sized papier-mâché *Two Women,* and a small Giacometti figure group). All of this is curiously traditional—the Mies-designed furniture can reasonably be classified as antiques in this context—while, at the same time, representative of a specifically twentieth-century style. It is aggressively contemporary in the sense that a glass wall is the popular image of the avant-garde in architecture; but it is nonetheless an antiquated building in several ways. Chief among these is its use of an already passé universal space to realize a kind of garden-residence on the order of certain eighteenth-century follies, such as the whimsical house-in-the-ruined-column of François-Racine de Monville in the garden near Paris known as the Desert de Retz.[23] Beyond all this interplay between past and present, the personal intellectualization of Johnson's methodology and the inevitable paradoxes and contradictions involved, comes within a hairbreadth of being the reverse of the Smithsons' wishful claim for Hunstanton: "A radicalism which owes nothing to precedent, and everything to the inner mechanisms of the Modern Movement." It is at least poetically true that the radicalism of the Glass House is due both to its author's recourse to precedent and to his rejection of the factual determinism of the "traditional" modern movement's inner mechanisms. Indeed, in his writing and statements, Johnson has, with ever-increasing vigor, denounced the entirety of the moralistic and mechanistic theory of modernism ranging from Ruskin, Morris, and Viollet-le-Duc to Gropius, Banham, and the Smithsons. The evolution of his style over the decade and a half since the Glass House was built only documents this sentiment.

Perhaps the most important feature of this epochal little building is one which cannot be so easily remarked except through contemplation of the plan. It is the visually concealed cross-axiality of the plan (which, significantly does not function spatially or for circulation) resulting from the placement of the four doors in the middle of each of the two long and two short sides of the Glass House. This feature figures more prominently in the spatial organization of other houses designed by Johnson in the early 1950's, notably the Hodgson House, New Canaan, 1951 (Figs. 86, 87, 229), where the main body of the structure is placed around a central court and the circulation system is based upon a monumental vestibule (which doubles as dining area!) with passages at right angles.[24] This centralizing, inward-oriented manner of relating spaces, with its evocation of Palladianism and of the academic tradition, can be seen in Hunstanton as well, and indeed is perhaps a part of the significance of the huge central lagoon in Saarinen's General Motors, which its architect maintained was to function as a unifying and reinforcing visual element in the design. This emphasis upon the inward coalescence of visual and spatial features, together with a tendency to a more or less regular, static organization of individual areas, becomes more and more apparent in the architecture of the succeeding decade. This is the nature of the transformation of architectural composition today; this is the irrepressible reaction to the boundless, dynamic spaces of the first half of the century, spaces that overran their nominal enclosures by virtue of their sliding and hovering planes that expanded outward from fixed inner cores. Johnson's Glass House stands on the brink of this transformation, looking both forward and backward.

The architects discussed in this chapter have in common the taking of Mies's late style and developing it in one or another direction. In the works of Saarinen, Kahn, Johnson, and the Smithsons, a variety of reactions seems to take place both in forms and in ideas, all of which seem to have the common feature of gradually, but inevitably, creating a new pattern of spatial organization. This adventure in architectural composition, however, seems to be a specifically individualistic one, a growth open to the widest imaginable diversity of justification, as well as to the most unusual formal embodiments. Indeed, between the forthright

228. Philip Johnson. Johnson House, Guest House. New Canaan, Connecticut, 1953.

229. Philip Johnson. Hodgson House. New Canaan, Connecticut, 1951.

formalism and traditionalism of Johnson, expressed both in word and in buildings, and the "inner motivated" materialism and factuality of the Smithsons, there seems to be a gaping chasm which would defy reconciliation. Where Johnson would take the vocabulary of the new tradition to create an architecture of the future, the Smithsons would presume that the working method of the recent past was the means by which the next step could be realized. These are polar opposites, magnetic points of controversy, but if they are not susceptible of reconciliation, they are issues which can be argued and debated with some purpose and benefit. It has been controversies of this magnitude which, in the past, have generated the necessary ardor, a basic prerequisite, for sustained creation.

Cutting across this debate between form and technique is one concerning the inner significance and meaning of architectural form. This issue has been raised, but in a befuddled fashion, by Saarinen's desire to express the nature of the program and even the character of the client (with Saarinen, the client is always corporate, never an individual) in the outward shapes of his buildings. The search for an appropriate image finds a certain echo in the slowly evolving ideas of Louis Kahn, ideas that did not really take shape until late in the 1950's, though already, in 1955, he could write:

Art is a form making life in order—psychic
Order is intangible
It is a level of creative consciousness forever becoming higher in level
The higher the order the more diversity in design
Order supports integration
From what the space wants to be the unfamiliar may be revealed to the architect.[25]

Rather than settle for the subjective literary expression of content, a state of things which seems to have satisfied Saarinen, Kahn sought the building's character by willing the process of design to be one of growth, of becoming. He externalized the creative workings of mind and eye in order to permit the building to have a unique kind of progressive self-fulfillment, one revealed to the architect only with increasing awareness of the problem of the moment. Here, indeed, abstruse though the language may be, we find nobly expressed longings of a kind comparable, perhaps, to those sentiments of the Smithsons concerned with "inner mechanisms." Kahn expressed them, however, also in the hope: "From what the space wants to be the unfamiliar may be revealed to the architect." It is in the search for the unfamiliar that Kahn rises beyond Saarinen and the Smithsons to a vision of the integration of form, technique, and content that has eluded most of the architects of his day. Since this profound synthesis was not yet possible in the still-Miesian oriented period of the early 1950's, it perhaps accounts for Kahn's lack of success and even commissions at the time. The recognized successes of the early and mid-1950's belonged to the commercial firms who had stabilized the quality and character of their design early in the decade, to an architect of selective discrimination and keen taste like Johnson, who knew what suited him, as well as how to use it, and to Eero Saarinen, a more restless, searching architect who would play a significant, distinctive role at a moment in the evolution of contemporary architecture during which its growing pains would be sharper than ever before.

# Chapter V
## Crisis and Reorientation: Theaters, Churches, Concert Halls, and Arenas in the Middle and Later 1950's

"The mistakes of great architects are always significant," tartly observed Bruno Zevi, apropos Eero Saarinen's Auditorium and Chapel at Massachusetts Institute of Technology, Cambridge, 1953–56 (Figs. 230–233).[1] Patronizing as this comment may be, it nonetheless points up the nature of the controversy that surrounded these fascinating and then unusual buildings. By any critical standards, whether modernist or academic, these structures are flawed, especially with respect to structural considerations and detailing. In the end, they are satisfactory only on the basis of their over-all concept, and even there one finds ample scope for controversy. Despite the valid criticism, however, they stand out as the most prescient inventions of the mid-1950's.

Indeed, the literary qualities of Saarinen's work which were latent at G. M. are here, at M. I. T., infinitely more conspicuous, chiefly because of the stark domical form, a form inevitably burdened with a historical suggestiveness that not even a novel structural technique could conceal. Zevi tellingly identified the nature of the crisis apparent in Saarinen's change of form between G. M. and M. I. T.: "I believe that the M. I. T. group is significant of today's figurative impasse, perhaps even of today's moral crisis. . . . The idea of a universally valid form separate from function . . . is the old classical, or better neoclassical, idea: a myth of the Romantic Age. In this kind of architectural philosophy, geometry prevails over psychology, abstraction over reality, symbols over men. The resulting building derives its value from the idea it represents, not from what it is."

Zevi, of course, viewed this crisis in terms of a status quo that he, himself, had so succinctly defined a decade earlier, of an organic theory poised in opposition to both the machine aesthetic and academic formulas. When viewed in retrospect, this same crisis seems to pose itself in a rather different context. From the vantage point of the early 1960's with its new architecture, Saarinen's M. I. T. buildings seem to stand as a source of much that has since been designed and constructed in an increasingly formalistic manner. M. I. T. represents a point of departure, a shift in emphasis toward academic, even arbitrary, composition schemes. The controversy concerning the propriety of this tendency within the broad context of modern design, or within the frame of reference of contemporary needs, has not yet subsided. The passage of a decade, however, has clarified the issues and the critic today is perhaps as inclined to praise Saarinen for his abstract, geometric forms at M. I. T. as Zevi was inclined to blame them in 1956.

The background of Saarinen's innovation is, of course, complex. Stark, simple forms had long been present in the work of Mies, whose academicizing propensity goes back to his association with Peter Behrens around 1910, and these patterns of organization and control were made more explicit by Johnson in his 1947–49 Glass House (Figs. 223–227). But it remained for Saarinen to direct the new form-making tendency away from the decidedly original spatial concepts of orthodox modernism. Because he was trained at Yale and at Cranbrook in two different, yet traditional, manners, he was perhaps unconsciously predisposed to this new kind of eclecticism. Where Johnson's academicism was an outgrowth of his desire to rephrase the Miesian manner in an aristocratic, fastidious way, Saarinen was much less closely identified with an established point of view. This independence facili-

230. Eero Saarinen & Associates. Massachusetts Institute of Technology. Cambridge, Massachusetts, 1953–56. Site plan. Auditorium (1), Chapel (2).

231. Eero Saarinen & Associates. Auditorium, Massachusetts Institute of Technology. Cambridge, Massachusetts, 1953–56.

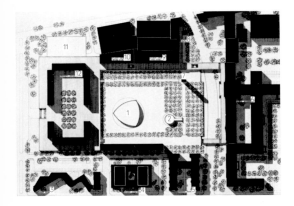

tated his role as a proponent of change, although it also made him the butt of much hostile criticism—criticism which tended to emphasize technical flaws in the execution of M. I. T. in order to damn the unfamiliar, over-all concept.

Unlike Johnson and others, Saarinen had little difficulty or compunction in casting off his rather casually adopted Miesian mantle. Moreover, in contrast to the reticent, self-effacing forms characteristic of his father's more romantic designs, he asserted himself as a designer of striking images. With M. I. T., Eero broke away from his father's predilection for rambling façade composition, but, significantly, not from his eclectic methods. He also broke with the modular regularity of the Miesian precedent, which had imposed a ruthless unity of scale and size, although he now adapted Mies's tendency toward precisely articulated forms. Indeed, he exaggerated this feature, substituting variety of form and material for uniformity, employing circular shapes in plan and silhouette where once there had only been trabeated right-angle relationships. In this pair of buildings, which is not nearly so visually satisfactory as his General Motors Technical Center, Saarinen knew rather well what he was doing: "Here ... in the middle of a crowded city campus ... the question was how to relate the auditorium to these buildings. ... We believed that what was required was a contrasting silhouette, a form which started from the ground and went up, carrying the eye around its sweeping shape. Thus, a domed structure seemed right. There were other reasons too ... there was the large dome of Welles Bosworth's central building at M. I. T."[2] The architect arrived at his dome by subjective association; but once the decision was taken, he proceeded to work it out from an anti-functionalist point of view, using Mies as the means: "Though function has to be respected, it seemed equally justifiable to let the basic form come from the structure. Thus, in developing the design of this building, we felt very strongly guided by Mies's principle of architecture—of a consistent structure and a forthright expression of that structure."[3] Though still cluttered with some of the debris of familiar machine age theory, these observations were perspicacious. They were not so outspoken, however, as Philip Johnson's recognition of the new formalism which he perceived, almost alone in 1954, in Wright's late work as well as in Saarinen's M. I. T. complex: "Where form comes from I don't know, but it has nothing at all to do with the sociological aspects of our architecture"; and to "sociological," Johnson could easily have added "functional and technical" in this context. He concluded, "We'll fit [form] to our sociological buildings, as Saarinen did to his buildings at M. I. T., and sooner or later we will fit it so it can be used."[4]

Johnson's beliefs and Saarinen's intuitions, as expressed in the Auditorium and Chapel, were already well removed from both the materialism of the previous generation and attitudes prevalent among other architects in the mid-1950's. Bruno Zevi reported that Nervi's reaction to the publication in Italy of the M. I. T. complex was hostile, quoting him as follows: "I could demonstrate that structural thought and common sense have been allied in all ages. Today structural ideas are invaded by extravagance, and they are deprived of all justification."[5] Thus did the master of twentieth-century concrete vaulting techniques disassociate himself from the emerging American formalism. Zevi himself, though with a certain equivocation, tended toward the same point of view, referring in particular to the Chapel as a building that "will excite the curiosity of M. I. T. students and visitors, but will be spiritually unsuitable and culturally misleading, as are all 'bright ideas.'"

These two buildings were greeted with a hail of abuse, only a part of which was justified, and much of which must have been provoked by the extraordinary way in which Saarinen seemed to renounce so many of the accepted truths of modernism. This pair of structures, a brick cylinder and a concrete-shell dome—each distinct form isolated upon its proper base, bounded on every side by nondescript buildings of greater mass—was the tentative opening statement of a new movement which sought its roots both in the familiar historical traditions of the past and in the new tradition of modernism. It was a necessary station on

232, 233. Eero Saarinen & Associates. Chapel, Massachusetts Institute of Technology. Cambridge, Massachusetts, 1953–56.

234. Pier Luigi Nervi. Municipal Stadium. Florence, 1930–32.

235. Pier Luigi Nervi. Aircraft hangar. Orvieto, 1935–36.

236. Pier Luigi Nervi. Exhibition Hall. Turin, 1948–49.

the way to Saarinen's later, and much less ambivalent, monumental buildings. More important, it provided the first widely publicized breach in the theoretical platitudes of modernism, and it simultaneously offered an even more original formal reply to the empirical ramblings of the 1940's than the answer provided by the more orthodox Miesian movement of the early 1950's.

In fairness to Saarinen's outspoken critics, and to history itself, some of the technical shortcomings of the M. I. T. designs should be pointed out. For example, when the forms of the dome were removed, the deflection turned out to be much greater than had been anticipated, and the mullions of the curtain wall had to be enlarged to act as secondary supports. It is perhaps for this reason that the circular brick podium upon which the building rests has settled in an irregular and displeasing fashion. Far more important are the visual shortcomings, notably the placement of the dome directly upon a stylobate, without some intervening form to "lift" the shell surface off the ground. If the extrados of a vault-form is to be used as the whole of a building's silhouette, it would seem mandatory that the curvature of the vault suggest a complex of tension and compression forces. As it stands, the dome of the M. I. T. Auditorium is much too static and the contact between ground and building much too abrupt. Finally, the dome, which in a traditional context serves as the climax of a space-volume crescendo, but which is here the totality of the form, is not able to provide a sense of culmination.

On the other hand, the positive aspects of these buildings must not be overlooked. After a half century of an architecture in which integration, continuity, and flux were nearly unquestioned ideals, and after the briefest of transitions in the wake of Mies's late style, the M. I. T. Chapel and Auditorium emerged as a full-blown realization of the exact opposite: two isolated, self-contained buildings, rather awkwardly placed in relation to each other and to their nondescript surroundings. As an ensemble, they react only in a static, ungainly, and tenuous way, instead of exhibiting a pronounced visual connection (in the form of a passageway or covered ramp) as would have been demanded by the so-called functional aesthetic. Reflecting if not a new wave of the future at least a profound disenchantment with the modernist status quo, both buildings are completely isolated from the ground, the chapel sunk in a round moat, the auditorium raised on its rounded brick platform. Furthermore, these features tend to overemphasize the dilute, emaciated character of the two contrasting masses. The blandness of the industrial-classic aesthetic, which still controls the detailing of the domical auditorium, is not modified to any great extent in the uniformly unbroken circular wall of the chapel, despite its somewhat Scandinavian execution in blackened clinker brick. Both buildings lack the sort of rhythmic punctuation that would have relieved surface monotony and, at the same time, would have provided the vital key for a scale relationship between the two.

Sympathetic though we may be to Saarinen's brave experiment, in the last analysis it must be granted that there is nothing especially logical, let alone inevitable or compelling, about the presence of these two buildings on the same site. This is a curious feature of many Saarinen buildings: a failure to communicate a sense of urgency or emotional involvement, in spite of the romantic subjectivity which seems to have determined the forms in the first place.

Saarinen, himself, several years later, in 1960, could write of these buildings with a curious detachment: "Looking back at this early work, I think the dome and chapel can be criticized as being too egocentric. The shapes of the buildings are closed. They do not contribute anything toward creating unity within an area which so badly needs unity. From the beginning, we conceived of these buildings on a great square, but neglected to define and crystallize exactly how it would be achieved. This we should have done."[6] Yet, in a certain historical sense, this may be his most crucial and revealing work, although not his most successful.

This dome and cylinder should be compared with a number of other monumental works of

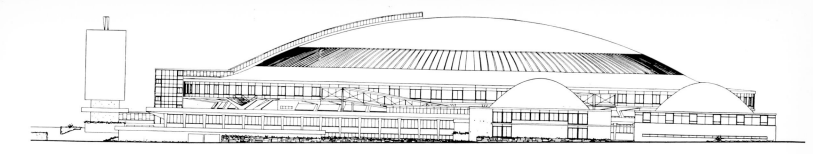

237. Pier Luigi Nervi. Project for a Sports Center in Vienna, 1953.

the mid-1950's in order to gain perspective on the ferment that was just beginning to disturb the modern movement at that time. There was a small rash of domical constructions toward the end of the decade, among the most satisfactory of which were the two domes conceived by Pier Luigi Nervi for the Olympic Games in Rome, the *Palazzo dello Sport,* 1958–60, and its companion *Palazzetto,* 1956–57 (Figs. 239–241). Neither structure resulted from especially new ideas; each was instead an outgrowth of earlier domical schemes, notably Nervi's 1953 competition entry for a Sports Center in Vienna (Fig. 237). That building was subsequently erected by a local architect, Roland Rainer (Fig. 238), in a manner more akin, in its jagged forms, to the neo-Expressionism of numerous German theaters and concert halls of the 1950's than to the constructive logic of the Italian engineer. Of all the major designers of our day, Nervi is the one who has perhaps yet to receive his full and just recognition. In considerable measure, this neglect has been due to the attitudes of purists of one sort or another, who maintain that, as architect, if not as engineer, Nervi's work does not merit consideration because his structures are not governed by the form-giving design aspects of architecture. Obviously, much of this argument is fanciful and unfortunately has only served to hide the nature of the role that Nervi has played in the history of recent architecture. A calm, unprejudiced survey of his work must lead to a recognition of his creative power as among the most fecund to appear in the period between the maturity of Mies and Le Corbusier and the ultimate emergence, in the late 1950's, of Louis Kahn.[7]

If only to explain his distinctive role in the evolution of architecture during the 1950's, a review of his career is in order. Born in 1891, Nervi is closer in age to the generation of modern pioneers than to the one which tardily attained its creative majority in the 1950's. Somewhat prophetically, after having taken his engineering degree at Bologna in 1913, Nervi did not participate actively in the first wave of modern Italian architecture, a wave that ranged from Sant'Elia's Futurist city projects, exhibited in Milan in 1914, to the elegantly refined works of Giuseppe Terragni in the 1920's and 1930's. His earliest significant work was the often reproduced Municipal Stadium, Florence, 1930–32 (Fig. 234), in which the constructive spirit so characteristic of his later inventions first saw the light of day. It was not until the design and construction of two aircraft hangars at Orvieto, 1935–36 (Fig. 235), that he had the opportunity to create a significant interior space. This commission proved to be the kind of

238. Roland Rainer. Municipal Hall. Vienna, 1954–58.

239. Pier Luigi Nervi. Palazzo dello Sport. Rome, 1958–60.
Detail of the dome.

monumental opportunity that few other twentieth-century architects had been offered (one has to go back to Eugène Freyssinet's World War I Orly hangars to find a true precedent). Here a cast-in-place, intersecting rib structure spans 132 feet. The marvel of the construction, however, was the fact that its open front required but one intermediary support in an otherwise clear opening that ran for its entire 330-foot length. This design was subsequently improved upon in six hangars of the same dimensions, built at Orvieto, Orbetello, and Torre del Lago, 1939–41, where the entire vault was then made of prefabricated concrete components which rested upon only six massive flying buttress-like concrete piers. The component parts were cast at the site in simple wooden molds, to be assembled into the vault frame.

The elegance and expressiveness of this utilitarian solution was surpassed in the postwar Turin Exhibition Hall, 1948–49 (Fig. 236), whose interior span of 240 feet and its seemingly elastic relationship between the precast vault elements and the diagonally placed abutting piers make this one of the most majestic of twentieth-century spaces. This same language of structural reciprocity was brought to the design and construction of the Olympic domes, the smaller of which, the *Palazzetto,* was perhaps Nervi's most successful realization. Unlike certain other of his works, where the exteriors were mutilated by collaborating architects, Nervi was able to produce the *Palazzetto* as an integrated, total building in which the causal relationships between interior and exterior, between structure, mass, and space were beautifully articulated. Clearly, this was a much more successfully realized

building, one which more clearly represented the principal theorems of contemporary orthodoxy, than Saarinen's M. I. T. dome. By the same token, however, it does not point toward the reorientation of modernism, as does the American building, despite its failure as a focused, explicit statement of that style-to-come.

Nervi's adventures in the shaping of large public spaces are the fulfillment of a long constructive tradition in modern architecture, a tradition that reaches back through the works of Perret, Freyssinet, and De Baudot, to Eiffel, Viollet-le-Duc, and Paxton in the nineteenth century, and ultimately joins with that wing of the neoclassic tradition represented by Soufflot, Rondelet, and Monferran. Paradoxically, Saarinen's contrasting intuitive approach to the creation of monumental forms and spaces also evokes aspects of the neoclassic aesthetic, but, naturally, aspects of a totally different character. Ancestors of these qualities are the symbolic, indeed structurally aberrant forms of Boullée and Ledoux. It has been this arbitrary evocation of Romantic Classicism on a form-making level, which is quite different in principle and in result from the candid structuralism of Nervi, that has led Saarinen along the path from M. I. T. to the Yale Hockey Rink, and finally to his neo-Expressionist air terminals in New York and Washington (Figs. 301, 301a, 303). These buildings, whose notably positive aspects and later dates demand consideration in a subsequent chapter, represent a more fully achieved realization of the novel architectural idiom that began its emergence in the mid-1950's.

In one way or another, much of Nervi's work has been flawed in execution as a consequence

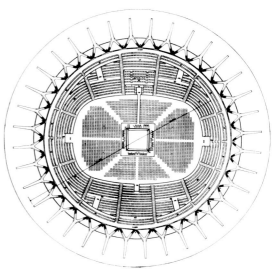

240, 241. Pier Luigi Nervi and Annibale Vitellozzi. Palazzetto dello Sport. Rome, 1956–57. View and plan of the hall.

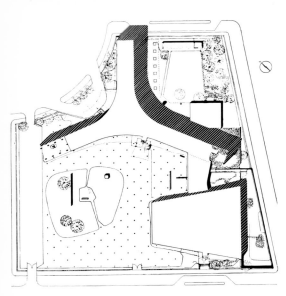

242, 243. Marcel Breuer, Pier Luigi Nervi, and Bernard Zehrfuss. UNESCO Headquarters. Paris, 1955–58. Site plan and façade detail of the Secretariat.

of his forced collaboration with other, frequently unsympathetic, architects. One of the most spectacular of these qualified successes was the *Centre National des Industries et Techniques,* Paris, projected in 1955 in collaboration with Camelot, de Mailly, Zehrfuss, and Jean Prové. This is a mammoth three-point groin vaulted structure with a clear span of 738 feet, formed of prefabricated concrete units, but enclosed by a huge glass curtain wall. Unfortunately, the structural concept did not lend itself to architectonic emphasis, as was the case in the Rome *Palazzetto,* with the result that from a moderate distance the over-simplified form of the *Centre National* lacks any real majesty and seems to be an awkward compromise between conventional academic pomposity and the mathematic elegance of machine-age techniques. In effect, this building has the same disarming thinness and blandness that one confronts in Saarinen's infinitely smaller M. I. T. edifices. In all three buildings, it is caused by a lack of suitably proportioned detail as well as by a much too simple effect of mass, owing, it would seem, to the lack of a deliberate climax.

In another large building in Paris, the UNESCO Headquarters, Place Fontenoy (opposite Gabriel's eighteenth-century *Ecole Militaire*) (Figs. 242–245), Nervi found a more stimulating partner in Marcel Breuer,[8] in collaboration with Bernard Zehrfuss. The UNESCO project goes back to 1953, though construction was delayed until 1955–58. In this work, the distinctive tendencies of Nervi's constructivism were blended with those of an architect steeped in the fundamental, central traditions of modernism. Breuer's career up to this juncture had been notably varied, including teaching at the Bauhaus and at Harvard, the designing of some of the most pioneering of all machine-era furnishings during the 1920's, and the building of a notable series of private houses in the United States during the 1940's. UNESCO was Breuer's first test as an architect on a monumental, official scale, and, as befitted the problematic period in which he produced the design, the result was interesting, if tentative. Its uncertainty of style—hovering indecisively between the polarities of Mies and Le Corbusier—is indeed a product of the period as well as the outgrowth of considerations relating to his own personal development. From the experience gained in this collaboration, Breuer—and, for that matter, Nervi as well—would be in a more favorable position for subsequent mature, large-scale work, toward the later 1950's.

Although the formal vocabulary of UNESCO is totally unrelated to M. I. T., there is a thinness of detailing, a certain arbitrary stiffnes in layout, and a survival in the detailing of certain overworked machine-era clichés, all qualities that can be found under a different guise in the Saarinen building. The plan of the principal office block of UNESCO

244, 245. Marcel Breuer, Pier Luigi Nervi, and Bernard Zehrfuss. UNESCO Headquarters. Paris, 1955–58. View of the Conference Building from southeast and southwest elevation.

is a curved "Y," a layout adopted in part so that one face of the building could adjust itself to the hemicycle shape of the Place Fontenoy, and also in order to create an effect of integration and flow among the wings of the building. This semblance of continuity is a survival of the formal concepts of the 1920's, although in a diluted transcription roughly equivalent to the earlier Lever House. Nevertheless, Breuer's work, brittle though it may be in its proportions and details, is not akin to the slick, sophisticated anonymity then cultivated by the American commercial firms. Instead of leaving the façade as a pristine curtain wall, Breuer constructed an "outrigging" of heat- and glare-resistant glass to help control the temperature and light of the office spaces. Visually, this detail tends to blur the otherwise sharp detail and glazed surface of the office wings, thus producing a peculiar, mirage-like effect. This leads to a lack of clarity where exact definition of over-all volume and individual detail is most expected, and therefore is largely responsible for the ambivalent effect produced. As the decade wore on, however, this became a lesson from which Breuer profited immensely.

The adjoining UNESCO assembly hall was, at least on the exterior, an eminently successful building. The roof structure of a "folded" concrete slab was carried through into the end walls, which themselves performed the crucial buttressing role, and the lower central portion of the reverse, inward-sloping roof is supported on isolated interior columns. The whole exterior form is a successful monumental transformation of the butterfly roof silhouette which Breuer had used in several of his houses of the previous decade, and which derived ultimately from Le Corbusier by way of Brazil and the works of Niemeyer and others. Indeed, this shape was a notable development out of such important Latin American structures as Reidy's small Rio de Janeiro Community Theater of 1950 (Fig. 246), where the same saddleback silhouette is used in combination with planar, rather than folded, roof and end-wall slabs.

In spite of its obvious shortcomings, Breuer was soon able to put his UNESCO experience to work in an independent design of his own, the chapel and free-standing belfry of St. John's Abbey and University, Collegeville, Minnesota, designed in 1953 but not completed until 1961 (Figs. 247, 248). Here the saddleback form was dropped, and the folded slab construction turned ninety degrees so that the ribs run athwart the space, and the side walls, rather than the end ones, continue the profile of the vault. While the form and the layout are not completely integrated (this is especially true with respect to the shape, of the baptistry, a low wing jutting out from the honeycomb façade wall, which nestles under the parabolic arches

246. Affonso Eduardo Reidy. Community Theater. Rio de Janeiro, 1950–51.

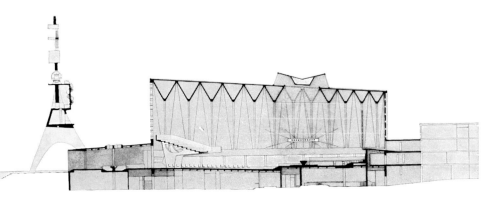

247, 248. Marcel Breuer. St. John's Abbey and University. Collegeville, Minnesota, 1961. View from northwest and longitudinal section.

of the open belfry), the result seems more completely under control than before. The de-tached belfry itself, with its splayed quadruped pylon (a concrete version of the Eiffel Tower, in whose shadow UNESCO was built), rises to grip a concrete slab containing the exposed carillon and, above this, a crucifix. It is a most startling blend of Christian iconography with machine-age symbolism, the latter invoked by the eccentric, arbitrary use of the slab. More recently, in 1961, Breuer carried his ideas a step further in the design for St. Francis de Sales Church, Muskegon, Michigan (Figs. 249, 250). The folded slab is replaced by a side-wall construction of hyperbolic paraboloids rising from a rectangular plan. This results in an unusual sloping, inverted, trapezoidal façade, as well as in a twisted mass of largely unpunc-tured concrete which is well set off by low parish buildings of an Egyptian, mastaba-like shape and simplicity. In this fashion, Breuer has continued to grow and develop in the last few years, and his designs have taken on a greater degree of assurance.

Having touched upon the works of three notable architects active in the mid-1950's—Eero Saarinen, Pier Luigi Nervi, and Marcel Breuer—and having noted their sharp disparity of intent, it is logical that, as the decade wore on, it appeared to be a period of increasing confusion, of individual wandering, with architects tasting, sampling, and rejecting a great variety of influences and possibilities. The monolithic unity of modern architecture, first cemented in the 1920's and 1930's and precariously put together again in the early 1950's, rapidly fell apart within the short space of five or six years. There occurred a mo-ment of confusion in which individuals and groups could establish momentary alliances based upon a certain restricted interest or transient cause, only to dissolve them at the first convenient moment either to form new associations or to strike out along new paths. Constancy ceased to be a significant feature in the new climate, which instead fostered an attitude that was even more fundamentally at variance with the International Style than the reactions of the 1940's had been. In spite of the ideals of Nervi, Kahn, and the Smithsons, all of whom sought to maintain at least a mystical faith in the old methodologies even while extracting new forms from the old procedures, the period was dominated by the works of men who were seeking new forms in a romantic, academic way. While Nervi was outside this movement, and Breuer at best was only on its periphery, Saarinen was at work in its very epicenter. Saarinen's limitations aside, he was the most popular architect of the 1950's. On April 26, 1953, *The New York Times Magazine* published an enthusiastic article, with illustrations of G. M. and M. I. T., by Saarinen's wife-to-be, Aline Louchheim; and the July 2, 1956, issue of *Time* carried Saarinen's portrait (with the plan of G. M. as back-ground) on the cover and published a long analysis in which his name was conspicuously associated with Wright, Le Corbusier, Mies, and Gropius. The Vitruvian epithet, "Well-building hath three conditions: Commodity, Firmness and Delight," was placed at the head of the article, which was smugly titled "The Maturing Modern." The ambiguous po-sition of Eero Saarinen, acceptably radical in his nominal espousal of machine technology, but also thoroughly safe in his willingness to provide an architecture of acceptable and understandable images, made him exactly the sort of culture figure cut to the measure of the powerful mass-circulation magazine industry.

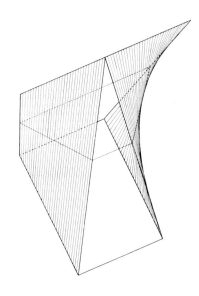

249, 250. Marcel Breuer. St. Francis de Sales Church. Muskegon, Michigan, 1961. Model and schematic drawing showing geometrical structure.

In this way, at least certain aspects of the new formalism of the 1950's found spontaneous popular, if not critical, acceptance, in contrast to the hostility that had greeted the mas-ters of the International Style. It would be unjust to insinuate that, by becoming the archi-tectural hero of the purveyors of mass culture, Saarinen and his work ceased to represent the continuing mainstream of avant-garde. In fact, a contrary situation existed, for the whole social and cultural substructure upon which the radical movements of the first half of the century were based seemed to perform a cartwheel in about 1950. Suddenly, it be-came fashionable to endorse the radical, to support the irregular, the outrageous, and the iconoclastic gesture. In Marxist terms, the bourgeoisie, economically more powerful and secure than ever before, suddenly became willing and eager to pay for seeing its values flaunted in the forms of contemporary art. Although architects could not go to the same

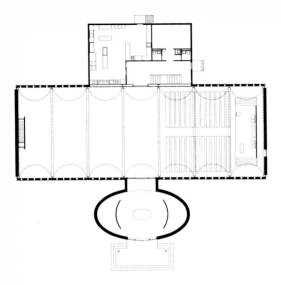

251–253. Philip Johnson. Kneses Tifereth Israel Synagogue. Port Chester, New York, 1956. Floor plan, exterior and interior views.

negative extremes as the painters (though the Smithsons would seem to have entertained such notions), the new climate of mass culture made the acceptance of the modern architecture of Saarinen and Skidmore, Owings and Merrill a foregone conclusion.

There were other architects, however, who did not immediately share in the deluge of adulation. Philip Johnson, for instance, did not have his day in *Time* until 1959, even though his work of the mid-1950's formed a plausible parallel to the highly publicized works of others. Probably, this was due to Johnson's conspicuous alliance with the old European pioneers Behrens and Mies, contrasted with Saarinen's more homely Scandinavian origins. On the other hand, Johnson's buildings contemporary with UNESCO and M.I.T. display an intellectual security and a creative sureness that were almost unknown to others of his generation during the mid-1950's. Quick to grasp analogies, impatient with doctrinal platitudes, Johnson was temperamentally equipped to evolve from a Miesian style to a more personal style with a smoothness quite unlike the shifts and jumps of Saarinen's career. This Johnsonian facility is well illustrated in the Kneses Tifereth Israel Synagogue, Port Chester, New York, 1956 (Figs. 251–253). Although not as obvious a break with the modernist tradition as Saarinen's new formalism, it nonetheless contains more specific, more comprehending references to the neo-classic tradition, but it does so within a Miesian context.

As a result, Johnson's transitional work does not suffer the same thinness of effect that Saarinen's sometimes does, though it does share an epigrammatic succinctness.

The exterior of Johnson's Port Chester Synagogue is composed of two connected, but contrasted, geometric elements: a domed oval vestibule set against a higher, steel-framed, precast concrete rectangular form. On the interior, the principal space is subject to an engaging, but arbitrary, modulation of surface and light. The inflection of the space is dominated by a suspended canopy vault of plaster whose scale is determined by the module of the black steel columns, visible on the interior and on the exterior. The walls come close to meeting the Brutalist requirement of seeming to be what they really are in terms of structure; but a strongly anti-Brutalist note is struck by the canopy overhead, which directs light downward against the white precast concrete walls, whose severe purity is relieved by slots of varicolored glass. The mixture of cold and warm light produces an extraordinary effect, and the entire configuration of space reveals itself as simultaneously Miesian and neo-classic. Johnson's elegant, intellectualized creation stands up nobly in comparison with other individual religious buildings of the mid-1950's, as Saarinen's round brick M. I. T. Chapel cannot.

A contemporary German church in the Rhineland, Rudolf Schwarz's Saint Anne, Düren, 1953–56 (Figs. 254, 255), approximates the ideals of New Brutalism even more closely than either of the American examples cited.[9] Moreover, it fulfills, in some measure, Schwarz's timeless ideals concerning church symbolism, and, in most respects, is a direct, emotional response to an ecclesiastical program. Its high, unpunctured rubble wall (built, as was Ronchamp, from the remains of a war-damaged church) and its total lack of subtlety in lighting reveal none of the niceties of history or the elegance of luminous spatial effect so seductively featured in both American churches. Yet this raw, almost uncouth building is meant to serve a traditional religious institution in a symbolic, indeed poetic way, evoking a sense of awe and of devotion. Latent in this polarity of religious architecture there is a fine controversy, but one which has not yet been effectively joined. Irrespective of the divergent merits of each case, both paths here illustrated bespeak a perceptive, satisfying enrichment of modern architecture, to the point where it can deal in a ready fashion with the challenges of monumental ecclesiastical architecture.

Some of Rudolf Schwarz's other churches are less astringent and brutal in conception than Saint Anne, and although harsh in aspect, they nonetheless reveal a formalist quality oriented both toward a burly Rhenish Romanesque tradition and toward a poetic Christian symbolism. The best known work in this vein is St. Michael, Frankfurt-am-Main, 1954

254, 255. Rudolf Schwarz. Saint Anne's Church. Düren, 1953–56. Exterior and interior views.

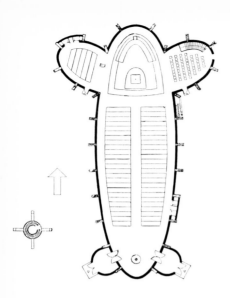

256, 257. Rudolf Schwarz. Parish Church of St. Michael. Frankfurt-am-Main, 1954. Floor plan and view.

258–260. Rudolf Schwarz. Church of Mary the Queen. Saarbrücken, 1956–59. Exterior and interior views, floor plan.

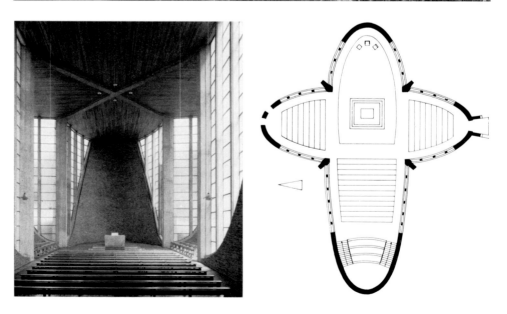

(Figs. 256, 257), where, from an unusual oval plan, the nave culminates in a very free, simple variation of the trefoil apse. The exterior elevation of the apsidal mass creates a veiled but unmistakably Romanesque effect, except for such details as the concrete buttresses, glass brick windows, and flat roof. The interior is stark and regular, its curving walls in sharp contrast to the almost unrelieved flat plane of the ceiling. Even more lyrical and integrated in its effect is the Church of Mary the Queen, Saarbrücken, 1956–59 (Figs. 258–260). In a form based upon the symbolism of the Chalice and the Mystic Rose, this handsomely situated church is of a simple four-lobed plan, constructed of concrete, glass, and red sandstone. The larger arm of the church forms the nave, which points downhill, and is built above a crypt which also serves as vestibule, so that the entrance to the church proper is gained in a dramatic fashion up a flight of stairs. Inside, the areas of glass are concentrated at the crossing, where the altar is placed (leaving a great void behind). In the walls that extend outward from the crossing, there is an inverted parabolic arch that rises to the height of the ceiling slab toward the end of each lobe-shaped arm. Above this inverted arch is glass; below is a red sandstone wall, extending outward and upward as would the petals of the symbolic rose. Inconographically, the result is at the opposite pole from the agnostic, more academically specific, historicism of Saarinen and Johnson, or even from the modernist, Bauhaus-oriented traditionalism of Breuer at Collegeville. The formal clarity, the regularity, and focused coherence of the Saarbrücken church establish it as an achievement equal to the nascent American formalism.

In this context, two representative Italian churches of the 1950's manage to echo the formal tendencies of simplicity and concentration, and at the same time make a successful effort to reconcile the modern idiom with the traditions of the early Church. Ignazio Gardella's 1957 church at Cesate (Figs. 261, 262) does this in a fairly obvious fashion.[10] Of a simple rectangular plan with no side aisles or transept, but with a high gabled lantern just in front of the sanctuary, the concept as well as the realization in brick and concrete suggest both historical tradition and regional vernacular, without making specific references. The vague Early Christian effect that Gardella gains in subtle terms at Cesate was stated with even greater force by Luigi Figini and Gino Pollini in their Church of the Madonna dei Poveri, Milan, 1952–53 (Figs. 263–265). Its rugged concrete forms are Brutalist in effect, but produce an ensemble of spaces that are accentuated by an extremely complex, romantic play of light. By providing a striking variety of light intensities, the architects deliberately created an atmosphere of meditation in the dark side aisles contrasted with one of exaltation in the brilliant area of the altar under the lantern tower. These variations are enriched by

261, 262. Ignazio Gardella. Church at Cesate, 1957. View and floor plan.

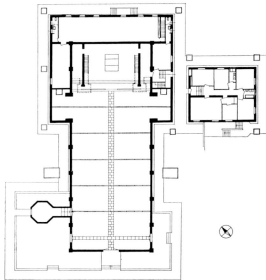

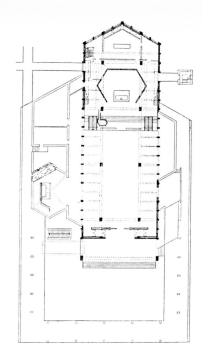

small, deeply recessed apertures high in the nave wall, openings that direct irregular patterns of light across the rugged, if somewhat artificially conceived, concrete surfaces. In marked contrast to the open, sweeping spaces of Schwarz or Johnson, Figini and Pollini here achieved an articulation and a degree of privacy rare in contemporary ecclesiastical architecture.

The cavernous, rather primitive ambiance of the Madonna dei Poveri, the result of awkward forms and raw surfaces, combined with an almost baroque, variegated lighting, is far removed from another equally vivid concrete church of the same epoch, Notre-Dame-de-Royan, France, 1954 (Figs. 266, 267). The work of the architect Guillaume Gillet, with the active collaboration of the engineers René Sarger and Bernard Lafaille, this elliptical church is covered by a suspended thin-shelled concrete vault. The vault is supported by a rugged structure of concrete piers which, together with the tall slits of glass between each pier, form the entirety of the wall, inside and out. The result is both original and satisfying, in spite of some tasteless interior furnishings, and is still another demonstration of the almost endless variety possible in monumental concrete structure. More contrived in their expression of structure and space are such widely acclaimed churches as Santa Maria Miraculosa, Mexico City, by Félix Candela and Enrique de la Mora, or the Presbyterian Church, Stamford, Connecticut, by Harrison and Abramovitz in collaboration with the engineer Felix Samuely. Both of these are typical of the forced and elaborate compositions that have become hallmarks of so much religious architecture since the mid-1950's, in which banal rhetoric (the Stamford Presbyterian church is in the form of a fish) takes the place of genuine structural and ecclesiastical expression. Eschewing this sort of design, the small, modestly shaped church by Van den Broek and Bakema at Nagele, Holland (Fig. 268), is a direct outgrowth of its simple concrete block structure. Its harsh aspect is similar to that of the recently completed Unitarian Church, Rochester, New York, by Louis Kahn, 1962 (Figs. 374, 375), but the simple cubic masses of the characteristically Dutch church seem much closer to the generation-old tradition of Dutch modernism as originally stated by Oud, Dudok, and their contemporaries than to the highly personal theories of the American architects.

It is curious that these varied churches by a number of different architects have tended to reflect aspects of New Brutalism while simultaneously exhibiting certain arbitrary

263–265. Luigi Figini and Gino Pollini. Church of the Madonna dei Poveri. Milan, 1952–53. Interior views and floor plan.

266, 267. Guillaume Gillet. Church of Notre-Dame-de-Royan. 1954–59.

formalist qualities. The church by Alvar Aalto at Vuoksenniska, near Imatra, Finland, 1957–59 (Figs. 269, 270), illustrates still another aspect of Brutalism, namely its endorsement of antidesign, of non-picturesque accidental features such as those incorporated in the Smithsons' Sheffield project (Fig. 216). In contrast to the vigorous patterns and congeries of order so characteristic of other churches during the 1950's, there is a casual, almost disinterested quality in all of Aalto's work.[11] These qualities reveal themselves in the bulky, irregular silhouette, random organization of plan, and free-form surfaces of the interior space at Vuoksenniska. They mark an attitude formed very early in Aalto's career as a reaction to the formal exactitude of the machine aesthetic. In his famous country house, the Villa Mairea, 1938–39 (Fig. 36), this tendency to dissimulate points of contrast and articulation, to round off forms where others would leave them square, was already manifest. In his post-World

268. J. H. van den Broek and J. B. Bakema. Church at Nagele, Noordoostpolder (Netherlands), 1960.

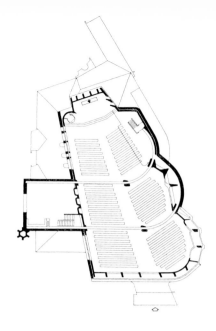

269, 270. Alvar Aalto. Church at Vuoksenniska, near Imatra, 1957–59. View and floor plan.

War II projects, the consistent use of a subjective, undulating form stirred memories of the old Expressionist movement, which from its heyday in Central Europe during the early 1920's had gradually declined and was finally engulfed by the geometry of the International Style.

It is in Aalto's House of Culture, Helsinki, 1955–58 (Figs. 271, 272), that we begin to see a resurgence of Expressionism in contemporary European architecture. Here, as in Baker House, M.I.T., 1948 (Figs. 95 96, and 336a, a monument of the postwar *détente,* whose romantic brick surface certainly influenced Saarinen's choice of material in his chapel there), the entire exterior effect is based upon a freely undulating wall. In its way, it is startling, for its formlessness placed it out of phase with the new design discipline emerging at that time. The formlessness, the organic sprawl of this building is duplicated in much of the German architec-

271, 272. Alvar Aalto. House of Culture. Helsinki, 1955–58.

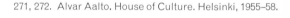

ture of the mid-1950's, an architecture that in some of its most interesting monumental complexes, notably theaters and concert halls, was in clear opposition to the harmonious, frequently classic order of Mies, Johnson, Saarinen, or the more structurally disciplined order of Nervi. There is some degree of similarity between this architecture of resurgent Expressionism and the improvised forms of Le Corbusier, notably Ronchamp. No matter how incalculable his forms became, however, the Franco-Swiss master never renounced his characteristic Cartesian certainty, nor did he abandon his classic Mediterranean trait of passion disciplined by intellect, of impulse in equipoise with reason.

In contrast to Le Corbusier's fixed, mensurate character, the new German architecture, of which Hans Scharoun is one of the most articulate spokesmen, is more Nordic and irrational.[12] To some degree, this is also true of the Aalto buildings discussed above and of his Cultural Center, Wolfsburg, Germany, 1962 (Figs. 273, 274). The accentuated individuality of Aalto's work, however, is distinctly personal and idiosyncratic, and did not result from the formulation of a conscious, literary doctrine, as was the case in a number of recent German examples. Instead, it was produced almost by personal taste alone.

273, 274. Alvar Aalto. Cultural Center. Wolfsburg, 1962. Ground floor plan and exterior view.

Far different is the case with Hans Scharoun's Philharmonic Hall, Berlin, 1956–63 (Figs. 275–277), where the placement of the orchestra "platform" in the center of the audience owes something to Gropius' concept of the 1920's for a Total Theater (a concept well-known to Scharoun, who was a veteran of the heated controversies of that period). Both in plan and in elevation, the shape of the interior is irregular, and this is reflected in the pliant contours of the exterior, where the folds of the roof suggest the wind-swept shapes of sand dunes. As if to extend this willful abandonment of order, the cluster of subsidiary shapes spreads out in a series of random yet somehow expressive forms, all of which provide the visual substructure from which the bulky, ungainly volume of the auditorium, with earth-tugging reluctance, painfully rises. This tortured silhouette is a world removed from the assured, confident, always expanding forms of Le Corbusier at Ronchamp or at the Chandigarh Assembly Building. In comparison, the masses characteristic of Scharoun and his German followers seem more passive and inert, despite their undulating surfaces and organic contours. Beside such expressive forms, the random, casual shapes of Aalto assert a cheerful spirit, while the cool elegance of Mies and his followers seems to belong to another century altogether, responding to a totally different set of emotional and material circumstances.

275–277. Hans Scharoun. Philharmonic Hall. Berlin, 1956–63. Interior and exterior views, section.

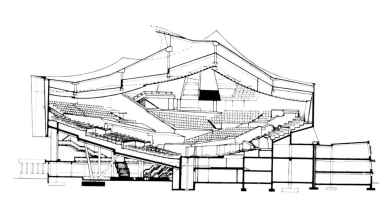

278. Hans Scharoun. Apartment Tower Romeo. Stuttgart, 1957–59.

A brief look at Scharoun's origins, however, will help to explain this striking antipathy between two types of contemporary monumental architecture. Born in 1893, he participated in a number of the group efforts in avant-garde German architecture in the late 1920's and early 1930's. Moreover, in spite of his youth he played an important role during the Expressionist period immediately after 1918. He built a house on the Weissenhof, Stuttgart, in 1927, and in 1930 he built several flats in Berlin, part of the Siemenstadt development, where two of his co-workers included Walter Gropius and Hugo Häring. In spite of his pronounced inclination to curved and somewhat bulbous forms, he was able to accommodate himself into the general frame of the ubiquitous white-surfaced abstract architecture without surrendering his individuality. After 1933, unlike many of his colleagues, he remained in Berlin, largely without work, and subsequently, after 1945, the unique fate of Berlin further hampered his opportunities. In a most unusual sense, then, Scharoun's current work is a belated, fossilized manifestation of the more romantic trends of the 1920's—trends that were submerged first by the triumph of Bauhaus rationalism, and subsequently by the academic reaction of the late 1930's. In the meantime, modern architecture had shifted its balance and its centers of activity, passing through two or three stylistic mutations before Scharoun had a chance to stage a comeback with the construction of a monumental work on the scale of the Berlin Philharmonia. Whether this re-emergence of a bypassed stem of the modern tradition will again contribute to the main line of contemporary developments is still a subject for some debate. On the basis of Scharoun's other new works—the multifaceted "Romeo and Juliet" apartment towers at Stuttgart, 1957-59 (Fig. 278), or the Girls School, Lünen, 1956–62 (Fig. 279), which are typically provocative ideas, rather poorly executed—as well as on the basis of his present influence, there seems to be a certain promise. Among recent works in the wake of Scharoun's concepts, Siegfried Wolske's Beethovenhall in Bonn, 1959 (Fig. 280), deserves special mention, not because it is a flawless instance of multi-hall planning, but because of the very freedom, looseness, and lack of preconception with which the various elements are handled. Here again, the principle of anti-design obtrudes, especially in the arrangement of the three smaller auditoriums at one side of the large concert hall, whose bulk determines the exterior mass. Least successful is the visual aspect of the acoustical ceiling in the large hall, which, in its fussy, small-scaled way negates the spirit behind the larger contours of the plan and mass of the building. On the same order of design is the Liederhalle, Stuttgart, 1955–56, by Adolf Abel and Rolf Gutbrod (Fig. 281). Although its generously

279. Hans Scharoun. High School for Girls. Lünen, 1956–62.

proportioned exterior mass is all but ruined by atrocious detailing, the terraced approaches nonetheless provide an excellent opportunity to perceive the changing aspect of formal relationships among the several masses of the building. On the interior, the execution and detailing of the foyers and halls are sufficiently restrained to allow the irregular, fluent spaces to make their point.

Opposed to the free shapes and undulating contours of these concert halls is the more rigid design and articulation of some of the newer theaters and opera houses in Germany. Notable in this respect is Gerhard Weber's National Theater, Mannheim, 1954–57 (Fig. 282), a distinguished edifice containing both a large and a small hall. The large hall contains a flexible stage and excellently conceived foyer and access spaces, which are reached through the glazed basement located at the center of the building's long side, underneath the twin stage area. Yet, in spite of this admirable planning, the building's exterior is dour in color and somewhat unsympathetic in mass, and it suffers by comparison with the widely publicized project submitted by Mies van der Rohe for this same theater in 1953 (Fig. 283),

281. Adolf Abel and Rolf Gutbrod. Liederhalle. Stuttgart, 1955–56.

where glass was to have been used to great effect on the exterior in a form that was both crystalline and structurally expressive. No doubt it was Mies who inspired the Gelsenkirchen Municipal Theater, 1958–59, by Werner Ruhnau, Ortwin Rave, and Max von Hausen (Fig. 284), a small, widely admired building. Its chief feature is a massive glass curtain wall that shelters a large foyer, a feature more commercially American than truly Miesian in excution. Although elegant and artistic in its dreary manufacturing town setting, its detailing is nevertheless not up to transatlantic standards of refinement. At the other end of the design spectrum is Wilhelm Riphahn's Cologne Opera, 1957 (Fig. 285), a regular monster of a building which, in an era of refined sensibility, manages the unusual feat of looking even larger than it really is. The forms and details are a rather incoherent mixture, randomly selected from the vast repertoire of modernism. Even the accumulation of various materials is meaningless. The result is a building of an old-fashioned monumentality, without the saving grace of intelligent academic-classic detailing, in which both modernism and the academic tradition are pilloried.

In America, there was no real counterpart to the casualness or the expressiveness of European architecture of the mid-1950's, though there are many parallels to the kind of stuffy neo-official architecture represented by the Cologne Opera. Only one major building, Paul Rudolph's Mary Cooper Jewett Art Center at Wellesley College, Wellesley, Massachusetts, 1956–58 (Figs. 286, 287), reflects some of the skeptical, questioning attitude that opened the way for these recent developments in German theater design. Its outward form of soft pink brick was meant to conform somewhat to a neo-Gothic campus; specifically, it had to complete a neo-Gothic quadrangle designed early in the twentieth century. Rudolph, in his first large-scale building, was looking for ways of expanding his structurally expressive concepts that had earned him a success with his Florida cottages of about 1950. Therefore, the concrete frame was brought to the exterior of the building in several places, notably on the downhill side of the structure. The taste of the day demanded a glass curtain wall, and one was included in the studio wing, but its adverse effects were tempered by the use of a metal grill or screen constructed upon an outrigger frame, a form which considerably modified the silhouette as well as the texture of the building. Right angles were avoided by giving a blunt beveled shape to the end walls. Admittedly the result was ingenious and intricate, perhaps in an effort to avoid some of the oversimplified character of the period's standard modernism, but the effects were not so much analogous to Teutonic neo-Expressionism as they were parallel manifestations of a gradually rising dissatisfaction with the slick, sparse detailing of contemporary commercial architecture.

Additional relief from this pervasive, brittle uniformity was provided by the work of Edward D. Stone, which suddenly blossomed in the second half of the decade.[13] After a desultory career, begun with promise in the 1930's—he had been a co-designer of The Museum of Modern Art, New York, 1939, and a popularizer of the International Style for expensive country houses in the pre-World War II period—Stone enjoyed a great popular success with his design for the American Embassy, New Delhi, India, 1957–59 (Fig. 288), and followed this with the controversial, but still widely admired, American Pavilion at the Brussels Exposition, 1958 (Fig. 289). Both of these buildings, the former rectangular and the latter circular in plan, had similarly detailed façades, with thin, emaciated columns and scaleless, all-pervasive perforated screens. Doubtless, a design of such chic was immensely appropriate for the temporary Brussels exhibition structure, but the Embassy is another matter altogether. That building was one of the first to be built under a worthy U. S. State Department program to construct a series of buildings abroad that would be of contemporary distinction in design, while reflecting something of the character of the host country. It was a praiseworthy aim, but one that was possibly delusory, based as it was upon the curiously bureaucratic assumption that an architect can somehow, Aladdin-like, produce a design "expressive" of a culture which, at best, he can only know

282. Gerhard Weber. National Theater. Mannheim, 1954–57.

283. Ludwig Mies van der Rohe. Project for the National Theater. Mannheim, 1953.

285. Wilhelm Riphahn. Opera. Cologne, 1957.

284. Werner Ruhnau, Ortwin Rave, and Max von Hausen. Municipal Theater, Gelsenkirchen, 1958–59.

286, 287. Paul Rudolph. Mary Cooper Jewett Art Center, Wellesley College. Wellesley, Massachusetts, 1956–58.

secondhand. Even worse, it is to accept the old fallacy, as Eero Saarinen was wont to do, of assuming that concern with the special circumstances of a particular situation will result in a distinctive and appropriately expressive design, and that this will be *the* right and meaningful one. This fantasy has been, and remains, one of the bugaboos of contemporary architecture, one that is particularly difficult to dispel because it is based upon well-intentioned sentiments, upon "right thinking," and upon a desire to find a point of common interest and agreement through compromise.

No doubt Edward Stone has been a victim of this type of muddled thinking, which has reduced so much of contemporary architecture to the level of trivia. He has also contributed to its already shallow aims by the nature of the order that he has superimposed upon his designs, irrespective of function or location. What is at issue here is not the propriety of conceiving a more or less universal formal solution, and then working a variety of programs into it—after all, this is the sanctified Miesian way—but rather of approaching the problem with judgment, discrimination, and taste.

Suddenly, architects had to find aesthetic criteria for selection of form, for sizing, shaping, and giving proportion to their designs, where only a few short years before they had operated upon the assumption that architectural form came from anywhere—from program, technology, or structure—except pure creative imagination. After a half century of seeking form in a causal fashion, there began a new search, in which imagination would have to be regulated and disciplined on the basis of taste and reason. In effect, this change reflected the shift from "form governed by function" toward a nineteenth-century academicism. In reality, this is the challenge to which Stone and many of his contemporaries have failed to respond with dignity and discrimination. The New Delhi Embassy and its notorious screen façades are, in the last analysis, quaint and even foolish, not so much because of miscalculations with respect to function and to climate, nor because of any lack of inner motivation in the design, but because the form is trite and lacking in dignity. Embodied in an Exhibition Pavilion at Brussels, its qualities of commercial styling and the flair with which it smugly displayed the affluent society made this perforated screen idiom acceptable. But this certainly is not the image that an embassy—especially one in a country which has yet to sample the benefits of a highly productive industrial and consumer society—should seek to display. Even some of Eero Saarinen's works of the 1950's had been afflicted by this crisis in taste and discrimination, but in the end he managed to avoid the worst of its consequences by his endless search for the appro-

pri... form. Through experience, he was able to provide his designs with an increasing certainty. Stone, however, was satisfied to rest with his screen façade, with consequences that need no further comment.

One other notable architect strayed into this developing academicism without, it would seem, adequate background or sufficiently resilient temperament to do more than achieve a series of questionable popular successes. He was Minoru Yamasaki, whose Wayne State University Conference Center, Detroit, Michigan, 1957, inaugurated a career that continued with the Reynolds Metals Building, Detroit, 1958 (Figs. 290, 291), the Science Pavilion at the Seattle World's Fair, 1961–62, and the design for the New York Trade Center, a series of commercial blocks in an area to be redeveloped in lower Manhattan, New York.[14] More the master of elegant pictorial effect than Stone, as well as being adept in the invention of pseudo-sophisticated "precisionist" detailing, Yamasaki has appealed to that segment of popular taste which, at the moment, desires richly ornamental modernist designs—if only to manifest its dissatisfaction with a half century of simplicity. Yamasaki has been

289. Edward D. Stone. U.S. Pavilion at the Brussels Exposition, 1958.

290, 291. Minoru Yamasaki. Reynolds Metals Building. Detroit, 1958.

quite vocal in maintaining that he wishes his buildings to express the spirit of their times while simultaneously introducing some unfamiliar elegance. This aim can be appreciated in the small-scaled gold-anodized aluminum screen of the Reynolds buildings, a form analogous to similar features in the more uniform work of Stone. After one or two applications, however, it is quite clear that this sort of exterior detailing can swiftly descend to the level of thoroughly unarchitectural "exterior design."

The major buildings of Lincoln Center, New York (Fig. 293), the design for which began in 1957 (although the first element, Max Abramovitz' Philharmonic Hall was not opened until the fall of 1962), avoid this species of exterior decoration, but they are by no means free of the superficial, updated academicism that became prominent in the late 1950's. The over-all design was coordinated by Abramovitz' partner, Wallace Harrison, who was also responsible for the new Metropolitan Opera House. Other architects responsible for individual buildings include both Philip Johnson and Eero Saarinen. The three largest halls of the complex, the Metropolitan Opera in the center, the Philharmonic Hall to the north, and the New York State Theater to the south (Figs. 292, 294, 296), are grouped around a large rectangular plaza, while other elements are disposed in odd corners of the site. The general plan is thus of extreme simplicity, even somewhat stiff, and given the extremes of weather in New York, the approaches are unduly open. Of the three major designs, the New York State Theater, Johnson's contribution, seems to offer an excellent solution, given the restrictions of the situation. It is a forthright classical layout with a glass façade set behind thin, paired concrete piers. The interior space of the foyer is one of the largest of this sort ever to have been constructed in the United States and contains, two monumental figures done to the designs of Elie Nadelman. The superiority of this building lies in the stately measure of its proportions, both interior and exterior, qualities of architectural design that Johnson learned in principle, though not in detail, from Mies. They have been the stabilizing elements of his recent, formalistic work, providing a sure, knowing touch that is, for the most part, unequaled by other architects who seek to explore this way of achieving a new design synthesis.

Of the other works at Lincoln Center, notably Harrison's Opera and Abramovitz' Philharmonic Hall, little need be said, for they merely attempt what for Johnson is second nature. At best, the results are awkward and stilted; at worst, the details are trite, and the

292. Max Abramovitz. Philharmonic Hall, Lincoln Center. New York, 1962.

various elements and spaces are not always successfully integrated. As far as the ensemble of buildings is concerned, they represent a tentative, but altogether superficial, effort to achieve a new pattern of order in architectural composition. Regrettably, the result is premature. Clearly, Lincoln Center, the buildings and the whole concept behind them, represents the most immediate consequence of the shift away from the architecture of unstable formal relationships that engendered a sense of flux and of "becoming" in its spaces. This shift made an early appearance in Saarinen's 1953 design at M. I. T., after having been predicted in the various Miesian developments of about 1950. However up-to-date the design of Lincoln Center may be, its over-all image seems weak and hollow, and its very stiffness would seem to offer no chance of further development along these lines.

293. Lincoln Center. New York, begun 1957. Model.

294. Philip Johnson. New York State Theater, Lincoln Center. New York, 1964.

295, 295a. Jørn Utzon. Opera. Sydney, 1966 under construction. Site plan and model.

296. Wallace K. Harrison. Metropolitan Opera, Lincoln Center. New York, 1966.

The winning competition design of 1956 for the Sydney Opera by Jørn Utzon (Figs. 22, 295, 295a), now approaching completion in 1966, is a concept worthy of comparison with Lincoln Center. Underneath a superficially expressionistic profile of shell vaults, it suggests a spatial discipline that seems to combine some of the permissive aspects of recent German architecture with the brittle, academic American designs. While it would be rash to advance any undue claims for this eye-catching design until it has actually been completed, nonetheless it appears that the architect was not content to rest with the creation of an outer image of impetuosity. The funnel-like, overlapping concrete shells seem to be conceived on the order of a tent floating above a huge terrace, upon and within which the spaces, circulation patterns, and working areas have been conscientiously worked out. Such a monument is, in truth, no more a new departure than those around the square of Lincoln Center, but it does seem to make fuller use of a number of architectural themes stemming from the recent past. As such, the shell-vaulted interior spaces of the Sydney Opera should make an interesting contrast with the simple and grand rooms created by Philip Johnson for Lincoln Center.

In any event these numerous structures of public congregation, designed or built in the mid-1950's, clearly defined the nature and scope of the crisis at that epoch—a crisis concerning the genesis of architectural form—and through their tentative, incomplete solutions, pointed towards the more assured styles of the subsequent decade.

# Chapter VI
## New Patterns of Order: The Architecture of the 1960's

The historian sees the creation of his own day in terms of a dialogue between the present and the past, often to the chagrin of the architect who, understandably, has his eyes set on the future. While many architects of the 1960's are prepared to recognize the ancestry of their efforts in the work of the heroic 1920's, and a few are even eager to acknowledge their debt to a more distant past, certain of today's designers understandably resent historical interpretations of their work. However, no period can escape the shadow of its immediate past. While the new architecture of the 1960's does indeed mark a fresh stage of stylistic evolution, one which promises even more radical changes of technique and procedure in the near future, it nonetheless also represents one more stage in the polishing and rounding out of a revolution begun earlier in the century—a revolution which, itself, was predicated upon countless subversive tendencies of the previous one hundred years. Hence, to speak of a "new order" for the 1960's is perhaps premature, given the extensive prehistory of our current "new forms", together with the likelihood that by the time these lines are read further developments will have shifted and perhaps blurred the image of recent architecture which seems, at the moment of writing, to be relatively clear.

Nevertheless, it is true that many of today's buildings seem to confront the beholder with a certainty and confidence that was quite lacking only yesterday. By 1960, the tentative, cautious designs that had so quickly followed the dissolution of the Miesian stereotypes were giving way to stronger, more cohesive statements. For the most part, the important architects were the same from one stylistic period to the next, except for the sad, premature death of Eero Saarinen in 1961. This continuity of personnel further demonstrates that the frequently indecisive designs of the mid- and later-1950's formed a transitional moment. Buildings such as those built by Saarinen from 1954 to 1961 now appear, in retrospect, to have been the connective tissue between an earlier climax of postwar design and the present emergence of yet another new architecture which historians of the future may well regard as the characteristic style of the third quarter of our century. This same struggle to find a new creative identity can likewise be found in numerous works of Johnson and Rudolph during the late 1950's, at a time when both architects were making the difficult switch from the design of small houses to large public and institutional buildings.

The new forms of the 1960's are bulkier, their spaces more emphatically shaped, and their structures visually more pronounced than before. Grandiloquence has replaced subtlety, while the compact, uniform sheath has given way to looser, form-revealing fashions. Le Corbusier, in his work since the late 1930's, anticipated this phenomenon, but his rugged personalism does not dominate this new epoch as forcefully and completely as Mies's elementary mode had overwhelmed the earlier one. By 1960, the culture and tradition of modernism was coming to be appreciated for its diversity rather than its rigidity, and the mainstream of twentieth-century architecture ceased to be the fragile, hybrid stem that it once was. If strict design discipline and a narrow range of choices had been a salutary thing in the early 1950's, it produced only frustration a decade later.

Understandably, a considerable amount of precious and brittle architecture, which had been familiar as a fashion of the late 1950's, persists into the current decade. Anodized

297. Philip Johnson. The Museum of Modern Art, new East Wing. New York, 1962–64.

298. James Stirling and James Gowan. Engineering Laboratories, Leicester University. 1960–63.

metal screens and columns, as well as the perforated concrete screens popularized earlier by Stone and Yamasaki (and once used even by Rudolph) after 1960 became a vernacular in the United States. They are widely employed as a badge of up-to-the-minute fashion by architects from every strata of the profession, though their use is often shallow and frequently only due to a desire to find an antidote to the glass wall. The curtain wall itself remains, and even Philip Johnson, who had turned to more solid and tactile modes of design by the late 1950's, produced an elegant "period" glass façade for the new wing of The Museum of Modern Art (Fig. 297), New York, in 1962–64.

The broad development of architecture, however, has generally ceased to be based upon plane surfaces and simplified contours. This earlier mode has now been supplanted by a more positive concern for particularized volumes and individual spaces, with tubes and retorts, ducts and pipes all playing a major role. These elements are no longer considered as mere architectural machinery, something to be concealed or prettified, but as ways for visualizing a new kind of design. Long ago, Mies had brought the skeleton of the building to the surface, at least in a figurative way; his successors have gone even further by bringing the circulatory and visceral systems of the building to the surface. Saarinen had tried to fashion his buildings according to symbolic, even literary, concepts, according to a vision that he chose to discover in each individual project or program. Subsequent architects were determined that the outer envelope of a building would be more explicit, would, in fact, reflect inner content and workings in a more objective and factual way. The "buttery hatch" aesthetic ascribed to Louis Kahn is almost too quaint a way to describe this type of design (a new shorthand to visualize the interconnections of usable space in any given building), but it is descriptive of a new concern to render visible the movements of people and things within buildings, using these patterns of movement as suggestions for the shaping and relating of distinct architectural volumes.[1] Despite its newness, however, there is much here that is both Futurist and Functionalist in origin. Indeed, the "buttery hatch" aesthetic seems to be a machine age restatement of a long-discredited academic procedure, the circulation diagram, which had been utilized well into the twentieth century by Beaux-Arts planners for the composition of huge and often quite unfunctional spaces which, nonetheless, dramatized corridors, foyers, and other connecting spaces. It is almost as if Louis Kahn has applied this nearly forgotten procedure to the integration of ducts and machinery in his new buildings, especially when he observed: "I do not like ducts; I do not like pipes. I hate them really thoroughly, but because I hate them so thoroughly, I feel they have to be given their place. If I just hated them and took no care, I think they would invade the building and completely destroy it. I want to correct any notion you may have that I am in love with that kind of thing."

Such emphasis on tubes and pipes as an integral part of design frequently results in forms that are, to one degree or another, clusters of towers. Credit for this belongs largely to Kahn, and was first evident in his Richards Medical Research Building, 1957–61 (Figs. 371–373), at the University of Pennsylvania in Philadelphia. A secondary or complementary role, however, was played by Saarinen's two new residential colleges, 1957–61 (Fig. 342), at Yale, where towers were used and a clustered effect achieved in an almost purely picturesque manner. In the space of a half-decade, this mode has become one of the most widespread of design clichés, used and misused by architects all over the world. Originally employed in buildings of a scientific or research nature, duct-tower effects are now found in buildings of a non-mechanistic, indeed even of a religious, nature. In fact, this pipe-fitter's and plumber's architecture has become very nearly universal in the early 1960's.

Beside it, of course, are various survivals from fashions of the 1950's, notably the manner in which Skidmore, Owings and Merrill has continued to use the glass curtain wall, even though concealed behind an exterior apparatus of concrete. Their Banque Lambert, Brussels, 1958–62 (Figs. 206, 300), and Tennessee Gas Building (Fig. 299), Houston, Texas, finished 1963, illustrate their efforts in this direction. Alternately, there are a few national schools, best represented by the Japanese who have enthusiasticlly embraced the Corbusian idiom, though maintaining their own ethnic identity in the process. There are English architects like Stirling and Gowan, creators of exceptionally provocative designs, who seek to wed nineteenth-century Victorian brick technology to the idiosyncracies of a 1920's machine aesthetic (Figs. 298, 378). There is Paul Rudolph, whose cartwheel plans and flowing spaces evoke the authority of Frank Lloyd Wright, but are expressed in a concrete style all his own. There are the Smithsons, gifted polemicists, who seem destined to remain the gadflies of contemporary architecture. There is the articulate Philip Johnson, creator of monuments that might better have served a more disciplined, form-conscious society in the past, and may well survive to serve another in the future. There are architects of new city halls (Toronto and Boston, Figs. 382–385), of new university quadrangles (Cambridge). All are participating in a vast movement that is continuing and perpetuating the architectural upheaval of the earlier twentieth century, in spite of many strong individual efforts to achieve a personal identity of style. In one fashion or another, however, the diverse efforts of all are resolved by common interests in sturdy structures and supports, vivid and unambiguous spatial drama, and strongly accented distinctions between individualized volumes. The evanescent spatial flux and structural ambiguity of the 1920's was transformed into the static universal spaces of the 1950's, only to be subsequently twisted and molded into the ducts, towers, and flaring roof shapes of the 1960's. Each successive crystallization of this evolving modern tradition has, however, preserved the vestiges of its predecessors, often in sufficiently strong quantities to confound or even refute the most artfully formed generalizations.

Conflict and controversy are an integral part of the development of modern architecture, no less today than yesterday. The last few years have seen the development of a spirited and sometimes acrimonious dialogue between the champions of a new American architecture, on the one hand, and the tenacious defenders of a more orthodox modernism in England.[2] The former assert a formalistic independence for their compositions, at least in speech and print, while the latter hold to ideologies that grew out of the debates and new schools of the 1920's.

An early glimmer of our new architectural order can be found in Saarinen's concrete air-

299. Skidmore, Owings & Merrill. Tennessee Gas Building. Houston, Texas, 1963.

300. Skidmore, Owings & Merrill. Banque Lambert. Brussels, 1958–62.

port terminals at New York and Washington. The first of these, the Trans World Airlines Terminal, John F. Kennedy International Airport, 1956–62 (Figs. 301, 301a), is a freely curved, low cross-vault constructed of a reinforced concrete shell.[3] Le Corbusier had himself used a curved shell vault at Ronchamp, although he had not pioneered in this technique. Nor did shell structures play a predominant role in the work of such constructor-architects as Perret and Nervi; instead they were first introduced by others, notably Eugène Freyssinet, Robert Maillart, and Eduardo Torroja. Such forms were closer in spirit to the characteristic vocabulary of Expressionism than to that of the customarily rectilinear International Style. Furthermore, these curved surfaces became commonplace only in the late 1950's as a part of the expanding repertoire of modernist forms.

In the T.W.A. building, the undulating surface continuity—itself a metamorphosis of the unstable flux inherent in the spaces of the International Style—played straight into Saarinen's predictable desire "to design a building in which the architecture itself would express the drama and specialness and excitement of travel." In a spirit of objective self-criticism, he stated: "We wanted to counteract the earthbound feeling and the heaviness that prevails too much in the M.I.T. auditorium. We wanted an uplift. For the same reason, the structural shape of the columns was dramatized to stress their upward-curving sweep."[4] Indeed, what the architect sought was an updated *architecture parlante,* not a style but, in a curious return to eighteenth-century methodologies, a literary architecture that would arouse emotions and affect sentiments. For some critics, not only did Saarinen fail to give the building a soaring aspect, but his very aim was misguided. To others, however, his intent of suggesting both movement and transition seems appropriate as a theme; certainly, it is much more intelligently related to the material aspects of the program than were his ideas with respect to General Motors. Debate will always exist on the subjective level of how well these shell forms suggest or anticipate the sensations of travel but, in the abstract, this interior is one of today's finest creations of monumental space, and the entire form is one of Saarinen's most effective and consistent. The flaws in the building lie elsewhere: Its size may not prove satisfactory for easy circulation under peak loads (a major functional flaw that may not be entirely the fault of the architect); and certain details, notably the metal balustrades, do not carry out the theme of undulating flux in so easy a fashion as they should. Perhaps the most significant feature of the T.W.A. terminal is that it creates a sharp, penetrating, memorable image in the fashion of the great railroad concourses and sheds of the previous century, something that no other airport building before had achieved.

301, 301a. Eero Saarinen & Associates. TWA Terminal, John F. Kennedy International Airport. Idlewild, New York, 1956–62.

The expressive spirit of the T.W.A. terminal carries over into the Dulles International Airport, 1958–62 (Fig. 303), outside Washington, at Chantilly, Virginia, though the image of the building could scarcely be more different. Here a vital, monumental effect is produced by the tensely-profiled structure (adapted from an early sketch of Eric Mendelsohn), and results in façades of extraordinary nobility. Indeed, this is one of the few monumental buildings of the period that can stand comparison with Le Corbusier's two "portico" façades at Chandigarh (Fig. 302). Unlike the T.W.A. terminal, the shape of the Washington building does not seem to grow out of a consideration of circulation and movement; the clichés of an *architecture parlante* are here left behind. Nothing in the architecture suggests movement on a transient, personal level, but the soaring roof, supported by the out-flung piers that hold it in tension—itself an exaggerated expression of the structural system—provides a heroic statement of the theme that the architect had in mind. Stripped of its literary complications, however, it at last becomes a form of universal strength. It is, indeed, extraordinary that Saarinen finally arrived at this triumph, having traversed the strange, uncertain path started a decade before. The monumentality of Dulles Airport is in distinct contrast to the conspicuous weakness of much contemporary formalist design. This virtue, as well as a suppleness of the shapes, leads to the conclusion that, in the process of evolving from a Miesian to a Corbusian position over the period from 1950 to 1960, Eero Saarinen did more than reflect the changing tastes and passions of his time: he truly found himself as an architect and as an individual.

If Saarinen, in some of the last buildings of his short, hectic career, proved that there still remained original ways of arriving at the sublime within the frame of twentieth-century architecture, that the paths of the hallowed masters were not the only ones possible, other architects were also involved in the same search. Temperamentally at the other end of the scale, more painstaking and cautious in his step-by-step growth, was Philip Johnson. In at least one instance, however, he was tempted by the same attractions of impulse and action. The Nuclear Reactor (Fig. 304) designed for the Israeli Government at Rehovot, finished in 1961, is largely an about-face from the architect's previous work. A characterful, rugged form is allowed to dominate in place of the usually restrictive geometry that gives Johnson's work a steadiness and solemnity. This sturdy, liberated form-making seems not to have been Johnson's specific goal, as it had been with Saarinen. Rather, it was a momentary yet necessary transition between his Miesian and post-Miesian designs of the 1950's, and his more personal yet no less regulated forms of the 1960's. There will be occasion to mention these recent works later.

302. Le Corbusier. Assembly Building. Chandigarh, 1959–62. Entrance Portico.

303. Eero Saarinen & Associates. Dulles International Airport. Chantilly, Virginia, near Washington, D.C., 1958–62.

The role that the new architecture in Japan has played, or better, is, perhaps, about to play, in this world-wide development of the early 1960's, is most difficult to assess. The problem is complicated not only because of the still tentative stage at which developments stand, but also because of certain recent historical precedents of a rather ominous cast. In the mid-1930's, the enterprising younger generation in Brazilian architecture adopted the style of Le Corbusier, and for the following three decades diligently explored its possibilities in combination with certain indigenous features freely derived from their own Baroque colonial traditions. The result was the creation of a regional style which, over the last decade, has given more and more evidence of fruitless introversion and creative stultification, in spite of a certain cheerful outward chic in its compositions, whether domestic or monumental. The issue came to a head in Oscar Niemeyer's designs for the government buildings of Brasília, 1958–60 (Figs. 188–192, 305, 353).[5] There, one is struck by an extraordinary paucity of substance and texture in forms of monumental aspiration. A typical example is the legislative chambers, where the form of the dome is used twice, once in normal fashion, and again by standing the form on its head, inverting the shell of the dome to produce a saucer-like shape. The idea in itself might possibly have been sustained, had the execution provided a sense of scale and size through the use of details or distinctive surface features, but the stone facing of these domical forms was as smooth as possible, and the forced simplicity of the design rigorously excluded consideration of detail that might have provided a sense of palpable reality to this curiously incoherent idea. This type of surface quality that deliberately abstains from detail (characteristic of much North American architecture in the late 1950's) is simply a travesty of the original source for this kind of formal inversion: Le Corbusier. Although by no means all recent Brazilian architecture has fallen into this shallow translation of a once-promising impulse, the seriousness of the failure in a large, national project is clearly ominous.

This is one of the dangers that now confronts the evolution of Japanese architecture: its almost exclusive reliance upon a single source for the development of a local modernist idiom.[6] Once again, Le Corbusier is the fountainhead, but the emphasis is on the fully developed style of his old age rather than the more smoothly finished early works. Architects like Tange, Mayekawa, and Sakakura have been more interested in the raw, coarse aspects of the Corbusian vocabulary than in the smooth white surface which the Brazilians swiftly metamorphosed into the sinuous, succulent forms dominating their recent buildings. In terms of pure taste, the discipleship of the Japanese is a more courageous gesture, one that implies an interest in more than the epidermis of form. By the same token, its borrow-

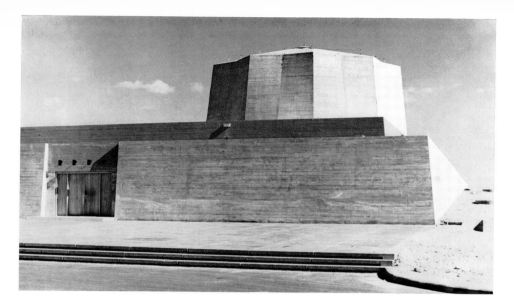

304. Philip Johnson. Nuclear Reactor. Rehovot (Israel), 1961.

ings have occasionally taken the shape of rather superficially rationalized mannerisms. Finally, the evidence of the Miesian wave which swept America in the early 1950's offers a different and more hopeful precedent, suggesting that even narrow imitation can frequently lead to ultimate and significant creation. In the hands of most commercial architects, the style of metal and glass curtain walls provided a dead end; but in the hands of the best designers, it provided the matrix out of which their subsequent and more independent work could evolve.

The pace of development which has been sustained in Japan over the last decade actually bears some relationship to the world-wide pattern of evolution. The difference arises from the fact that until the second half of the 1950's, developments there were of purely local significance in terms of quality and orientation. When seen beside Kunio Mayekawa's Tokyo Metropolitan Festival Hall (Figs. 306, 307), completed in 1961, the works of five or six years before seem thin and puny. In this massive, vigorously shaped building, containing two halls as well as vast cavernous circulation areas, one finds a distinctive touch, yet one which remains respectfully within the orbit of Le Corbusier. The *béton brut* possesses a different, more calculated crudity, and the forms that it molds are stiffer and more ungainly. Certain

305. Oscar Niemeyer. Senate, Secretariat, and Assembly Building. Brasília, 1958–60.

details, such as the small moat surrounding much of the portico of the Festival Hall, are inspired by some of the features of traditional Japanese architecture, although (as also in the work of Tange) these never obtrude as literal historical clichés. Instead, these motifs are filtered through an unmistakably Western style, and rendered in one of the most challenging, refractory materials provided by the revolution of the machine era.

On the outside, the high space of the larger hall and its abrupt intersection with the lower space of the foyers is manifested in the studied clumsiness with which the battered, pre-cast concrete walls of the former are partly surrounded by the almost totally unrelated lower form, with its glass walls almost hidden, so deeply are they recessed behind boldly projecting, upturned slabs of the huge roof. These roof forms, however, do not spring from the core of the building, uncoiling outward in a rising, elastic thrust in the manner of Le Corbusier at Chandigarh (Figs. 176–185). Instead, there is the effect of massive, almost in-supportable, weight bearing down—in effect, upon nothing, since the rather shapeless columns are deeply recessed. To Western eyes, educated by the constantly active dialogue of structural forces apparent in any kind of building, this inert superstructure is perplexing, when not actually disagreeable. It is, however, perfectly explicable; it is a frequently en-countered phenomenon in recent Japanese work, largely accounted for, as might be ex-pected, by the tendency of traditional Japanese wood structure to emphasize the mass and bulk of a roof system placed upon diminutive and seemingly insufficient supports.

How different this massive, self-possessed building by Mayekawa seems in comparison with the more brittle designs of the mid-1950's, of which Kenzo Tange's Tokyo City Hall, 1952–57 (Fig. 308), is representative.[7] A tall office slab with concrete frame exposed on the lower floor, but enclosed with a system of *brises-soleils* above, it invokes simultaneously the "façade in depth" of Le Corbusier's *Unités* while, in its rather thin, emaciated proportions, it resembles the more delicately scaled detailing of the *Miesschüler*. This ambivalence, which is more satisfactory in the realization than in pure theory, is of course parallel to the pattern in American and European architecture in the mid-1950's, which displayed much uncertainty and hesitancy, but which ultimately revealed a desire to break with many of the ingrained patterns of design. Shortly afterward Tange found a more integrated, confident, and original means of handling the problem of structural expression in concert with the creation of shadow-producing forms in the Kagawa Prefecture Office, Takamatsu, 1955–58 (Figs. 309–313). There the mass of the various structural elements was given a notable em-phasis by projecting the horizontal concrete beams outward to form the underpinning of a system of balconies, whose silhouette was made especially robust by the massively simple balustrade. The result was aggressively constructive, yet relatively free of any Corbusian mannerism. The concrete post-and-beam system was treated in a way which, by emphasiz

306, 307. Kunio Mayekawa. Metropolitan Festival Hall. Tokyo, 1961.

308. Kenzo Tange. City Hall. Tokyo, 1952–57.

ing the horizontal members, produced a certain procedural analogy with traditional Japanese methods of exaggerating the structural features of wooden architecture.

It was only in a subsequent monumental edifice, the Kurashiki City Hall, 1958–60 (Figs. 314, 315), that elements of the Franco-Swiss master's style were incorporated almost decoratively into an otherwise honest, forthright essay in concrete constructivism.[8] Tange persisted in his technique of piling up a mass of interlocking beam-like forms to emphasize the horizontal at the expense of the vertical, but the projections of beam ends were used more sparingly. The result is a closed, disciplined volume on the exterior. The welcome sense of order and clarity of composition that dominate the whole is in sharp contrast to the rambling discursiveness of so much of Mayekawa's contemporary work and, also, of Tange's own previous work. The side façade, facing the square, has a major tripartite division marked by the pylon-shaped *pilotis* of the basement, and by the projection of major transverse structural beam ends in the cornice. This cornice, together with the ribbon window directly underneath, disciplines the somewhat fortuitous, indeed impressionistic, rhythm of window slits in the face of the wall. The pylons at the corners are single, but those toward the middle, separating the central from the outer thirds of the façade, are doubled, creating a strained, elastic rhythm which is echoed in the wider separation of the projecting beam ends in the cornice slab. This variation is in accord with the placement of the council chamber in the interior, whose undulating Ronchamp-inspired space (Figs. 315, 316) projects above the cornice and is enclosed by the ramp-like superstructure on the roof-terrace. Below, in the entrance hall directly underneath the council chamber, is a marvelously decorated wall making free, if somewhat indiscriminate, use of the funnel-shaped openings created for the thick wall of Ronchamp. In large measure, the interiors of Tange's Kurashiki City Hall produce more of an effect of undigested Corbusian mannerisms than any building by Mayekawa, although its exterior remains the most striking instance of what will perhaps become the disciplining order of new Japanese building. This is especially noteworthy since it was Mayekawa who was actually an associate in Le Corbusier's office (in the 1930's), while Tange, who never studied abroad and who, being younger, was still a student of architecture during the 1930's and early 1940's, is much more exclusively the product of postwar Japan.

309–313. Kenzo Tange. Kagawa Prefecture Office. Takamatsu, 1955–58. Views, plans of ground floor and first floor.

In contrast to the striking cohesiveness which has been coming progressively to the fore in the work of Tange, Mayekawa's many large works betray a rambling, sometimes even

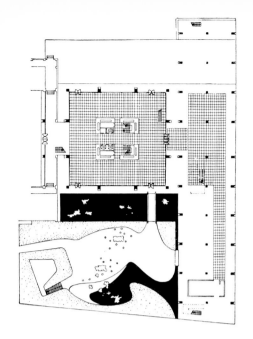

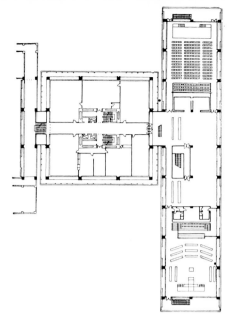

314. Kenzo Tange. City Hall. Kurashiki, 1958–60.

shapeless, quality which clearly distinguishes his designs from those of Tange. Notable in this respect is the Kyoto Kaikan (Fig. 317), a new concert hall completed in 1960 in the traditional Imperial capital. In spite of its location, with the heritage of the past literally pressing in from every direction, Mayekawa produced a somewhat noncommittal yet still recognizably Corbusian building. The huge purple brick or tile covering so much of the exterior is its most distinctive feature. The structure is handled rather dryly, with the flair in the roof-cornice being much less drastic than in the nearly contemporary Tokyo Festival Hall. In contrast, the structural underpinning is handled with greater emphasis, with the result that the balance of load and support in the building is less disconcerting than was the case at Tokyo. The one oppressive feature here is the shapeless mass of the auditorium, which projects, rather unenthusiastically and with a certain weariness and inertia, above the flared cornice. An earth-born clumsiness dominates the form, altogether in contrast not just with the galvanic character of Chandigarh's Assembly, but also with the powerful, outward thrust of Saarinen's Dulles Airport structure.

Nonetheless, all of these new Japanese buildings manifest a probing, searching effort to discover a new architectural language based upon the shapes and technology of Le Corbusier. The indigenous quality, however, is introduced not for chauvinistic effect, but to achieve a particular innate character and distinction. Based upon the achievement eviden in the work of the last few years, it would seem that Mayekawa and Tange, as well as other prominent designers of less consistent taste, have produced a potent offshoot of the Corbusian strain of modernism. This has been done without allowing it to remain a simple, undernourished hybrid, as seems to have been the case in South America.

The forceful, aggressive quality of Japanese architecture is rather at odds with the situation in Germany, once the homeland of the contemporary idiom. There is, as has already been pointed out, a gifted architect of the old generation, Hans Scharoun, whose deeply felt and profoundly thought-out messages continue to be largely unrecognized, and who is still working in the Expressionist past. Alternately, other German architects, notably Egon Eiermann or Hentrich and Petschnigg (Fig. 320) are influenced by International Style models. These men have designed excellent offices and administrative buildings in a brittle, elegant, rather Americanized idiom, and their debt to Mies, given the present climate of opinion, is almost too painfully evident. Their work stands at a historical level approximating that of the best commercial practitioners in New York of five years before. It

315. Kenzo Tange. City Hall. Kurashiki, 1958–60. Council chamber.

316. Le Corbusier. Notre-Dame-du-Haut. Ronchamp, 1950–54.

is not simply a matter of fashionable imitation. Indeed, Eiermann's work offers an inevitably thoughtful exterior aspect, and in certain ways his hyper-refined manner of handling metal stanchions and railings has a distinctiveness all its own. This is true of his German Pavilion (Fig. 318) at the 1958 Brussels Fair (the cool, rational elegance of which can instructively be compared with the decorative, rather unarchitectonic elegance of Stone's American Pavilion, Fig. 289, at the same fair), or of the fenestration and balcony details in his small five-

317. Kunio Mayekawa. Concert Hall. Kyoto, 1960.

story office building for the Müller Steel Construction Company, Offenburg, 1960 (Fig. 319). If the latter is representative of a new moment of clarity, definition, and order in recent German architecture, however, it is a representative which, in spite of its buoyant effortlessness of structural effect is burdened both with the memory of an earlier day in European modernism, and with a point of view which in other parts of the globe has given way to more robust proportions. In this respect, its timid structural fragility deserves comparison with the brash, indeed almost overblown, articulation of elements in Tange's Kagawa Prefecture, a building which also uses balconies to shade a glass curtain wall, or with the exteriorized steel structures of Saarinen's John Deere and Stirling's Dorman Long offices.

If, in their respective ways, Scharoun and Eiermann provide an indication of the tentative, unsure attitudes rampant in German architecture, even among personalities of established taste, the diversity of form—indeed, the veritable chaos of the plan—in the Hansaviertel, Berlin, 1957 (Fig. 321), represents the problem from a different angle. Here, fifty-three architects from all over the world—the list reads like a who's who: Le Corbusier, Gropius, Aalto, Niemeyer, Arne Jacobsen, Kay Fisker, and van den Broek and Bakema, along with old Berlin hands like Wassili Luckhardt—were given individual tasks within the frame of a loose over-all scheme, somewhat on the order of the 1927 Werkbund development on the Weissenhof (Fig. 26), Stuttgart, but much vaster and in a location fraught with political implica-

318. Egon Eiermann and Sep Ruf. German Pavilion at the Brussels Exposition, 1958.

319. Egon Eiermann. Administration Building for the Müller Steel Construction Company. Offenburg, 1960.

320. Helmut Hentrich and Hubert Petschnigg. Phoenix-Rheinrohr skyscraper. Düsseldorf, 1957–60.

tions. It would be futile to try to evaluate even a small number of the apartment blocks that grew out of this project for, unlike the unanimity of form and intent on the Weissenhof in 1927, the 1957 Hansaviertel showed the greatest divergence not just in dwelling concept, but in outward architectural appearance. Even the greatest of those involved, Le Corbusier, was the victim of his clients and contractors, with the result that his plans and intentions were seriously mangled in execution. The level of other work there generally invites the epithet "average."

Actually, there are a number of large residential blocks and groups completed in the last few years in Great Britain which, by dint of quality, deserve mention at some length. The tradition of the modern flat had achieved a certain *succès d'estime* with the construction of High Point I, London, 1935, by the Tecton Group, which had, among its partners, Berthold Lubetkin. After the ravages of the World War II blitz, however, the new architecture was utilized on a massive scale and with a certain success not only by the architectural staff of the

321. Hansaviertel. Berlin, 1957.

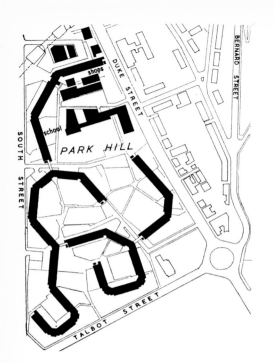

Greater London Council, long led by Sir Leslie Martin, but also in the Churchill Gardens housing group by Powell and Moya, which comprised thirty-six elements when finished (the competition was won in 1946), or in the more recent, more literally Corbusian, Roehampton Estate (Fig. 324), a huge grouping of duplex slabs and point blocks, coherently planned, if not invariably consistent in detail, by the architects of the Greater London Council. The new English architects make a virtue of employing of the less flamboyant aspects of the rich Corbusian legacy, and in ways altogether different from the sturdier Japanese or more ebullient Brazilians. More eye-catching, and perhaps a portent of a coming variety of plan and visual aspect in mass housing construction, is the unusual point block of Denys Lasdun's Bethnal Green Housing (Figs. 325–327), London, completed in the late 1950's. With its almost as strikingly shaped lower companion units, it forms one of the most aggressively detailed complexes to be found anywhere. The irregular articulation of the various "wings" in the tower creates a sense of rather arbitrary, pictorial fragmentation,

322, 323. The Sheffield Corporation City Architect's Department (J. L. Womersley). Park Hill Estate. Sheffield, 1961. Site plan and view.

324. Greater London Council (Hubert Bennett). Alton Estate West. Roehampton Lane. London, 1955–59.

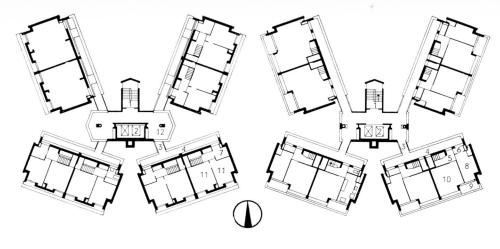

325–327. Denys Lasdun and Partners. Cluster Block. Bethnal Green, London, 1956–60. Floor plans with living and sleeping floors of the duplex apartments, exterior view.
  1 Main stair
  2 Elevators
  3 Bridge
  4 Access balcony
  5 Hall
  6 Toilet
  7 Bathroom
  8 Dining-kitchen
  9 Private balcony
 10 Living room
 11 Bedroom
 12 Drying platform

though the separation of elements can also be justified through functional reasoning as well. Whatever the case may be, these works of Lasdun serve as a reminder that urban housing ought to escape the bureaucratic mold of sameness without slipping into the equally grievous error of trite, picturesque variety. Even more original in layout is the vast Park Hill Estate, Sheffield, completed in the early 1960's (Figs. 322, 323). The elevations are severe and even homely, and, unlike the open planning in the manner of Le Corbusier's *ville radieuse* employed at Churchill Gardens and at Roehampton, the various elements are inwardly oriented around large-scaled courtyards of grass and pavement. Consequently, a sequence of enclosed outdoor spaces results, rather than the open, park-like environments characteristic of most housing estates of the last two decades.

Quantitatively, the Smithsons have contributed very little to the gradual accumulation of significant contemporary buildings in England, devoting much of their effort to polemic and teaching instead. But their one major completed work of the 1960's, the Economist Building (Figs. 328, 329) in the heart of London's West End, is a distinctive addition to the historic skyline of that metropolis, and thereby represents a significant contrast to the banal highrise offices that have sprouted recently in the British capital. The strong, disciplined severity of this design, which adapts itself as well to the narrow streets as it does to the skyline, is more self-contained and regular in mass than other recent English works which are at least expressively if not conceptually Brutalist in character. Whereas Roehampton was indebted to the *ville radieuse* formula of Le Corbusier, the first notable work by James Stirling and James Gowan,[9] a row of flats at Ham Common, 1958 (Fig. 330), seems to derive from the Jaoul type,[10] with its visible concrete slabs, brick walls, and irregular window openings. The dark brick shapes at Ham Common form an interesting parallel with the chunky masses of Louis Kahn's Richards Medical Research Building, 1957–61 (Figs. 371–73), and the brick-veneered forms of Paul Rudolph's Married Student Housing, Yale University, 1961 (Fig. 332). Here is a striking instance of three buildings designed in the late 1950's by three architects of considerably different background and philosophy which coincidentally yet significantly reveal common stylistic features.

Stirling and Gowan's more recent housing at Preston, though larded with one or two Corbusian clichés (notably the exterior ramps between levels), is more closely tied to a native brick technology and seeks, within the framework of twentieth-century social responsibility, to reproduce something of the dense visual effect of Victorian row housing. The particular brick shapes here belong to a more all-encompassing family of contemporary forms, and

in addition to the Kahn and Rudolph examples just cited, van den Broek and Bakema's 1957 multi-family housing at Rotterdam, Aalto's Pension Institute (Fig. 331), Helsinki, and a number of designs by the new German architect, Oswald Mathias Ungers (particularly a housing project in Cologne, 1959, Fig. 333) must be mentioned. While the doctrine of design and form which is at the heart of Louis Kahn's recent buildings points towards a particularly self-conscious new aesthetic discipline, the remainder of these designs seems to have grown out of a less deliberate search for a philosophy of form, and their characteristics are attributable to more materialistic or even functional considerations.

Not only does this contemporary and very internationally distributed vernacular contain features related to the willful shape-making of Le Corbusier, but it seems to contain also an empirical admixture, one which may owe a specific debt to the Aalto of the 1940's, as exemplified by the Baker Dormitory at M. I. T., a building which played so ambivalent a role in determining certain features of the Saarinen buildings there. In the context of these English and related developments of the last few years, few buildings are more significant than the new structures for Caius College (Figs. 334–336), Cambridge, by Sir J. Leslie Martin in association with Colin St. John Wilson, finished in 1962. Ranged around a paved terrace is a regular quadrangle of buildings, three stories high, with setbacks for terraces on the second and third levels, and major entrance openings at two neighboring angles. It is the ungainliness of one of the exterior façades, where a bundle of stairs descend from the flush brick wall of the upper floor, and behind a row of what can only be termed *pseudo-pilotis*,

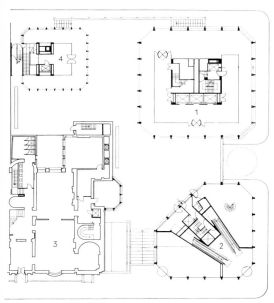

328, 329. Alison and Peter Smithson. Economist Group. London, 1960–64. Exterior view and plan of the ground floor.
1 Economist Tower
2 Martin's Bank
3 Boodle's Club (existing)
4 Boodle's Residential Building

330. James Stirling and James Gowan. Row of flats. Ham Common, Surrey, 1958.

which places this design in the realm of Brutalism. Here is manifest not just the now well-digested Corbusian influence, but, somewhat more openly (in part because of the brick surfaces), the Aalto line as well (Figs. 336a, 336b). However conflicting the design principles of these two masters may seem, they have curiously met in this building.

Perplexing as are all of these recent English developments in terms of what they signify for future growth and evolution, they nonetheless are a considerable contrast to the many academic and formalistic patterns of order evident in the works of the most prominent American architects during the late 1950's and early 1960's. A great many American architects at this juncture were searching for a formula to replace that of the glass-sheathed surface, one which would possess a certain degree of novelty and elaboration, but which would, however, preserve the sense of modular regularity. Thus, while many British architects were testing numerous possibilities for composition of a Brutalist or neo-functionalist sort, American architects were searching for ways of enriching the package alone, leaving aside, for the most part, the challenge of interior-exterior relationships. The special contributions of Stone and of Yamasaki, among others, catered to this development, since they offered new decorative and even structural patterns for the exterior shell of the building, patterns which enriched but did not alter the regularity of form or affect the sometimes forced simplicity of internal layouts. For most architects, this neo-academic pattern of design turned out to be a cul-de-sac. However, for the stronger and more assertive like Johnson and Saarinen, even though they ecountered a variable success in many of their

331. Alvar Aalto. Finnish Public Pension Institute. Helsinki, 1956.

332. Paul Rudolph. Married Student Housing, Yale University. New Haven, Connecticut, 1958–61.

333. Oswald Mathias Ungers. Block of flats. Cologne, 1959.

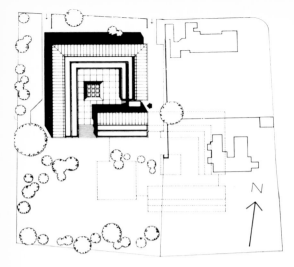

334–336. Sir J. Leslie Martin and Colin St. John Wilson. Caius College. Cambridge, 1960–62. Site plan and views.

works of the transition, they were able, under favorable circumstances, to create works of major importance within the confines of the prevailing formalism of about 1960. Indeed, the vigorous, purposeful-seeming masses of their best buildings often made them comparable in strength if not in philosophy with the more aggressive English designs. So while modernism in Anglo-American architecture at this juncture formed itself into two distinct camps, it is possible to find certain relevant points of comparison if not of reconciliation.

It is indeed, entirely possible that the new champion of a reunited modernism is already here in the person of Louis I. Kahn. Before the merits of this argument can be considered, a further examination of the new American formalism ought to be made. An aspect of this tentative academicism, one roughly parallel, but certainly not equivalent, to the various international Corbusian enthusiasms of 1960, is seen in Saarinen's two airport buildings. A totally different side of the phenomenon can be recognized in the same architect's Embassy Chanceries in Oslo, 1955–59, and London, 1955–60. The London Embassy (Fig. 337) met with a hail of abuse, often for reasons quite outside the realm of architecture or even aesthetics. However, the basic fact that Saarinen was determined to build a monument, that in fact he approached the design with the kind of deliberation that would have done justice to a Charles McKim or a Sir Herbert Baker, has perhaps caused more chagrin than any of the building's individual details, which in themselves are puzzlingly original, even eccentric in several respects. Whereas the half-century constructive tradition of modernism provided Saarinen with a matrix in which to evolve the ordered designs for his airport terminals, the very nature of the embassy problem, with no useful precedents whatsoever, left him vulnerable and exposed. It is futile to argue that another, less self-conscious master would have found a better way. The fact remains that at London, in the context of a Grosvenor Square that was scheduled to be rebuilt in a rather overscaled neo-Georgian style, Saarinen produced what he felt would be a distinctive and fitting building. While the Harrison and Abramovitz buildings at Lincoln Center (Figs. 292, 296) may indicate the sterile side of things, Saarinen's embassies, together with many of the new buildings and projects of Philip Johnson, indicate the possibilities of growth that are latent in firm but not rigid design discipline. In the face of much of the clumsy, accidental, or pseudo-accidental features in architecture elsewhere, this clarity and visual rationale has been most welcome. True, Johnson's Atomic Reactor building at Rehovot (Fig. 304), discussed earlier as an example of relatively subjective form-making (in spite of its structural sense), is, in part, an exception to its architect's more customary design rationale. However, transgressions of this sort are an indication that the dividing lines separating the several branches of international modernism in the 1960's are easily crossed; indeed that the distinction between the formalists on the one hand and the post-Brutalists on the other is, itself, something of an oversimplification. Moreover, this distinction was equally unclear during the 1950's when an historically-inspired building like Johnson's Glass House (Figs. 223–227) could simultaneously appear to exemplify certain Brutalist precepts *avant la lettre*. Around 1960, Johnson began to substitute a novel, subtly shaped pier and arch form as the regular exterior module of his buildings in exchange for the familiar Miesian one.

This new language is used in several different schemes as a stereotyped vocabulary of order, notably in the dwarf-scaled pavilion, finished in 1962, situated in the midst of the miniature lake immediately below Johnson's now charmingly antiquated 1949 Glass House. The same "order" is employed, but this time in travertine rather than in precast concrete and on a larger scale, in the Sheldon Art Gallery, Lincoln, Nebraska, 1960–63 (Figs. 338, 339). In other designs, notably the recently finished gallery addition for Dumbarton Oaks, Washington (Fig. 340), Johnson has made use of a traditionally Byzantine grouping of domes (nine in a square with, in this case, the central one omitted to make place for an open court) to produce a still different, if somewhat anachronistic, effect. Finally, as a part of the expanding science facilities at Yale University, New Haven, Johnson designed the fourteen-story Kline

336a. Alvar Aalto. Senior Dormitory, Massachusetts Institute of Technology. Cambridge, Massachusetts, 1948.

336b. Le Corbusier. Monastery of La Tourette. Eveux, near Lyon, 1957–60.

337. Eero Saarinen & Associates. U.S. Embassy. London, 1955–60.

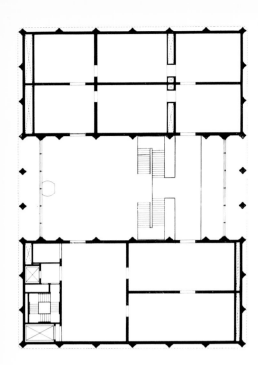

338, 339. Philip Johnson. Sheldon Memorial Art Gallery, University of Nebraska. Lincoln, Nebraska, 1960–63. Plan of the first floor and view.

Tower (Fig. 341). It is both a provocatively negative reaction to the brittle Miesian idiom of the 1950's, by virtue of the robust plasticity of mass, produced by its stout cylindrical columns, and a distinctive effort to come to terms with the collegiate eclecticism already dominating the surrounding architectural landscape. Johnson achieved the latter not by imitating its forms or its rhythms, but by producing collateral effects of color and texture.

In this effort, Johnson was following on the heels of Saarinen who, in his designs for two new residential units on the same campus, Stiles and Morse colleges, 1958–62 (Fig. 342), had also sought out an accommodation. Johnson's result, however, in achieving much the same end, was altogether different from the fantasy and touching personal romanticism of his contemporary's irregularly planned buildings. Not only must the irregular planes and surfaces

340. Philip Johnson. Art Gallery. Dumbarton Oaks, Washington, D.C., 1962–64.

of Saarinen's Yale colleges be contrasted with the more frankly tectonic group by Johnson, but they must also be set against the work of Martin and St. John Wilson at Caius (Figs. 334–336). These three alternate ways of shaping new collegiate environments within the frame of a traditional, localized context is but one more illustration of the breadth of possibility present in the architecture of today. In particular, the new Saarinen buildings at Yale seek to perpetuate a collegiate environment which, architecturally speaking, had been established by the fanciful, luxurious early twentieth-century neo-Gothic buildings of James Gamble Rogers—buildings which were still quite new when Eero Saarinen was a student during the early 1930's in the Yale architectural school, then a stronghold of historicism. It is this particular and personal understanding of the special Yale ambiance that governs so much of the character, if not the letter, of Stiles and Morse colleges.

At the same time, these faintly fantastic, near-expressionist designs seem to close a personal family circle inaugurated by Eero's father in the 1904 design for the Helsinki Station (Fig. 211). To be sure, there is no real influence, no basic resemblance of form, between the two, even though both exhibit a tendency to rambling, loosely articulated façades. In effect, the early station and the late colleges stand at opposite ends of the high machine era of modern architecture. They underscore both the father's reluctance to participate in this phase of modernism and the son's frequent uncertainty in making use of its particularly demanding style. The relationship here, a matter of character, of sensitivity to rough surfaces and dusky colored materials, indicates the reappearance, disguised and totally metamorphosed by the passage of time and events, of a long submerged anti-mechanistic romanticism. This is true despite the use made of a modified concrete technology in the creation of the irregular rubble-aggregate wall surfaces in the Yale colleges.

The personal ancestral complications that have made Saarinen's role in contemporary architecture so difficult to appreciate and so illusive in character are not found in Johnson's recent turn to more overt historic modes, since he has continued to operate in a detached cerebral way just as he did earlier. Consequently, he has always been the master of almost any design situation, whereas Saarinen has frequently been its creature, relying upon the program to provide not merely guidance but the very ideas and images of the composition itself. In this respect, Saarinen resembles Louis Kahn, who also seeks the image of the building from the conditions of the program, but with a different, almost purist,

341. Philip Johnson. Kline Tower, Yale University. New Haven, Connecticut. Project, 1962.

342. Eero Saarinen & Associates. Stiles and Morse colleges, Yale University. New Haven, Connecticut, 1958–62.

ascetic fervor which is a world removed from the genial literary expressionism of the former. Still a different method of finding the form and shape of the building is practiced by Marcel Breuer. Perhaps the most conservative of modern architects now practicing—if by this we mean not those who rely upon history or upon academic methods of order but instead those who persist in the compositional methods of a generation ago—Breuer, like Mies and Le Corbusier, proves that the heritage of the International Style is a still viable source. This can be seen to best advantage in a complex of four buildings for the University Heights Campus of New York University, 1956–61 (Figs. 343–345). Here the familiar geometries of the 1920's are maintained both in mass and detail, even though the variety of surface is rather more vigorous than would have been true of Bauhaus design. Most eye-catching in silhouette is the lecture hall, the outer mass of which is a concordance of space, surface, and volume in the best functional tradition. At that time, such a treatment would more likely have been found in Japan, Brazil, or Venezuela. Breuer's more recent large buildings, however, notably the I.B.M. Research Center, La Gaude, Var, France, 1960–62 (Figs. 346–348), manifest a development in which the over-all composition is regularized, the details given a more monumental, tactile proportion, and the curtain wall principle of structure and surface separation is abandoned. These walls are made of prefabricated folded con-

343. Marcel Breuer. Auditorium, University Heights Campus, New York University. 1956–61.

344. Marcel Breuer. University Heights Campus, New York University. 1956–61. Site plan.
1 Gould Hall of Technology
2 Auditorium
3 Community Building
4 Dormitory

345. Marcel Breuer. Community Building and Dormitory, University Heights Campus, New York University. 1956–61.

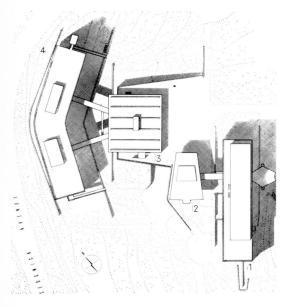

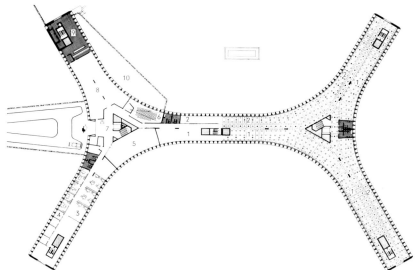

346–348. Marcel Breuer. Research Center of IBM-France. La Gaude, Var, 1960–62. Total view, detail of the façade, and plan of main floor.
1, 2 Laboratories and research offices
3, 4 General and administrative-executive offices
5 Exhibition and display
6 Auditorium
7 Lobby
8 Cafeteria
9 Kitchen
10 Terrace

crete elements, which, individually, form the window embrasures and, altogether, comprise the structural web of the building. These folded concrete shapes not only act as *brises-soleils* but also, within their hollow forms, they contain pipes and conduits. Thus, Breuer has rather belatedly arrived at a new integrated building order, one which, appropriately for a person of his generation and experience, is different from the lyrical sculptured forms of the older Le Corbusier, yet simultaneously at variance with the more academic system of arches, domes, and porticoes dominating the work of the younger Philip Johnson or the unique amalgam of structure and surface present in the work of Louis Kahn.

Peripheral to the distinctive work of Breuer, but roughly at the same stage of stylistic development throughout the 1950's, is the work of Carlos Raúl Villanueva in Venezuela. The various buildings at the University in Caracas, notably the Aula Magna (Figs. 350, 351) and the architectural school (Fig. 349), are among his most distinctive works in a concrete idiom drawn from sources that seem to be notably eclectic. More impressive in its scale and extent is the Cerro Piloto Housing Development in Caracas (Fig. 352), the work of a large staff of architects headed by Guido Bermudez. Here we have a series of multi-storied residential slabs, of quality but of little original distinction, set on a series of hills between the city below and the mountains beyond. To a degree, they capture something of the spirit

349. Carlos Raúl Villanueva. School of Architecture, University of Caracas. 1957.

350, 351. Carlos Raúl Villanueva. Aula Magna, University of Caracas. 1952.

352. Guido Bermudez, with Carlos Raúl Villanueva, Carlos Brando, Juan Centella. Cerro Piloto Housing Development. Caracas, 1954.

of Le Corbusier's great North African urban projects of the 1930's. It is in the buildings of Affonso Eduardo Reidy in Rio de Janeiro, notably the Museum of Modern Art (Figs. 354, 355), begun in 1954 but as yet unfinished, that one finds some of the most stimulating instances of a development of characteristic International Style design methods surviving from the 1920's. At the same time, in spite of the articulated composition which rigorously distinguishes one element from another (while sustaining a unity through low connecting passages), the gallery itself is given a degree of monumental spatial and structural clarity that at least anticipates a new and more rigorous pattern of order. This is brought about by suspending the gallery spaces within a structural cage of diagonal struts which dominate the exterior by their formal mass. Their measured rhythm, and the fashion by which they provide the exterior with an authentic, original sense of monumentality do credit to the architect. Indeed, when compared to the somewhat softer, less realistic forms of Niemeyer at Brasília, notably in the Presidential Palace, completed in 1959 (Fig. 353), one contemplates with satisfaction the combined structural-formal effect of Reidy's Museum. It is a more wholly integrated architectonic conception than the patently chic but thin works of his contemporary.

Museums have been one of the most frequently encountered building types in the last decade, and have offered one of the most fruitful areas for the expansion of the contemporary idiom, especially with respect to the handling of space and structure in large-scale monumental ways.[11] While some American museums are among the most successful

353. Oscar Niemeyer. Presidential Palace. Brasília, 1959.

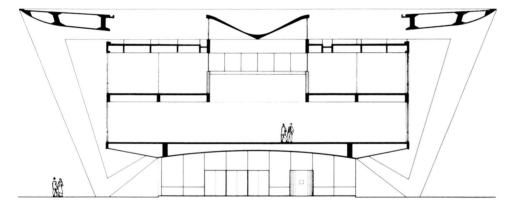

354, 355. Affonso Eduardo Reidy. Museum of Modern Art. Rio de Janeiro, begun 1954. Transverse section and view.

356–358. Carlo Bassi and Goffredo Boschetti. Gallery of Modern Art. Turin, 1954–59. Exterior view, transverse section and ground floor plan.

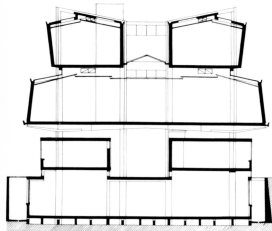

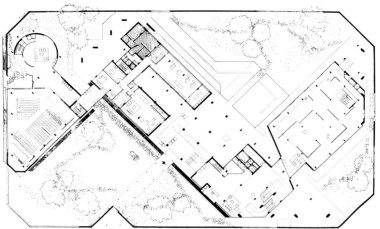

359. Kiyonori Kikutake. Shimane Prefecture Museum. Matsue, 1959.

formalist structures built since the close of the neo-classic period, others go to opposite extremes. Notably informal, indeed almost labyrinth-like, is the Gallery of Modern Art, Turin, 1954–59 (Figs. 356–358), by Carlo Bassi and Goffredo Boschetti. Although on a rectangular site, the plan is a zigzag. The main block stretches diagonally across the site, the gallery thereby enjoying a better angle with respect to natural light, which is admitted through overhead skylights. The location of these lights determines the unusual shape and profile of the interior spaces and structure; but in spite of this interior rationale, the entire building preserves a rambling, informal character. More forceful and outwardly disciplined is the new (1959) Shimane Prefecture Museum (Fig. 359), Matsue, Japan, designed by the rising young architect Kiyonori Kikutake (born 1928), largely because the main lines of the structural frame are so visible. Here the main rectangular exhibition space is boldly thrust up from the ground by a rugged substructure two stories high. Its top-heavy quality is akin to Mayekawa's Tokyo Festival Hall (Figs. 306, 307), but the structural clarity of Kikutake's Museum, with its distinction between the load at the top and the support underneath—two clearly contrasting elements—gives the younger man's design a coherence that is frequently missing in even the best works of his compatriot Tange.

At first glance, nothing might seem further apart than the recent architecture of Japan and Italy. Yet there is at least one striking Italian scheme that seems to parallel the omnipresent *brut* concrete of Japan, namely Vittoriano Viganò's Marchiondi Institute, Milan, of 1957–58 (Fig. 361). This blend of massive concrete outrigging with a neat surface of glass behind is something of an anomaly on the Italian scene, as are, for that matter, the uniquely structured halls and arenas of Pier Luigi Nervi. A more balanced picture can be obtained in examining two edifices of the past few years where the problem of bringing the structure of the building to the surface is solved in lively, quizzical, if somewhat awkward ways. The first is one of Europe's early skyscrapers, the Torre Velasca, Milan, 1954–58 (Fig. 360), by Lodovico Barbiano di Belgioioso, Enrico Peressutti, and Ernesto N. Rogers. The second is the department store in Rome, the *Rinascente,* by Franco Albini, projected in 1957 and finished in 1962 (Fig. 362). Neither possesses an especially focused over-all form, though the awkwardness of surface and support in each does insure a strong image. No doubt these are transitional works—in the sense in which the word was applied to the designs of Eero Saarinen—yet from these original efforts, we may still see a bold new architecture emerge from Italy after, it would seem, so many false dawns.

Many, if not all, of the architects recently mentioned—Breuer, Villanueva, Reidy, and Nie-

360. Studio architetti BBPR (Lodovico Barbiani di Belgioioso, Enrico Peressutti, and Ernesto N. Rogers). Torre Velasca. Milan, 1954–58.

361. Vittoriano Viganò. Marchiondi Institute. Milan, 1957–58.

362. Franco Albini. La Rinascente Department Store. Rome, 1957–62.

meyer, the Japanese, and even some of the Italians—have displayed mounting interest in the diverse work of Le Corbusier's old age. Similarly, the recent work of Paul Rudolph carries this tendency even further, but with a more personal vision and with a deeper cultural base that takes into account not just Le Corbusier alone, but Wright and, perhaps, Kahn as well.[12] Rudolph is without doubt the most distinctive of all those who have been moved by Le Corbusier's big concrete forms, yet he arrived at this vocabulary relatively late in his career, having undergone a very representative pattern of development from the late 1940's onward. His first houses were already quite original, though they owed their brittle, efficient proportions and structural clarity to a very individual appreciation of the lesson of Mies van der Rohe. From these, Rudolph proceeded to the design of the Wellesley College Art Center (Figs. 286, 287), a building of rather transient importance marking a difficult point in his evolution. That pattern became much clearer with the design and construction of the Sarasota, Florida, High School, 1958–59 (Figs. 363, 364), where, in a favorably sultry climate, Rudolph was able to design an open-air foyer on the order of the Chandigarh High Courts. Even the use of *brises-soleils* on the Sarasota School indicated the new sense of plasticity that was beginning to inundate American architecture in the late 1950's. These forms were used by Rudolph with an intriguing originality. Rather than underscore the mass of the structure and the volume (in the best Corbusian tradition), the architect seemed more concerned with the play of intersecting and parallel surfaces. This quality is emphasized in the way in which the *brises-soleils* are suspended out and away from the main volume instead of being integrated with it.

Nevertheless, this was still a tentative work in which Rudolph seems to have been shedding the Miesian structural lesson and gradually assimilating new ideas about mass, volume, and their integration with the spaces of the building. It is with the design and construction of the new Yale art center, 1959–63 (Figs. 365–368, 370), adjacent to Kahn's Art Gallery Extension, that Rudolph at last emerged as a major architect. The profoundly thought-out relationship between the mass of variously sized and shaped interior spaces and the ruggedly formed exterior mass is a satisfactorily picturesque and monumental culmination to a very difficult fringe site between the college campus and the townscape proper. Furthermore, it is a challenging statement of original contemporary design. Its plan is based upon the cartwheel idea first given currency in twentieth-century architecture by Wright, though in rather different form, and its vertical section reveals an amalgam of spaces disposed about a central area which vaguely resembles Wright's Larkin Building (Fig. 369) as well as suggesting certain compositional ideals concerning the characteristic identities of space

363, 364. Paul Rudolph. High School. Sarasota, Florida, 1958–59.

365. Paul Rudolph. Art and Architecture Building, Yale University. New Haven, Connecticut, 1959–63. Detail of the façade.

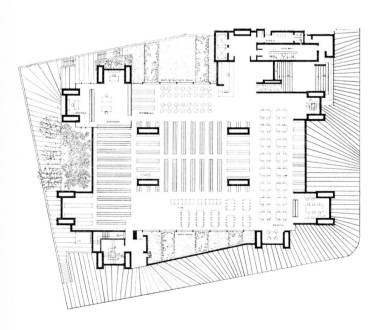

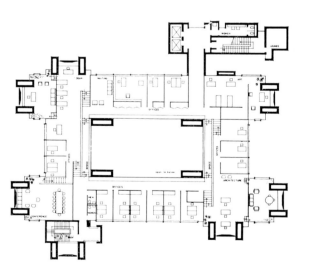

that are cherished by Louis Kahn. On the exterior, the casual observer will understandably be reminded of Le Corbusier, though the scored surface of the concrete is a device unique to Rudolph, and the distinctive effect of the surfaces and openings seems to be concerned with intersecting planes rather than with dense, impenetrable sculpturesque volumes. The building has a vague, eclectic aura about it, and there is no doubt that its author both consciously and unconsciously evoked more than a few skeletons from the closet of the modern tradition. He has done so, however, in a building that also reveals that his forms and spaces have an individual personal quality uniting a sense of practicality with one of sumptuousness—features only too rarely encountered in contemporary building.

Throughout the pages of this chapter, we have had occasion to refer to Louis Kahn in order to explain certain specific tendencies of one or another architect. Indeed, he would seem, more than anyone else in the mid-1960's, to be the architect of the hour, the rallying point at which much of the diversity of the epoch can be reconciled on the level of theory as well as of practice. He is certainly not the only major and significant inventor of new architectural forms presently at work, but the explicitness of his creative technique (made manifest both in the buildings and in his writings) throws his work into high relief. Because of this, his work seems to combine, in an archetypal fashion, those formal qualities of the emerging second half of the twentieth century, qualities which are in explicit reaction to the geometries of continuity and flux of the recent past. At the same time, his attitudes toward design seem to preserve that almost legendary sense of self-identity, of creative individuality, which made the masters of the early twentieth century the unique figures they were and have remained. In this latter sense, no other architect of the most recent generation seems, at least yet, entitled to this accolade, though certain ones are pressing close to the boundary. It is thus only fitting that a consideration of Kahn's recent works should dominate the concluding passages of this tentative history of the most recent phases of the modern movement, not just for reasons of the clarity of his stand, but because that very stand may well be the springboard for the immediate future.

As a historic personage, Kahn is something of an enigma, for he denies the reasonable supposition that a creative personality makes itself felt in an unmistakable fashion some time before early middle age. It was not until after his fiftieth birthday that Kahn, born in Estonia in 1901, constructed his first distinctive building: the addition to the Yale Art

Page 188:

366–368. Paul Rudolph. Art and Architecture Building, Yale University. New Haven, Connecticut, 1959–63. Exterior view, plans of ground floor and third floor.

369. Frank Lloyd Wright. Larkin Building. Buffalo, New York, 1904.

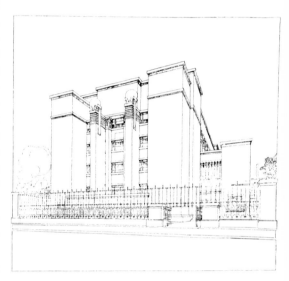

370. Paul Rudolph. Art and Architecture Building, Yale University. New Haven, Connecticut, 1959–63. Interior view of the library.

Gallery, 1952–54 (Figs. 218–220). Even after that building, all was not clear sailing. There were still several more lean creative years, and it was not until the design of the Richards Medical Research Building at the University of Pennsylvania (Figs. 371–373) that the pieces fell into shape. The building was not finished until 1961, and although its construction was closely followed by the architectural magazines, Kahn's international reputation in effect dates from 1961, which witnessed his sixtieth birthday. A curious record indeed.

Beyond this, Kahn's architecture possesses a distinctive kind of magic: an ability to shed light upon the work of his contemporaries as well as to illuminate, by analogy, certain works of the past, both near and remote. In this respect, his work acquires the sort of seminal importance that was the exclusive property of Wright, Mies, and Le Corbusier alone in the first half of the twentieth century. Indeed, Kahn's creative insight is of an order not regularly encountered at any given moment in history, and one searches in vain among the unending lists of talented architects of centuries as rich in creation and invention as the eighteenth and nineteenth without finding a single individual whose work held such universal implications. To a degree, it depends upon a kind of spontaneity, an instinctive rather than a rational or cerebral appreciation of the mission of architecture—here understood as an art capable of a sublime reconciliation of the most crass materialism with a transcendental formal idealism. By an implacable turn of fate, Louis Kahn possesses the requisite mixture of innocence and insight to furnish the necessary response.

These properties perhaps stemmed from his background, his education, and the very way that as a young man he somehow refrained from exploiting his talent for the more obvious sorts of satisfaction and gain. Unlike Eero Saarinen, Kahn was not born into the profession. On the other hand, like the son of the veteran Finnish modernist, Kahn was not educated in the midst of the turmoil and excitement of the radical early twentieth-century ideologies. Instead, his background was strictly Beaux-Arts, and his first contact beyond the scholarly genteel tradition of the Schools was rather second-hand. His knowledge of the avant-garde in European architecture came slowly and, to some degree, was little more than an indirect by-product of his own experiences of hardship during the depression of the 1930's. At the end of this superficially unfruitful period, he formed, in 1941, an association with George Howe, a once-fashionable architect of luxurious, sentimentally historical mansions, who had braved the currents of commercial architecture in the late 1920's and early 1930's to realize the first modern tall office building in America, the Philadelphia Savings Fund Society Building, finished in 1932. Contacts of this sort were, however, only elements of accumulated experience; the creative release would come only much later. The Yale Gallery was a kind of false dawn, for the real arrival of Kahn's talents was destined to be delayed still a bit longer.

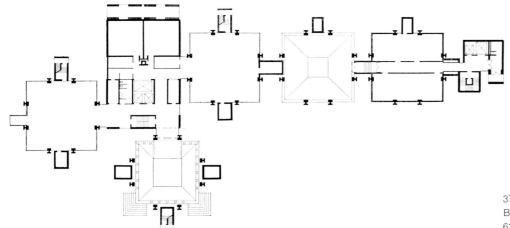

371–373. Louis I. Kahn. Richards Medical Research Building, University of Pennsylvania. Philadelphia, 1957–61. Exterior views and plan of typical laboratory floor.

374, 375. Louis I. Kahn. Unitarian Church. Rochester, New York, 1959–62. Floor plan and view.

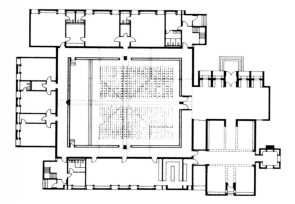

The Richards Medical Research Building and the Rochester Unitarian Church (Figs. 374, 375), the latter designed in 1959 and finished in 1962, represent the materialization of a quest that goes on today in a series of new Kahn projects. The very nature of the profession and of its clientele has, of course, never permitted a particularly comfortable place to be made for this restless and questioning kind of designer. Lacking the extroverted temperament and monumental self-assurance of a Wright or a Le Corbusier—Kahn is reticent if not actually shy—for a long time Kahn suffered from a real lack of an audience. Indeed, at the moment of contemporary architecture's greatest popular success in the early 1950's, he was more cut off than ever from a public that could admire the well-tailored designs of Skidmore, Owings and Merrill or even the more difficult to appreciate, sculpturesque idiosyncrasies of Wright or of Le Corbusier. Even now, at the peak of his career, Kahn's buildings are not especially palatable, and much of his success is due to that certain snob appeal which difficult and perplexing art forms sooner or later acquire. It is his harsh vigor that still sets his work apart, for in his hands the epithet "brutal" takes on a meaning that was only partly intended by those who first made it a current term of approbation in architectural criticism. Unlike Rudolph's new buildings, which offer strong pictorial similarities with such early examples of the modernist tradition as Wright's Larkin Building (Fig. 369), Kahn's compact, towered structures resemble that now-hallowed masterpiece less from any "stylish" motivation than through a parallel method of ordering and inventing spaces to fulfill a variety of distinct, specific deeds and services.

Kahn's work does not really require an outside apologia at this juncture. His buildings, tough and raw in appearance though they may be, are visually self-explanatory and, on a professional and creative level, his own writings, phrased though they are in a highly personal language, are the best exegeses that his structures could ask for. The Research Building was an essay in the articulation of "servant" and "served" spaces, where it is not enough that this functioning interrelationship merely work, but where it must be made manifest in the character of the spaces and the forms themselves. The early sketches for this laboratory complex show that Kahn had the tower cluster in mind from the start. Subsequently, he polished and made more explicit his first idea through a consideration of program and structure. In the end, it was the structural solution, with its interlocking web of precast ceiling and floor elements that determined much of the external and internal fabric. The clarification and ultimate separation of parts into a series of interconnected tower elements produced no mere essay in functional composition, any more than the New

Brutalist endeavor to breathe new life into the old dogmas of the 1920's produced a duplication of form and effect.

The differences between Kahn and his contemporaries at home and abroad are only partly due to his sheltered education in the grand tradition with its emphasis upon large, formal compositions. The Unitarian Church in Rochester was his first opportunity to create a monumental space, and in its design the architect constantly sought for a result that would not be generalized and universal, but that would be unique and specific. Its uniqueness had nothing to do with landscape and site, as had been the case a few years earlier at Ronchamp; indeed, the site in Rochester is a characterless suburban wasteland. Exterior form and interior space enjoy a reciprocal relationship characteristic of so much recent architecture. The central meeting room, with its four corner towers providing through their windows a stark, cold, shadowless light, altogether at odds with the rich chiaroscuro of a Wright or Le Corbusier space, makes itself felt as the centralmost and topmost exterior volume. From this sustained, chordal climax, the forms descend to the two-story wings that surround each of the four sides of the central space. The silhouette is neither picturesque nor accidental, in the Brutalist sense. The order and discipline are all Kahn's own: stiff, stark, and ungainly; seemingly the work of a true primitive, one who is not naïve but who is able to employ mind and instinct simultaneously. The exterior is of

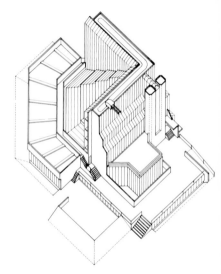

376, 377. James Stirling. History Library, Cambridge University. 1963–66. Interior view of model and drawing of exterior.

378. James Stirling and James Gowan. Engineering Laboratories, Leicester University. 1960–63.

379. Ludwig Mies van der Rohe. Federal Center. Chicago, 1964.

380 (Right). Paul Rudolph. Boston Government Service Center, Health, Education, and Welfare Building. Boston, Massachusetts. Project, 1964; under construction.

381. Philip Johnson. Henry L. Moses Research Institute, Montefiore Hospital. New York, 1963–65.

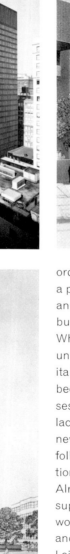

ordinary purple brick with terra-cotta along the cornice. This monochromatic purity is but a preparation for the *grisaille* effect of the interior, produced by the raw concrete surfaces and the walls of concrete block. The shells of the interior and the exterior match perfectly, but their distinctive role is made manifest in their individual surfaces and coloring.

While these buildings have been perfected through Kahn's endless search for the proper, unique balance between program, spaces, and forms, the final result possesses an inevitability and a stylistic consistency which make it seem as if the whole of the building had been the result of a sudden burst of inspiration. In short, Kahn's few executed works possess a creative certainty that the more numerous works of his peers have occasionally lacked. On this rarefied level of the invention of a personal, yet universal, vocabulary of new architecture, Kahn is nearly alone. Perhaps his example will produce others, not followers, but architects sufficiently self-effacing to put aside easily fashionable glib solutions and to peer deeply into the means of architectonic invention.

Already, in England, the work of Stirling and Gowan has lately crystallized into a style that supplements the implications of Kahn and his work.[13] Nonetheless, their new, large-scale work, the Engineering Laboratories at Leicester University (Figs. 298, 378), finished in 1963, and Stirling's History Library at Cambridge University (Figs. 376, 377), projected just as the Leicester building was being finished, owe nothing directly to Kahn's style and next to nothing to his manner of thought. In its own way, Stirling and Gowan's Leicester building

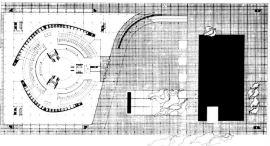

has its roots deep in the same modern tradition, and this accounts for the parallels. Its red brick walls may be only skin deep, as is the case with Kahn, but such surfacing takes us back to the Victorian era, to the times of William Butterfield, George E. Street, and Sir George Gilbert Scott. With Stirling and Gowan, however, there is a preoccupation with glass (a material that is only incidental in Kahn's work), both as a symbol and as the substance of their twentieth-century European heritage. Both build towers in the tradition of Wright's Larkin (1904; Fig. 369) and Johnson Wax (1936–50; Figs. 56, 57) buildings; that is to say, tall buildings that avoid the almost inevitably sterile image of the uniform commercial sky-scraper tower. Yet Stirling and Gowan find their own way, one that because of their fasci-nation with glass ultimately owes little either to Kahn or the followers of Le Corbusier. Varying situations demand a different treatment, and some of their glass is opaque, some translucent, and some clear. The elements of the buildings are sternly articulated, and

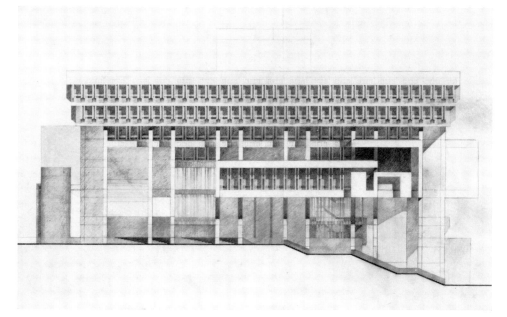

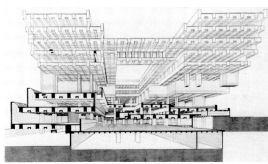

384, 385. Gerhard Kallmann, N. M. McKinnell, and E. F. Knowles. City Hall. Boston, Massachusetts. Competition project, 1961; under construction. South elevation and sectional perspective.

386. Skidmore, Owings & Merrill. Administration and Research Building, Emhart Manufacturing Company. Bloomfield, Connecticut, 1964.

387. Pier Luigi Nervi. Palace of Labor. Turin, 1960–61.

their separateness is compromised only in the open and much glazed circulation and stair spaces. Kahn's buildings and stairs *shelter,* as do Wright's, but Stirling and Gowan give us buildings where the inhabitants are left exposed in corridors, and passageways of glass are left vulnerable and visible (though most of the working spaces are traditionally enclosed). Such architecture puts a premium upon movement and action, drawing the individual around and about from one space to another, providing in the most direct, architectonic way, specific goals, fixed and allocated spaces of predetermined form and use, closed volumes that are reached by passing through spaces whose transparent, precarious character is meant to inspire and stimulate motion.

There is, understandably, no end to this new architecture. Boston, with a new City Hall (Figs. 384, 385) designed by Gerhard Kallmann, N. M. McKinnell, and E. F. Knowles (the winners of a competition), represents still another adventure into the unknown.[14] A few years hence, this unique contemporary civic monument will be backed up by a new civic center with its own enclosed plaza, the design of Paul Rudolph working in conjunction with several other firms (Fig. 380). The confident, robust masses of this complex, apparently improvised, but, in fact, carefully studied ensemble leaves the cool measured rhythms of Mies's I. I. T. far behind. Yet, ever imperturbably, Mies goes on today in his established vein: The new Federal Center in Chicago (Fig. 379) is only one of the most recent of his classic ventures that now seem timeless and outside of history. In the mid-1960's, these pristine forms seem little more than brilliant anachronisms, and yet, in a few years, they may once again become relevant.

Today, no individual building can completely represent the stylistic aspirations of our unsettled age; we are not about to build *our* Parthenon or Notre-Dame. No one shape or image typifies today's architectural vocabulary and syntax. Our culture is too diverse to provide one definitive monumental program, and our architects are too individualistic to be capable of working within the narrow stylistic limits that would be imposed by a single symbolic monument. Thus, we build both tall buildings, like Johnson's research center for Montefiore Hospital in New York City (finished in 1965; Fig. 381) or, alternately, long low buildings that seem to float above the ground, like the Emhart Manufacturing Company's research building at Bloomfield, Connecticut (Fig. 386), one of the most recent endeavors of Skidmore, Owings and Merrill. Although these buildings by two of Mies's important disciples are detailed with economy and restraint, their solid volumes and forthright

388. Eero Saarinen & Associates. Administration Building, John Deere & Co. Moline, Illinois, 1961–64.

expression of structure mark the significant changes in taste that have transpired since the mid-1950's when dissimulation of weight and mass was still the order of the day. Indeed, the expressive means by which the Skidmore, Owings and Merrill building is lifted off the ground—polygonal *pilotis* supporting radiating beams—can be compared instructively to the interior supports of Nervi's hypostyle hall for the Palace of Labor, Turin, 1960 (Fig. 387), where the Italian builder appears to have imparted a surprisingly classicistic image to his revealed structure. Taken together, these two designs suggest the sort of rapprochement that is, in the 1960's, possible between the formalist and constructivist wings of architectural design.

Other works of the past few years, notably Eero Saarinen's posthumus John Deere Administrative Building, Moline, Illinois, 1961–64 (Fig. 388), and James Stirling's project of 1965–66 for the Dorman Long Steel Works Administrative and Research building, Middlesborough, England (Fig. 389), are not only unusual in general mass, but offer unique and expressive means of displaying steel structure beyond, rather than simply upon, the exterior skin of the building. Parallel if less spectacular methods of "exteriorizing" the skeletal parts of a building can be seen in the *brut* concrete of Wurster Hall at the University of California, Berkeley, by Joseph Esherick, Donald Olsen, and Vernon De Mars (Fig. 390). Another tendency can be seen in the compact, stunted towers visible in so many of Kahn's recent buildings, like the Residence Halls at Bryn Mawr College, finished in 1965 (Fig. 391, 393), and in the original forms of Clowes Memorial Hall, a multipurpose theater designed by John Johansen and Evans Woollen at Butler University in Indianapolis, Indiana (Fig. 392). There also seems to be an inexhaustible variety of ways to reach the clouds, whether the means be the sail-like concrete shells of Jørn Utzon's Sydney Opera Theater (Figs. 295, 295a) or the two crescent-plan towers of Viljo Revell's Toronto City Hall (Figs. 382, 383). Both buildings, having been designed originally as competition projects in the late 1950's, are only nearing completion in the mid-1960's. Small as well as large municipalities the world over have sought to equip themselves with new public buildings, as is exemplified by the Civic Center of Bat-Yam, Israel (Figs. 394, 395), by Alfred Neumann, Z. Hecker, and E. Sharon. Halls and arenas continue to offer still other kinds of challenge to architects, most notably in recent years in the dramatically conceived structures of Kenzo Tange for the Tokyo Olympics of 1964 (Figs. 396, 397).

This is a heterogeneous as well as incomplete roster of recent buildings designed by

389. James Stirling. Project for an Office and Research Building, Dorman Long Steel Works. Middlesborough, 1965–66. Model.

390. Joseph Esherick, Donald Olsen, and Vernon De Mars. Wurster Halls, University of California. Berkeley, California, 1960–64.

variousa rchitects who, after a trying period, have at last freed themselves from the legends and myths of modern architecture that cramped developments through much of the 1950's. Happily, although the pseudo-romantic aura surrounding the designs of Wright, Mies and Le Corbusier has finally been dissipated, the useful lessons offered by the masters of the heroic generation have remained as a substantial and realistic basis of further development. The petty criticisms of early modern architecture as set forth by such movements as new empiricism and new humanism more than a decade ago have vanished without a trace. Diverse and personal as today's contemporary buildings may be, largely lacking the common-denominator quality of the late 1920's, these individual manners add up, remarkably, to a coherent emphatic, if ideologically somewhat insecure style. Although the vast majority of today's architects have not addressed themselves, in concert with public and private authorities, to many of the pressing constructive problems that have been closing in relentlessly upon a ceaselessly changing world, nevertheless they have made a dramatic and useful beginning.

Ours has been an era of doers, not of thinkers or dreamers. Individuality has become a special virtue, and we prefer to think of objects and events as unique, non-repetitive, and highly specialized, with the result that distinctiveness and originality have become inflated in value. We excel in making distinctions and are inclined to be impatient with efforts to establish discipline and community of purpose in the creative arts. Nevertheless, the ensemble of today's consequential buildings, those that are more than mere artifacts, reveals a surprising stylistic coherence and historical logic. This coherence has nothing to do with simple unanimity. Instead, it refers to the meaningful interrelationship of various trends and personal manners, the way in which these contrasts establish a fertile dialogue between divergent or convergent interests. The history of the past quarter-century is no monologue but is, rather, an animated and still unresolved conversation. Indeed, the very absence of a conclusive, definitive resolution to the many contradictions contained within contemporary architecture is the surest indication of a vigorous, creative future.

It would not be appropriate to postulate lessons and maxims for the future on the basis of recent events, as the eighteenth- or nineteenth-century historian might have done. It would be equally silly to star-gaze or peer into a crystal ball. It *is* feasible, however, to glimpse the possibilities and choices open to architects in the closing decades of our century. In particular, the exaggerated preoccupations, which have bounded from one extreme to another in the course of the last half-century, offer valuable clues to the future. Furthermore, the

391. Louis I. Kahn. Residence Halls, Bryn Mawr College. Bryn Mawr, Pennsylvania, 1961–65.

392. John Johansen and Evans Woollen. Clowes Memorial Hall, Butler University. Indianapolis, Indiana, 1963.

surviving contradictory fragments of our nineteenth-century heritage (mostly of a theoretical nature) also suggest certain incompletely explored areas of activity which might well be taken up by the next generation.

How valid for the future are the theories and ideals of the recent past? The nineteenth-century fanfare of modernist doctrine, as contained in the works of Morris or Viollet-le-Duc, spoke of creating a style appropriate to need and relative to material and technique, thus implying a rejection of thoughtless repetition or variations lifted from inherited models. A subsequent generation, that of Berlage, Wagner, and Loos, added the idea of a *new* style, a *modern* style, to the more analytical proposals of their predecessors. Their followers, in turn, produced the Futurist manifestoes, *L'Esprit Nouveau, Frühlicht,* and the other visionary tracts and projects of the heroic age. Today, these ideals of the 1920's remain largely unfulfilled. Their hortatory invocations, while still applicable to our architectural dilemmas, are increasingly remote, their naïve language evokes smiles of condescension or frowns of irritation. The problems they pose are too vast for brief analysis or easy comprehension; the solutions they offer (although they have influenced innumerable individual structures over the past twenty-five years) are too simple and general to be applied directly to the larger matter of the total environment. Specialization and the gargantuan proportions of today's megalopolis have made the graphic urban design of Le Corbusier (or Mies, or Wright) seem not so much outmoded as merely wanting in detail, a romantic, or Wellsian, fantasy rather than a concrete proposal for the present.

Although we are presently able to bask in the glow of a pragmatic modernism more fertile and prolific than ever before, we also find that our appetites are more readily sated, our senses more swiftly jaded. An ironic variant upon the principle of supply and demand seems to be at work, consuming talent at a prodigious and wasteful rate. Would this condition prevail under more intellectually disciplined or restrained circumstances of design? Having finally pulled down the old academic apparatus of architectural doctrine, an apparatus that had obstructed the development of style (if not theory) through most of the nineteenth century, we ought to be searching for a new touchstone. The ideals of the first machine age (to use Reyner Banham's terminology) gave much promise, but that particular creative and intellectual synthesis disintegrated in the 1930's. Once the war was over, it was no longer possible to go back and begin again, because the architectural crisis of the 1930's had been caused by a social as well as an aesthetic rejection of machine age universalism, a rejection of the very philosophical fiber of the International Style. True, it was possible, after a short breathing spell in the late 1940's, to pick up a few of the older pieces and,

393. Louis I. Kahn. Residence Halls, Bryn Mawr College. Bryn Mawr, Pennsylvania, 1961–65.

interspersing them with new cement, to approximate a reincarnation of modern architecture. This was a formalistic beginning, however, and was not at all comparable to the situation that had followed the armistice in 1918, when a new architecture was considered as just one aspect of a new social order. Part of the recent popular success of the modern building styles has, indeed, been due to their separation from other forms and manifestations of twentieth-century radicalism.

Somehow, if our new architecture is to continue to grow, rather than merely to change, its pragmatic attitude, concentrating as it does on the exigencies of individual designs at the expense of general concepts, must be encouraged to press toward the development of ideas and ideals. Mid-century architecture has sought its own particular solutions in an atmosphere contemptuous of idealistic, or universally valid formulae. Our current skeptical regard for images of a world of tomorrow has substantially aided the expansion of modern architecture from a single mainstream into several strong, complementary currents, since it freed designers from the limiting aspects of International Style doctrine and the monolithic quality of its austere style. In addition to aiding the personal development of a certain small band of able architects, however, this skepticism has also fostered a rash of imitations and has encouraged opportunism and anti-intellectualism.

The time may soon come for one more turn of the wheel. One hopes that it will be possible to reunite the creative aspect of early modern theory (particularly its aura of expectation, but freed from its fascination with simple, universal solutions) with the character and finesse of today's pragmatic architectural design. Perhaps, much of the energy that is now spent in an increasingly futile effort to produce new and startling form might be channeled into other activities. Since we already have a rich modern style, would it not be fruitful to consider how best to utilize what exists rather than compulsively (or arbitrarily) to increase its quantity and variety? Certainly, there is nothing implicit in our permanent architectural revolution that demands incessant change or revision of style. Creative effort need not be directed only toward sensual gratification, whether material or aesthetic. These energies might better be released in the direction of planning and developing a more comprehensive and satisfying environment for human life, one which would open a variety of heretofore unimagined benefits. Such an environment would not need to be restrictive and uniform, nor would it have to be flashy and vulgar.

Beyond these vague, tentative suggestions, the historian should not trespass, for this is the realm of the theorist or even of the law-giver. That a great, imponderable task remains to be defined and accomplished by the architects of the future is clear. An unprecedented effort will be necessary to prepare for this fulfillment. The Futurist and Internationalist visionaries have offered suggestions and provided sketches of a general order. Technologically, these schemes are, of course, already outmoded, although they will certainly remain valid as visual guides for some time to come. Throughout the middle years of the century, these ideas have remained dormant, but they have been carefully studied and nurtured by isolated groups or individuals in the hope that, after the present phase of predominantly formalistic architecture has exhausted its special appeal, it will be possible to embark upon a new adventure. Nevertheless, before a new generation of public officials, private patrons, building contractors, and architects can rise to the challenge of a renewed industrial and mechanical revolution, tremendous preparatory work is mandatory.

A new generation of prophetic, visionary theorists will have to come forth from the ranks of working architects. Beyond this, however, it will be necessary for many able architects to turn away from their arbitrary contrivance and gratuitous manipulation of space. Of course, they must not yield to a solution of architectural problems through social, technocratic, or economic devices alone. Indeed, to gravitate to that alternate extreme would, in effect, be a total triumph of philistinism. Instead, they must seek a more secure and integrated balance between the practical and aesthetic interests of architecture. Through this search, the achievements of the first two-thirds of the twentieth century will be consolidated and the future of modern architecture assured.

396, 397. Kenzo Tange. National Sports Arenas. Tokyo, 1963–64. Model and cross section of the smaller Sports Arena.

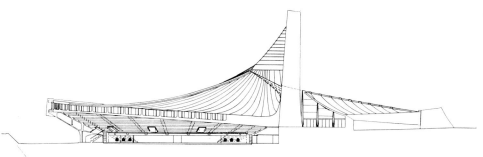

# Notes

**Chapter I**

[1] Marc-Antoine Laugier. Essai sur l'Architecture (Paris, 1752; 2d ed., 1755). The various architectural trends of this period are dealt with in great detail in: Emil Kaufmann. Architecture in the Age of Reason (Cambridge, Massachusetts, 1955); and in: Wolfgang Herrmann. Laugier and Eighteenth Century French Theory (London, 1962).

[2] This question is touched upon with great insight by: Rudolf Wittkower. Architectural Principles in the Age of Humanism (2d ed.; London, 1952), pp. 124—35.

[3] An approach to the methodology of revivalism and eclecticism that sympathetically proposes that these movements be considered as more original and self-expressive than is generally the case is to be found in Carroll L. V. Meeks, "Creative Eclecticism," Journal of the Society of Architectural Historians, XII, No. 4 (December, 1953), 15—18, and in the same author's "Picturesque Eclecticism," The Art Bulletin, XXXII, No.3 (September, 1950), 226—35.

[4] The classic presentation of the International Style is in: Henry-Russell Hitchcock and Philip Johnson. The International Style: Architecture since 1922 (New York, 1932). See also the exhibition catalog, Museum of Modern Art, New York. Modern Architecture, International Exhibition (New York, 1932), with texts by Alfred H. Barr, Jr., Henry-Russell Hitchcock, and Philip Johnson. The term itself was coined by the organizers of that exhibition, but it probably is indebted to the title of Walter Gropius': Internationale Architektur (Weimar: Bauhaus, 1925). Other discussions of this aspect of twentieth-century architecture are to be found in: Bruno Taut. Modern Architecture (London, 1929); Henry-Russell Hitchcock. Modern Architecture, Romanticism and Reintegration (New York, 1929), pp. 153—220; Alberto Sartoris. Gli Elementi dell'Architettura Funzionale (Milan, 1932); S. Giedion. Space, Time and Architecture (3d ed., enlarged; Cambridge, Massachusetts, 1954), pp. 425—564; Bruno Zevi. Storia dell'Architettura Moderna (Turin, 1950), pp. 117—207; Pierre Francastel. Art et Technique aux XIX$^e$ et XX$^e$ Siècles (Paris, 1956), pp. 163—207; Henry-Russell Hitchcock. Architecture, Nineteenth and Twentieth Centuries (Harmondsworth and Baltimore, 1958), pp. 363—91; Jürgen Joedicke. A History of Modern Architecture (New York, 1959), pp. 66—105; John Jacobus, "European Modern Movements. Architecture," Encyclopedia of World Art (New York, 1962), Vol. V; John Jacobus, "Modern Architecture," in: World Architecture (2d rev. ed., London and New York, 1966); Vincent J. Scully, Jr. Modern Architecture (New York, 1961); and Alison and Peter Smithson, "The Heroic Period of Modern Architecture," special No. of Architectural Design, XXXV, No. 12 (December, 1965). For the unique, often forgotten Russian contribution see: Vittorio de Feo. URSS Architettura, 1917-36 (Rome, 1963). There are also volumes on the architecture of the 1920's which illustrate not just the rational avant-garde, but also the subjective, expressionist side as well. See: Maurice Casteels. The New Style . . . A survey of its first phase in Europe and America (London, 1931). By way of contrast, see: J. G. Wattjes. Moderne Architectur (Amsterdam, 1927), which gives a thorough coverage of all creative facets of building in the 1920's except for the International Style itself. For a panorama of the decade 1929-39, during which the International Style withered, see the collection of fundamental papers presented at The Modern Architecture Symposium (MAS 1964), Columbia University, New York, edited by G. R. Collins and A. K. Placzek, under the chairmanship of Henry-Russell Hitchcock, published in the Journal of the Society of Architectural Historians, XXIV, No. 1, (March, 1965), 3-95. Reyner Banham's: Theory and Design in the First Machine Age (London and New York, 1960), considers the pre-world-war originis of the International Style as well as developments throughout the 1920's.

[5] Thus proclaims the title of Ozenfant and Jeanneret: Après le Cubisme (Paris, 1919). It should be pointed out that at this time Le Corbusier still made use of his own patronym, Jeanneret, in connection with his paintings and with his writings on painting.

[6] In contrast to the way in which the designers of expressionist sympathies veered towards a more rational International Style mode of expression in the later 1920's, a number of the leaders of the latter movement, notably Gropius and Mies, produced designs and buildings immediately after World War I that were expressionist in the dramatic, emotive character of their forms. Illustrating this tendency were Gropius' Sommerfeld House, Berlin, 1921, and Mies van der Rohe's Glass Skyscraper projects of 1919—21.

[7] These influences are amply testified to in the artistic catechism of Le Corbusier (Charles-Edouard Jeanneret-Gris). Vers une Architecture (Paris, 1923). This book mainly consisted of articles that had appeared in the periodical L'Esprit Nouveau. In its English translation by Frederick Etchells (London, 1927; New York, 1959), the title was softened to: Towards a New Architecture. Regrettably, the addition of the word "new" obscures the universality of the Purist aesthetic, at least as practiced by Le Corbusier, which was more spontaneously traditional than its predecessors, Cubism and Futurism. The section on the Parthenon appears in Part III under the heading "Architecture, Pure Creation of the Mind." With passages like this in mind, it is readily understandable that even at that

early date, Le Corbusier did not conceive of Purism as simply an incidental reaction to, or reordering of, the new twentieth-century aesthetic. Instead, he saw it as a movement of broader and more fundamental intentions, with determined links both to selected aspects of the remote past as well as to a gradually evolving contemporary tradition.

[8] Henry-Russell Hitchcock, "Frank Lloyd Wright and the 'Academic Tradition.'" Journal of the Warburg and Courtauld Institutes, VII (1944), 46—63.

[9] In addition to Viollet-le-Duc's: Entretiens sur l'Architecture (2 vols.; Paris, 1863—72), see also the articles "Architecture" and "Construction" in: Dictionnaire raisonné de l'Architecture Française du XIe au XVIe Siècle, Vol. I (Paris, 1854), 116—452, and IV (1859), 1—279.

[10] The best survey of the architecture of the period 1900—14, one that also follows its development down into the mid-1920's (at which point its growth was halted and then replaced by the new architecture of the International Style), is: G. A. Platz. Die Baukunst der Neuesten Zeit (Berlin, 1927; 2d ed., 1930), even though its coverage is restricted to Central Europe. For other architecture of the period, see: Arnold Whittick. European Architecture in the Twentieth Century (2 vols.; London, 1950—53), and: Nikolaus Pevsner. Pioneers of Modern Design (3d ed.; Harmondsworth, 1960).

[11] See note 7, above.

[12] The phrase "Une villa sur les dunes de Normandie," translated freely by Etchells as "sea-side villa," is used by Le Corbusier in the caption of an illustration of the Cunard liner Aquitania in: Vers une Architecture, p. 76 (Towards a New Architecture, p. 92). The detail of its aft superstructure bears a noteworthy similarity to the over-all exterior massing of the Villa Savoye, which was designed six years after the original publication.

[13] The relation of Picasso's paintings of the 1920's to the Purist, post-Cubist architecture of Le Corbusier does not end here. A lengthy and varied series of paintings of figures on the seashore seems to relate both thematically and stylistically to the most fully developed of these International Style villas. One thinks in particular of Picasso's great neo-classic "Pipes of Pan," 1923, and of the extraordinary "Seated Bather," early 1930, the latter in the collection of The Museum of Modern Art, New York. The "Seated Bather" is, in a profound stylistic way, a kind of hollowing out of the human figure, analogous to the treatment of form and space that occurs in the Villa Savoye. In the Picasso, we have a reconstruction of a human figure in which the approximately flat, planar representation of the body's limbs helps to define an incorporeal volume within the figure. Similarly, the thin walls and wind screens of the Villa Savoye create an unenclosed "interior" space. In effect, each form has been disemboweled and the normal idea of tangible solid has been inverted.

[14] Vincent Scully was the first to suggest the analogy between Le Corbusier's house plans (specifically the Citrohan types of 1920—22) and the Helladic megaron form. See his "Modern Architecture," College Art Journal, XVII, No. 2 (Winter, 1958), 140 (this article is also in: Perspecta, The Yale Architectural Journal, No. 4 [1957], 5—10, as "Modern Architecture: Towards a Redefinition of Style"); and: Modern Architecture (New York, 1961), pp. 42—43.

[15] Colin Rowe, "Mannerism in Modern Architecture," The Architectural Review, CVII (May, 1950), 289—99.

[16] A special number of Architectural Forum, LXVII (January, 1938), was devoted to a generous illustration of new work of this period, including Falling Water.

[17] Vincent Scully. Frank Lloyd Wright (The Masters of World Architecture Series) (New York, 1960), p. 28.

[18] This subject of the sun-breaker, or "brise-soleil," in the work of Le Corbusier is summed up in: Le Corbusier. Œuvre Complète 1938—1946 (2d ed.; Zurich, 1950), pp. 108—115. The form seems to have evolved in a series of buildings and projects from 1928—33.

[19] Le Corbusier and P. Jeanneret. Œuvre Complète 1934—38 (Zürich, 1939), p. 125, and: Le Corbusier 1910—1960 (Zurich and New York, 1960), p. 68.


## Chapter II

[1] Two illustrated books, which have received wide circulation, give a particularly apt picture of the more novel aspects of modern architecture at this time: Alfred Roth. The New Architecture (La Nouvelle Architecture; Die Neue Architektur) (Zurich, 1940); and S. Giedion. A Decade of New Architecture (Dix Ans d'Architecture Contemporaine) (Zurich, 1951). The latter volume was published at the behest of Les Congrès Internationaux d'Architecture Moderne, and covered the years 1937—47.

[2] The question of a modern style in architecture before 1939—45 is vexed by the fact that progressive design was in every respect a minority movement, and that the vast majority of buildings built in the 1920's as well as the 1930's were in one way or another reactionary or shallowly traditional. See Chapter XXIV, "Architecture Called Traditional in the Twentieth Century," in: Hitchcock. Architecture, Nineteenth and Twentieth Centuries (Baltimore, 1958), pp. 392—410.

[3] This theme is treated in detail by Vincent J. Scully, Jr., "Wright vs. the International Style," Art News, LIII, No. 1 (March, 1954), 32—35.

[4] See: Philip C. Johnson. Mies van der Rohe (New York, 1947), pp. 96–130; Le Corbusier and P. Jeanneret. Œuvre Complète 1934—38.

[5] A convenient literary landmark at this period is J. M. Richards, "The Next Step," The Architectural Review, CVII, No. 639 (March, 1950), 165—81.

[6] The first article in which the phrase itself was actually employed was "The New Empiricism: Sweden's Latest Style," The Architectural Review, CI, No. 606 (June, 1947), 199—204. Significantly, this phrase was not employed in a comprehensive article on recent Swedish architecture a few months earlier: E. L. Bird, "Swedish Architecture in 1946," Journal of the Royal Institute of British Architects, 3d series, LIII, No. 12 (October, 1946), 523—29, nor was it used in the special wartime issue on Sweden of The Architectural Review, XCIV, No. 561 (September, 1943). A subsequent presentation of the subject is Eric de Maré and others, "The New Empiricism," The Archi-

tectural Review, CIII, No. 613 (January, 1948), 9—22. See also: G. E. Kidder Smith. Sweden Builds (2d ed., revised; New York, 1957).

[7] See: Bruno Zevi. Verso un'Architettura Organica (Milan, 1945), the title of which implicitly called to account Le Corbusier's manifesto of Purism: Vers une Architecture. See also his: Storia dell'Architettura Moderna (Turin, 1950), especially Chapter VI, "Il Movimento organico in Europa," pp. 283—328, and Chapter XI, "Il Movimento organico negli Stati Uniti," pp. 477—523. In effect, the later publication is an expansion of the argument developed in: Verso un'Architettura Organica, five years earlier.

[8] The most famous of the periodicals that had publicized sympathetically the new architecture during the interwar period were: de Stijl, 1917—31; Wendingen, 1919—25; L'Esprit Nouveau, 1919—25; and L'Architecture Vivante, 1923—33. Also important were the numerous volumes published by the Bauhaus in the course of the 1920's. L'Architecture d'Aujourd'hui was one of the few avant-garde periodicals to survive World War II, but it had made its first appearance in 1930 after the heroic phase of modern architecture was nearly concluded.

[9] See particularly "Save us our Ruins," with a foreword by the Dean of St. Paul's, a text by G. A. Jellicoe, and drawings by Neville Conder, The Architectural Review, XCV, No. 565 (January, 1944), 13—17. Subsequent issues of the Review cited Sir Joshua Reynolds on "Picturesque Architecture," and Sir Uvedale Price on "Picturesque Planning," and supplemented the latter with reproductions of color and texture studies by John Piper, whose sensibility would seem to stand at the furthest extreme from the architectural aesthetic of the 1920's. To supplement these fragments were more extensive articles: H. F. Clark on "Lord Burlington's Bijou, or Sharawaggi at Chiswick" (concerning the picturesque gardens surrounding a neo-Palladian country house) and H. A. N. Brockman on "Fonthill Abbey" (the most outré instance of picturesque, neo-Gothic sensationalism dating from the early nineteenth-century). Finally, in the November, 1944, issue, Professor Pevsner provided a survey, anthology, and summing up of this tendency in "The Genesis of the Picturesque." These titles, by themselves, give some indication of the intensity with which the new interest in the eighteenth century was then pursued. It is striking to see how well these historical pieces fit in with the remainder of the Review's contents of that epoch, some of the typical features being concerned with Swedish schools (premonitions of new empiricism), war housing in the U. S. A., military camouflage, or numerous examples of recent Brazilian architecture. From the myriad riches of The Architectural Reviews of the 1940's, one is tempted to think that the two volumes (XCV and XCVI) of 1944 were never surpassed. See also John Piper, "Pleasing Decay," The Architectural Review, CII, No. 609 (September, 1947), 85—94.

[10] Henry-Russell Hitchcock. Modern Architecture, Romanticism and Reintegration (New York, 1929), p. 220.

[11] This term has been current since the publication: S. Giedion. Spätbarocker und Romantischer Klassizismus (Munich, 1922).

[12] The parallel character of architecture of 1800 with that of 1920 was first suggested by the title: Emil Kaufmann. Von Ledoux bis Le Corbusier (Vienna, 1933).

[13] See: Philip C. Johnson. Mies van der Rohe (New York, 1947), pp. 9—20.

[14] Wright's early buildings became widely known in Europe as the result of two publications issued by Wasmuth, Berlin: Frank Lloyd Wright. Ausgeführte Bauten und Entwürfe (1910); Frank Lloyd Wright. Frank Lloyd Wright; Ausgeführte Bauten; preface by Charles R. Ashbee (1911).

[15] The special issue of Architectural Forum, January, 1938, devoted to the work of Wright, contains the best illustrative survey of his buildings and projects of this period. Other general works on or by Wright to be consulted in connection with his works of the late 1930's and early 1940's are: Henry-Russell Hitchcock. In the Nature of Materials, The Building of Frank Lloyd Wright (New York, 1942); Frank Lloyd Wright. A Testament (New York, 1957); An American Architecture, edited by Edgar Kaufmann (New York, 1955); Drawings for a Living Architecture (New York, 1959).

[16] The analogy between the plan of Florida Southern and Hadrian's Villa was first noted by Vincent Scully, Jr. Frank Lloyd Wright (New York, 1960), p. 29.

[17] See Chapter I, note 8.

[18] For a survey of American architecture at this period which presents the buildings that will subsequently be discussed see: Built in U. S. A.—Since 1932, edited by Elizabeth Mock, foreword by Philip L. Goodwin (New York, 1945). Also of help in establishing the directions in domestic architecture at this time is a book published slightly after the period under discussion: Robert Woods Kennedy. The House and the Art of Its Design (New York, 1953).

[19] For a presentation of the Havens House (which was not included in: Built in U. S. A.) see: Architectural Forum, LXXIX (September, 1943), 77—87. For the architecture of this "regional school," see: John and Sally Woodbridge. Buildings of the Bay Area, A Guide to the Architecture of the San Francisco Bay Region (New York, 1960).

[20] For a survey of the career of Wurster, see: Richard Peters, "L'Architetto William Wilson Wurster," Casabella, No. 238 (April, 1960), 14—27.

[21] The first book on this subject is: Philip L. Goodwin. Brazil Builds (New York, 1943). More recent is a general survey: Henrique E. Mindlin. Modern Architecture in Brazil (New York, 1956).

[22] Stamo Papadaki. The Work of Oscar Niemeyer (New York, 1950) provides the most complete survey of the early work of this architect.

[23] In: Goodwin, op. cit., the amount of space devoted to Brazil's colonial architecture is almost equal to the space given to new architecture.

[24] See: Giulio Carlo Argan. Ignazio Gardella (Milan, 1959), pp. 79—81.

[25] See: Peter Blake. Marcel Breuer, Architect and Designer (New York, 1949); Marcel Breuer. Sun and Shadow, edited with notes by Peter Blake (New York, 1955); and especially for more recent work: Marcel Breuer—Buildings and Projects, 1921—1961, with an introduction by Cranston Jones (New York, 1962).

[26] See: Arnold Whittick. Eric Mendelsohn (2d ed.; New York, 1956), and Wolf von Eckardt. Eric Mendelsohn (New York, 1962).

[27] In effect, the new order had been prepared by certain academic or scholarly tendencies found in Johnson's

own 1949 New Canaan home. Because of its extraordinary personal qualities, this house is considered separately. See below, Chapter IV, pp. 122–125.

[28] This house is reproduced, along with other buildings that show the extraordinarily diverse character of the period in: Built in U. S. A. — Post War Architecture, edited by Henry-Russell Hitchcock and Arthur Drexler (New York, 1952), pp. 64—65.

[29] Esther McCoy. Five California Architects (New York, 1960) provides the most convenient introduction to the works of Maybeck and of Greene and Greene.

[30] See: Albert Christ-Janer. Eliel Saarinen (Chicago, 1948).

[31] Another academic commission in Cambridge, Gropius' Harvard Graduate Center, 1949—50, illustrated another aspect of the renewed vitality of contemporary architecture. See: S. Giedion. Walter Gropius (New York, 1954). Similarly, this vitality was evident in the continuing series of buildings, each one seemingly more exacting and elegant in detail, that Mies was designing for I.I.T. These works, however, can be more profitably discussed in the context of the late styles of these masters. See Chapter III, p. 74.

[32] Klaus Franck. The Works of Affonso Eduardo Reidy. Introduction by S. Giedion (New York, 1960), pp. 96—117.

[33] Edward D. Mills. The New Architecture in Great Britain, 1946—53 (London, 1953). A useful survey of this challenging period in Britain. On the subject of the Festival Hall, see especially pp. 107—28 and also the remarks of Sir John Summerson in his introduction to: Trevor Dannatt. Modern Architecture in Britain (London, 1959), pp. 18—20.

[34] Carlo Pagani. Architettura Italiana Oggi (Milan, 1955) provides a general survey of the first phase of post-World War II architecture in Italy. The Rome Terminal is presented on pp. 270—75. See also: G. E. Kidder Smith. Italy Builds (New York, 1955).

[35] Pagani, op. cit., pp. 78—81.

[36] The Works of Pier Luigi Nervi. Preface by Pier Luigi Nervi, introduction by Ernesto Rogers, notes by Jürgen Joedicke (New York, 1957).

[37] This traditional, even classicistic, trait in Perret's work has been given a detailed discussion in: Peter Collins. Concrete, The Vision of a New Architecture, A Study of Auguste Perret and his Precursors (New York, 1959).

## Chapter III

[1] The paramount issues of this period, as seen from the American point of view, are succinctly phrased by Arthur Drexler in his essay for: Built in U.S.A.—Post-War Architecture, pp. 20—37. A parallel view of the same situation is expressed by S. Giedion, "Aspects de l'Architecture aux Etats-Unis en 1953," L'Architecture d'Aujourd'hui, XXIV, Nos. 50–51 (December, 1953), 7–9. The evolution of the next few years, the mid-1950's, is described in: Ian McCallum. Architecture U.S.A. (London and New York, 1959); in: Trevor Dannatt, op. cit.; and in: G. Hatje, H. Hoffman, and K. Kaspar. New German Architecture (Stuttgart, London, and New York, 1956). All of these books, however, stop short of the new movement that is taking shape in the early 1960's.

[2] Rudolf Wittkower. Art and Architecture in Italy, 1600—1750 (Harmondsworth and Baltimore, 1958), p. 151. As yet, there is no satisfactory study of Wright's activity after 1941. In addition to the material cited in Chapter II, note 15, see: Arthur Drexler. The Drawings of Frank Lloyd Wright (New York, 1962).

[3] Lewis Mumford, "Skyline," The New Yorker, December 5, 1959, pp. 105—29, is illustrative of the friendly attitude of disillusionment. By way of contrast, see Peter Blake's knowledgeable and perceptive remarks in "The Guggenheim: Museum or Monument," Architectural Forum, CI, No. 6 (December, 1959), 86—92.

[4] The Solomon R. Guggenheim Museum. Architect: Frank Lloyd Wright (New York, 1960), pp. 16—17.

[5] See: Emil Kaufmann. Three Revolutionary Architects, Boullée, Ledoux, and Lequeu (Philadelphia, 1952); Helen Rosenau. Boullée's Treatise on Architecture (London, 1953).

[6] See: Henry-Russell Hitchcock. The Architecture of H. H. Richardson (New York, 1936; rev. ed., 1961), plate 99.

[7] The statement was first made in a lecture, "The Art and Craft of the Machine," delivered by Wright at Hull House in 1903. It was later printed in his: Modern Architecture, Chapter I ("Machinery, Materials and Man"), 1930; and reprinted in his: The Future of Architecture (New York, 1953).

[8] See Chapter VI, and also: Vincent Scully. Louis I. Kahn (New York, 1962), plates 60, 63.

[9] See: S. Giedion. Walter Gropius (London and New York, 1954); Gilbert Herbert. The Synthetic Vision of Walter Gropius (Johannesburg, 1959); James Marston Fitch. Walter Gropius (New York, 1960), as well as the special issue of L'Architecture d'Aujourd'hui edited by Paul Rudolph, XX, No. 28 (February, 1950).

[10] In addition to: Philip Johnson. Mies van der Rohe (New York, 1947; 2d ed., 1953), see: L. Hilberseimer. Mies van der Rohe (Chicago, 1956); Arthur Drexler. Ludwig Mies van der Rohe (New York, 1960); and the special issue of L'Architecture d'Aujourd'hui, No. LXXIX (September, 1958).

[11] See: Le Corbusier. Œuvre Complète, Vol. V: 1946—52 (Zurich, 1953); Vol. VI: 1952—57 (Zurich and New York, 1957); Vol. VII: 1957—65 (Zurich and New York, 1965). In addition, see the one-volume: Le Corbusier 1910—1960 (Zurich and New York, 1960); Le Corbusier. Creation is a Patient Search, introduction by Maurice Jardot (New York, 1960); and Françoise Choay. Le Corbusier (New York, 1960); special Le Corbusier No. of Aujourd'hui, No. 51 (September–November, 1965).

[12] See Le Corbusier's preface to a book of photographs: Joaquin Gomis and J. Prats Valles. Gaudí (Barcelona and New York, 1958). Le Corbusier dates his first encounter with Gaudí's architecture as 1928. See also: Salvador Dali. Dali on Modern Art (New York, 1957), pp. 29—47.

[13] The essential document on this building is: Jean Petit. Chapelle du Notre-Dame-du-Haut (Dessins et croquis de Le Corbusier), No. 8 in the series "Cahiers des Forces Vives" (Paris, 1957). See also: Le Corbusier. The Chapel at Ronchamp (London and New York, 1957); and the provocative remarks of James Stirling, "Ronchamp, Le

Corbusier's Chapel and the Crisis of Rationalism," The Architectural Review, CXIX, No. 711 (March, 1956), 155—61, an interpretation that differs basically from the one presented here.

[14] Le Corbusier. Towards a New Architecture, p. 153.

[15] Le Corbusier. Creation is a Patient Search, p. 166. See also Jean Petit, op. cit.

[16] See: Glyn Daniel. The Megalith Builders of Western Europe (New York, 1958), Plate III. On this subject, see also: Sibylle von Cles-Reden. The Realm of the Great Goddess (Englewood Cliffs, New Jersey, 1962).

[17] Vincent Scully first called my attention to this similarity. See his: Modern Architecture, p. 45, which also contains extremely vivid interpretations of other Le Corbusier buildings.

[18] See Colin Rowe, "Dominican Monastery of La Tourette, Eveux-sur-l'Arbresle," The Architectural Review, CXXIX (June, 1961), 400—410.

[19] See: François Cali and Lucien Hervé. Architecture of Truth, The Cistercian Abbey of Le Thoronnet in Provence, with a text by Rayner Heppenstall and a preface by Le Corbusier (Grenoble and New York, 1957). Le Corbusier remarks, in part: "Architecture as the unending sum of positive gestures, the whole and its details are one. . . . Light and shade are the loudspeakers of this architecture of truth, tranquillity and strength. Nothing further could add to it. In these days of 'crude concrete' let us greet, bless and salute, as we go on our way, so wonderful an encounter."

[20] I am indebted to Norma Evenson, whose unpublished doctoral dissertation: "Chandigarh, A Study of the City and its Monuments," Yale University, 1963, provides much information and insight with respect to these buildings.

[21] A quarter of a century earlier, Le Corbusier had designed extensive projects for the League of Nations, 1927 (see Chapter II, plate 54), and the Palace of the Soviets, Moscow, 1931, but neither of these was ever built. Similarly, the great urban schemes, which had consumed much of his energy from the 1920's to the early 1950's, were generally ignored.

[22] This similarity was pointed out by Vincent Scully in: Modern Architecture, p. 48. Compare his Plates 3 and 149.

## Chapter IV

[1] The most famous of the rivalries is the one concerning the influence of Theo van Doesburg upon the taste and style of the Bauhaus in Weimar during 1922—23. See: H. L. C. Jaffe. De Stijl, The Dutch Contribution to Modern Art (Amsterdam, 1956); Reyner Banham. Theory and Design in the First Machine Age (London and New York, 1960); Bruno Zevi. Poetica dell'Architettura neoplastica (Milan, 1953).

[2] It would be next to impossible to give a detailed list of publications indicating the growth of a popular audience for contemporary architecture over the past decade. As examples of the audience acceptance, however, I would point out that several books by the critic Lewis Mumford were available in paperback format to the American reading public by the mid-1950's, and that by early 1963 no fewer than five volumes of the writings of Frank Lloyd Wright were in print in the same format. The same is now true for almost all of the literature by and about Louis Sullivan.

[3] This characteristic of the architecture of the past two centuries was first made explicit by S. Giedion in: Space, Time and Architecture (Cambridge, 1941; 4th ed., 1962), although the nature of the split was already clearly recognized by Viollet-le-Duc in: Entretiens sur l'Architecture (Paris, 1863—72).

[4] The deliberation with which an almost traditional order was achieved by, for example, the Smithsons, is forthrightly recognized by Reyner Banham in "New Brutalism," The Architectural Review, CXVIII, No. 708 (December, 1955), 355—61, which cites the influence of Rudolf Wittkower's: Architectural Principles of the Age of Humanism (London, 1949; 2d ed., 1952). See also Banham's articles "Brutalismus" and "Neoclassizismus" in: Knaurs Lexikon der Modernen Architektur, edited by Gerd Hatje (Munich, 1963), pp. 54—57, 181—84. (Published in English translation as: A Dictionary of Modern Architecture [New York, 1964].) In a similar retrospective fashion, Philip Johnson, in: The Architectural Review, CVIII, No. 645 (September, 1950), 152—60, has cited the sources of his Glass House of 1947—49.

[5] See The Museum of Modern Art (New York) exhibition catalog: Skidmore, Owings and Merrill, Architects U.S.A., (Museum of Modern Art Bulletin, XVIII, No. 1 [Fall, 1950]). A comprehensive if selective survey of this firm's work from this epoch onward is: The Architecture of Skidmore, Owings and Merrill, introduction by Henry-Russell Hitchcock (Stuttgart and New York, 1962). The most revealing studies of American commercial architecture in the 1950's are William H. Jordy, "Formal Image U.S.A.," The Architectural Review, CXXVII, No. 757 (March, 1960), 157—65; and Vincent Scully, "The Precisionist Strain in American Architecture," Art in America, XLVIII, No. 3 (Fall, 1960), 46—53.

[6] See: William H. Jordy, "Seagram Assessed," The Architectural Review, CXXIV (December, 1958), 374—82; Thomas H. Creighton, "Seagram House Re-Reassessed," Progressive Architecture, XL (June, 1959), 140—45; and William H. Jordy, "Seagram House Re-Reassessed," a reply to the foregoing, Progressive Architecture, XL (August, 1959), 58. This exchange opens a fundamental quarrel between what might be called the academic, historically oriented criticism of architecture and the pragmatic, professional, marketplace variety. There is, needless to say, a place and a role for each to play, though I suspect that the passage of time will always tend to vindicate the former. In addition, see The Museum of Modern Art catalog: Buildings for Business and Government (New York, 1957), for further documentation on this commercial idiom. In effect, this exhibition was the canonization of this phase of postwar architecture in the United States. Superficially, the change that was about to set in was manifested by the extreme popularity of the same Museum's exhibition of the architecture of Gaudí, which also took place in 1957.

[7] See: Eero Saarinen on His Work. A selection of buildings dating from 1947 to 1964, with statements by the architect, edited by Aline B. Saarinen (New Haven and London, 1962); Allan Temko. Eero Saarinen (New York,

1962); and Walter McQuade, "Eero Saarinen, A Complete Architect," Architectural Forum, CXVI (April, 1962), 102—19.

[8] Eero Saarinen on His Work, p. 24.

[9] Ibid., p. 6.

[10] Ibid., pp. 6—7.

[11] Ibid., p. 14.

[12] Le Corbusier. Towards a New Architecture, p. 31.

[13] See also Chapter II, pp. 52—54, and plates 90—92, above.

[14] "School at Hunstanton: Architects, Alison and Peter Smithson," The Architectural Review, CXVI, No. 693, (September, 1954), 148—62, with comments by Philip Johnson. An exhaustive survey of the Smithson's career is found in: Jeremy Baker, "A Smithson File," special issue of Arena, The Architectural Association Journal, February, 1966.

[15] Reyner Banham, "New Brutalism" (see above, note 4). See also: "Conversation on Brutalism," with Alison and Peter Smithson, Jane Drew, and E. Maxwell Frey, Zodiac, IV (1959), pp. 73—81. A complete history of the origins, development and influence of the Brutalist movement is found in: Reyner Banham. Brutalismus in der Architektur, Dokumente, Vol. 5 (Stuttgart, 1966).

[16] Humanism was the concept most in favor in American discussions of the mid-1950's, based partly on a revived interest in Geoffrey Scott's iconoclastic denunciation of architectural moralism and historicism in his: Architecture of Humanism (London, 1914; 2d ed.; 1924; New York, 1954), and partly on the widely read and more scholarly: Architectural Principles in the Age of Humanism, Rudolf Wittkower's perceptive reinterpretation of Alberti and Palladio. See note 4, above.

[17] The origin of the phrase is amusingly detailed by Banham in "Brutalism," A Dictionary of Modern Architecture (New Jork, 1964), p. 54.

[18] This, and subsequent quotations, are from Reyner Banham, "New Brutalism." See above, note 15.

[19] See: Vincent Scully. Louis I. Kahn (New York, 1962); special issue of Progressive Architecture, February, 1962; and special issue of L'Architecture d'Aujourd'hui, CV, No. 33 (December, 1962—January, 1963), 1—39.

[20] See: George A. Sanderson, "Extension: University Art Gallery and Design Center," Progressive Architecture, XXXV, No. 5 (May, 1954), 88—101.

[21] Philip Johnson. Mies van der Rohe (New York, 1947; new ed., with an additional chapter, 1953). For accounts of Johnson's work, see: John Jacobus. Philip Johnson (New York, 1962); Kentiku, May, 1962; Perspecta, The Yale Architectural Journal, No. 7 (1961), pp. 3—8; and "Recent Work of Philip Johnson," Architectural Record, CXXXII (July, 1962), 113—28.

[22] Architectural Review, CVIII, No. 645 (September, 1950), pp. 152—60. See note 4, above.

[23] See: Osvald Sirén. China and the Gardens of Europe (New York, 1950), pp. 115—20, plates 81—89.

[24] See above, Chapter II, where Johnson's Hodgson House is used to illustrate the growth of order, discipline, and clarity that comes about in domestic architecture around 1950.

[25] Quoted from "Statement by Louis Kahn," Perspecta, The Yale Architectural Journal, No. 3 (1955).


## Chapter V

[1] This and the following quotations are from "Three Critics Discuss M.I.T.'s New Buildings," by Bruno Zevi, J. M. Richards, and Sigfried Giedion. Architectural Forum, CIV, No. 3 (March, 1956), 156—57.

[2] Eero Saarinen on His Work, p. 34.

[3] Ibid.

[4] Philip Johnson, in: Perspecta, The Yale Architectural Journal, No. 2 (1953), p. 48.

[5] See above, note 1.

[6] Eero Saarinen on His Work, p. 36.

[7] See: The Works of Pier Luigi Nervi. Preface by Pier Luigi Nervi, introduction by Ernesto N. Rogers, notes by Jürgen Joedicke (Stuttgart, Paris, London, and New York, 1957); Ada Louise Huxtable. Pier Luigi Nervi (New York, 1960).

[8] See: Marcel Breuer, Buildings and Projects. Introduction by Cranston Jones (Stuttgart and New York, 1962); and Whitney S. Stoddard. Adventure in Architecture: Building the New St. Johns (New York and London, 1958).

[9] See: Contemporary Architecture in Germany. Introduction by Ulrich Conrads, text by Werner Marschall (Stuttgart and New York, 1962); and Rudolf Schwarz. Vom Bau der Kirche (English translation: The Church Incarnate, The Sacred Function of Christian Architecture [Chicago, 1958]).

[10] See: Giulio Carlo Argan. Ignazio Gardella (Milan, 1959).

[11] See: Frederick Gutheim. Alvar Aalto (New York, 1960); Alvar Aalto. Complete Works, 1922—60 (New York, 1963).

[12] Margit Stäber. "Hans Scharoun, Ein Beitrag zum Organischen Bauen," Zodiac, X (1962), pp. 52—92.

[13] See: Edward Durell Stone. The Evolution of An Architect (New York, 1962).

[14] Strictly speaking, the Lambert Field Terminal, St. Louis, by the firm of Hellmuth, Yamasaki, and Leinweber, finished 1956, is the first prominent design by Yamasaki. However, its sequence of groin vaults of a certain dry monumentality, parallel to the effects of Saarinen's M.I.T. auditorium of the same epoch, do not prepare one for the intricate and, finally, prissy character of Yamasaki's work as it took shape about 1960—62.


## Chapter VI

[1] Reyner Banham, "On Trial, The Buttery Hatch Æsthetic," The Architectural Review, CXXXI (March, 1962), 203—06.

² See Monica Pidgeon's periodical: Architectural Design, which published as a special issue in December, 1962, the "Team 10 Primer 1953—62," edited by Alison Smithson, with important contributions by Aldo van Eyck, J. B. Bakema, Peter Smithson, S. Woods, and others. This collection of ideas and projects thoroughly documents the "orthodox" English and continental point of view. The new formalists as yet do not have a comparable publication.

³ See: Edgar Kaufmann, "Inside Eero Saarinen's TWA Building," Interiors, CXXI (July, 1962), 86—93.

⁴ Eero Saarinen on His Work, p. 60.

⁵ See: Zodiac, VI (1961), 129—39; Zodiac, XI (1963), 2—19, 36—47; L'Architecture d'Aujourd'hui, XC, No. 31 (June–July, 1960), 1—33.

⁶ See: Udo Kulterman. New Japanese Architecture (New York, 1960); and J. M. Richards, "Japan 1962," special issue of The Architectural Review, CXXXII (September, 1962).

⁷ See: Robin Boyd. Kenzo Tange (New York, 1962), pp. 29—30 and plates 52—60.

⁸ Philip Thiel, "City Hall at Kurashiki," The Architectural Review, CXXI (February, 1962), 106—14.

⁹ See: " 'The Functional Tradition' and Expression," Perspecta, The Yale Architectural Journal, No. 6 (1960), pp. 88—97.

¹⁰ In 1955, Stirling published a perceptive appreciation of these buildings, "Garches to Jaoul; Le Corbusier as Domestic Architect in 1927 and 1953," The Architectural Review, CXVIII (September, 1955), 145—51.

¹¹ See: Roberto Aloi. Musei, Architettura, Technica (Milan, 1962).

¹² See: Perspecta, The Yale Architectural Journal, No. 7 (1961), pp. 51—64; Architectural Record, CXXXV (February, 1964), 111—20; Architectural Forum, CXX (February, 1964), 62—83; Progressive Architecture, XLV (February, 1964), 106—29; Arts and Architecture (February, 1964), 26—29.

¹³ See: Architectural Design, February, 1964, special issue devoted to Leicester University Engineering Building.

¹⁴ For a notion of Kallmann's attitude to new forms, see his article " 'Action' Architecture of a New Generation," Architectural Forum, CXI (October, 1959), 132—37.

# Index

# Photo Credits

The publishers are indebted to all individuals and institutions listed below, and especially to: The Architectural Press Ltd., London; Droemersche Verlagsanstalt Th. Knaur Nachf., Munich; Albert Langen Georg Müller Verlag, Munich; Prestel Verlag, Munich; The Museum of Finnish Architecture, Helsinki.

A. C. I., Brussels 24
Michel Aertsens, Rio de Janeiro 101
Agenzia Fotografica Industriale, Venice 186
Albright-Knox Art Gallery, Contemporary Art Collection, Buffalo, N. Y. 29
Alinari, Florence 32
Anderson, Rome 133
The Architects' Journal, London (Photo Wm. J. Toomey) 328
Architectural Forum, New York, N. Y. 127, 128
The Architectural Press Ltd., London 11, 12, 53, 268, 306, 317, 335, 336, 359
The Architectural Review, London 212, 214, 215, 323

Bibliothèque Nationale, Paris 119
Bildarchiv Foto Marburg 4
Alfred Brandler 352
Brecht-Einzig, London 298
British Features, Bonn 103
de Burgh Galwey 53, 212, 214, 215, 323
René Burri—Magnum, Paris/New York 172, 174

J. Cellard, Bron 171
Chicago Architectural Photo Co., Chicago, Ill. 117
Chicago Heritage Committee, Chicago, Ill. 2
Lucca Chmel, Vienna 238
Connecticut Life, West Hartford, Conn. 219

Robert Damora, New York, N. Y. 40, 134
Dandelet, San Anselmo, Calif. 130, 131
John Donat 335, 336
Jean-Pierre Dumont, Royan 266, 267

Edizione S. A. F.—Fotocelere, Turin 104
Walter Ehmann, Klettenburg, near Cologne 333

Roy Flamm, San Francisco, Calif. 390
Fortunati, Milan 263, 264
Fotogramma, Milan 361
John D. Fowner 332
Reinhard Friedrich, Berlin 276

P. Gasparini, Caracas 349–51
Marcel Gautherot, Rio de Janeiro 43, 74, 75, 190–92, 305, 353
Alexandre Georges, New City, N. Y. 147, 148, 224, 252

Gerlach, Vienna 3
Gherardi-Fiorelli, Rome 240, 241
Giraudon, Paris 9
Gomis-Prats, Barcelona 156
Gottscho-Schleisner, Inc., Jamaica, N. Y. 72
Greater London Council, Architect's Dept., Photographic Unit, London 324
P. E. Guerrero, New York, N. Y. 80
The Solomon R. Guggenheim Museum, New York, N. Y. 115

Lee A. Hanley 247
C. Hartzenbusch, Junkersdorf, near Cologne 285
Robert D. Harvey Studio, Boston, Mass. 232
Heikki Havas, Helsinki 269, 271, 272, 331, 382
Hedrich-Blessing, Chicago, Ill. 48, 50, 51, 52a, 58, 111–13, 143, 144, 146, 149–53, 194, 217, 283, 379
H. Heidersberger, Wolfsburg 274, 318
W. Heller, Telgte 53a
Klaus Herdeg, Zurich 185
Lucien, Hervé, Paris 1, 25, 30, 34, 35, 44, 46, 54, 107, 110, 157–61, 173, 180, 181, 184, 193, 243, 244, 336b
Ch. Hirayama, Tokyo 308
Jan Hodgson 216
George Holton, New York, N. Y. 304
Franz Hubmann, Vienna 164

John Jacobus 182a, 375, 391, 393
Josef Josuweck, Cologne 16

Akio Kawasumi, Tokyo 306
G. E. Kidder Smith, New York, N. Y. 105, 268
Kolmio 36
Baltazar Korab, Birmingham, Mich. 154, 290, 291, 337

Lennart af Petersens, Stockholm 196
Lincoln Center for the Performing Arts, New York, N. Y. 293
Erich Locker, New York, N. Y. 203
Luckhaus Studio, Los Angeles, Calif. 8

Manchete 188
Massachusetts Institute of Technology, Office of Public Relations, Cambridge, Mass. 336a
Peter Mögenburg, Leverkusen 284
Lucia Moholy-Nagy 13a
Moisio, Turin 106, 236
Joseph W. Molitor, Ossining, N. Y. 286, 287, 365
Moncalvo, Turin 387
Paolo Monti, Milan 356
Moss Photo Service, New York, N. Y. 202
F. Murasawa 309, 312, 313
The Museum of Finnish Architecture, Helsinki 36, 90–92, 211, 269, 271, 272, 331, 382